THANK YOU SABRES

MEMORIES OF THE 1972-73 SEASON

By Sal Maiorana

Foreword by Northrup Knox

Quality Sports Publications

For information write:

Quality Sports Publications
24 Buysse Drive
Coal Valley, IL 61240
(309) 234-5016
(800) 464-1116

Duane Brown, Project Director
Melinda Brown, Designer
Susan Smith, Editor

Printed in the U.S.A.
by
Master Litho
Neenah, Wisconsin

ISBN 1-885758-10-3

**Cover photo: The 1972-73 season was the birth of
The French Connection – Gilbert Perreault, Rene Robert
and Rick Martin. (Photo courtesy of Ron Moscati)**

**Right: 1972-73 Buffalo Sabres: (Left to right)
FRONT ROW: Angelo Nigro, trainer; Dave Dryden;
Tim Horton; Joe Crozier, Coach; Gerry Meehan;
Gil Perreault; Roger Crozier; Frank Christie, trainer.
SECOND ROW: Rick Martin; Tracy Pratt; Don Luce;
Jim Schoenfeld; Larry Carriere; Steve Atkinson.
THIRD ROW: Mike Robitaille; Larry Hillman;
Randy Wyrozub; Craig Ramsay; Butch Deadmarsh.
FOURTH ROW: Larry Mickey; Rene Robert;
Jim Lorentz; Paul Terbenche.**

CONTENTS

Dedication

To Christine,
Taylor and Holden:
You are my heart, soul and
inspiration. How can I ever
thank you?

I would like to thank the following people whose efforts were instrumental in the writing, editing and publishing of this book.

First to the writers who covered the Sabres in that magical 1972-73 season: Dick Johnston, Jim Peters, Steve Weller, Phil Ranallo, Wayne Redshaw and Jack Gatecliff. Because I was 10 years old and still quite a few years away from breaking into the sportswriting business, it was the detailed accounts of the games and the interviews with the players and coaches that these men provided which helped me relive 1972-73 and bring back to life the accomplishments of the Sabres that year.

To fellow authors Budd Bailey (*Celebrate the Tradition*), Scott Young (*Heaven and Hell in the NHL*, co-written with Punch Imlach) and Ross Brewitt (*Sabres - 26 Seasons in Buffalo's Memorial Auditorium*), whose books were invaluable resources; to Randy Schultz, who provided many of his feature stories which were a huge help; to Ron Moscati and Robert Shaver, whose captivating photos are displayed on these pages; to John Murphy, who sent me an informative Newschannel 7 video celebrating the Sabres' 25th anniversary which included footage from the 1972-73 season that allowed me to hear the "Thank You Sabres" chant; and to Jim Kelley, a good friend and the most knowledgeable hockey man I know, who lent perspective, guidance and friendship to this book.

Many thanks to the Sabres alumni relations director Larry Playfair, and to the Sabres media relations department including Gil Chorbajian, Bruce Wawrzyniak and John Isherwood, who answered all my questions and let me poke through old media guides, reference books and photo files.

Special thanks to Christye Peterson for her tireless efforts at the beginning to get this project off the ground. Christye was my first contact with the Sabres, she believed in the idea and helped facilitate its production.

Thank you to the wonderful people at Quality Sports Publications. To my publisher, Duane Brown, who in addition to being a great publisher, has become a trusted friend; to designer Melinda Brown, who had it a little easier than the last time we worked together, but nonetheless treated this project with just as much care and flair; to Susan Smith for her skillful editing; and to Mick McCay for his dazzling cover design.

Of course, thank you to the players and coaches who were interviewed for this book: Joe Crozier, Gilbert Perreault, Rick Martin, Rene Robert, Gerry Meehan, Jim Schoenfeld, Craig Ramsay, Jim Lorentz, Don Luce, Mike Robitaille, Larry Carriere, Danny Gare, Jerry Korab, Fred Stanfield, Denis Potvin, Ed Westfall, Bob Clarke, Brad Park, Marcel Dionne and Terry O'Reilly. Without the time these men gave me, not to mention their uncanny recollection of events that took place 25 years ago, this book would not have been possible.

And lastly, thanks to my wife Christine and my two children, Taylor and Holden. We made it through another book unscathed. Thanks so much for your patience, your love and your understanding.

Sal Maiorana

ACKNOWLEDGEMENTS

A few years back, I was interviewed by Ross Brewitt for a book he was writing about the Buffalo Sabres entitled *Sabres - 26 Seasons in Buffalo's Memorial Auditorium*, and I reflected on what it was like to watch Gilbert Perreault play in the early 1970s.

"One of the things that was a constant source of enjoyment for the people sitting behind and near the Sabres bench was watching the reaction to things Gilbert Perreault did on the ice," I told Ross. "He'd come barreling up the ice with those powerful strides and make some of his best moves in the neutral zone right in front of both benches. Teammates and opponents would look at each other, sometimes roll their eyes or shake their heads in amazement."

I have been associated with the Sabres since their birth in 1969 and the wonderful memories are certainly not limited to watching Gilbert skate circles around the National Hockey League's greatest players.

For instance, there was the 1972-73 season which Sal Maiorana has so eloquently captured in the pages of **THANK YOU SABRES: *Memories of the 1972-73 Season***. What a year that was as the Sabres took myself, my late brother Seymour, and the great fans of Western New York and Southern Ontario on a magical ride that none of us will ever forget.

In just our third year of existence in the NHL, the Sabres qualified for the Stanley Cup playoffs, an achievement almost unheard of. And once we got there, we stared defiantly at the mighty Montreal Canadiens and won two games in the best-of-seven series before their abundant talent finally overcame us.

But I do not remember that loss to Montreal as much as I do the wheeling and dealing of general manager Punch Imlach, and the teaching and emotional leadership behind the bench of Joe Crozier; the eye-popping skating and passing skills of our Hall of Fame center, Gilbert, the wicked slap shot of Rick Martin, and the scoring touch of Rene Robert; the incessant checking and penalty-killing of Don Luce and Craig Ramsay, and the bone-rattling checks of Jim Schoenfeld; the coolheaded captaincy of Gerry Meehan, and the acrobatic goaltending of Roger Crozier and Dave Dryden; the nonstop grinding of Jim Lorentz, Mike Robitaille, Tracy Pratt, Larry Hillman, and of course, the veteran poise and ultimate professionalism of Tim Horton. There are so many memories of all of our players!

We enjoyed our greatest success as a franchise two years later in 1975 when we made it all the way to the Stanley Cup finals against the Philadelphia Flyers, but as I look back a quarter century to that 1972-73 season, I am reminded that success is not measured solely in wins and losses, but also in the gratification of setting goals and accomplishing them.

Hearing the fans in Memorial Auditorium chant "Thank You Sabres" that glorious night of April 12, 1973, when that season came to an end is an image forever burned in my heart and soul. It provided an exclamation point on a year filled with laughter, joy and satisfaction.

As we celebrate the 25th anniversary of that beloved 1972-73 team, I say again, "Thank You Sabres."

Northrup R. Knox

Northrup R. Knox

FOREWORD

Photo courtesy of Ron Moscati

Prologue

Thank You Sabres!

It started in the upper balcony of Memorial Auditorium, the orange-colored seats where fans were afforded a panoramic view of the ice surface at the expense of a nose bleed.

"Thank You Sabres" they chanted as the final minute of the magical 1972-73 season ticked away on the big royal blue scoreboard that hovered over the center faceoff circle.

Like lava pouring from a volcano, the chant slid down to the blue seats, and then to the reds.

"Thank You Sabres, Thank You Sabres" they sang in unison, the decibel level increasing with each verse until the folks in the upper and lower golds had joined the chorus, and then it couldn't get any louder.

"Thank You Sabres, Thank You Sabres, Thank You Sabres." Over and over it reverberated throughout the arena, a passionate, appreciative and heart-warming salute that puddled the eyes of those who were being thanked – Gilbert Perreault, Rick Martin, Rene Robert, Roger Crozier, Jim Schoenfeld, Tim Horton, Craig Ramsay, Don Luce, Gerry Meehan and the rest of the Buffalo Sabres.

It did not matter that on this night – April 12, 1973 – the Sabres were about to be eliminated from the Stanley Cup playoffs by the powerful Montreal Canadiens. All that mattered was that this young, energetic hockey team had given the citizens of Buffalo – people in desperate need of an escape from the harsh realities of a failing economy, horrid weather, and a pitiful National Football League team named the Bills – a reason to smile, a reason to put their troubles aside.

"Thank You Sabres."

"I'll never forget it," said Robert, emotion gripping his voice nearly a quarter of a century later. "I've never experienced anything like that in my life. Here we are, getting beat out in the playoffs, and the fans are cheering, 'Thank You Sabres.' This is something that I'll always remember, this is an experience that someone has to have somewhere down the road. It brings tears to your eyes."

Martin interrupted this outpouring of gratitude when he scored with 12 seconds left to play to make the final score 4-2, but soon after the fans had finished celebrating the last goal of the season, they picked up the chant and serenaded their beloved Sabres throughout the traditional post-game handshakes.

"It just had a nice warm feeling," Martin recalled. "When 16,000 people get up and cheer, it's electric, it's a hard feeling to describe, it's like this energy glows around you. We all had that feeling that night. It was great, it made us feel so good. Everyone likes to be appreciated. We got beat by a good team, and it was nice that the people appreciated the effort that we put out. We entertained them pretty good."

Said Schoenfeld, "It was kind of the signature of the Buffalo people. They identified very strongly with their athletes and their teams and if you gave them an honest day's effort, that's all they asked for. Everybody would like to be associated with a championship team and everybody wants to identify with a winner, but these people went beyond that. If you gave them everything you have, that was enough to satisfy them and they felt that season that we had given everything we had and this was their way of showing their appreciation for that effort.

"I'll tell you what, it was well-received by the players and it was a very emotional time for us. It meant a lot to us. It's not something you see in modern-day athletics nearly as much, if ever."

Despite the unfavorable outcome on the scoreboard, the sellout crowd at Memorial Auditorium stands as one and chants "Thank You Sabres" as the Sabres and Canadiens go through the traditional playoff handshake line. (Photo courtesy of Ron Moscati)

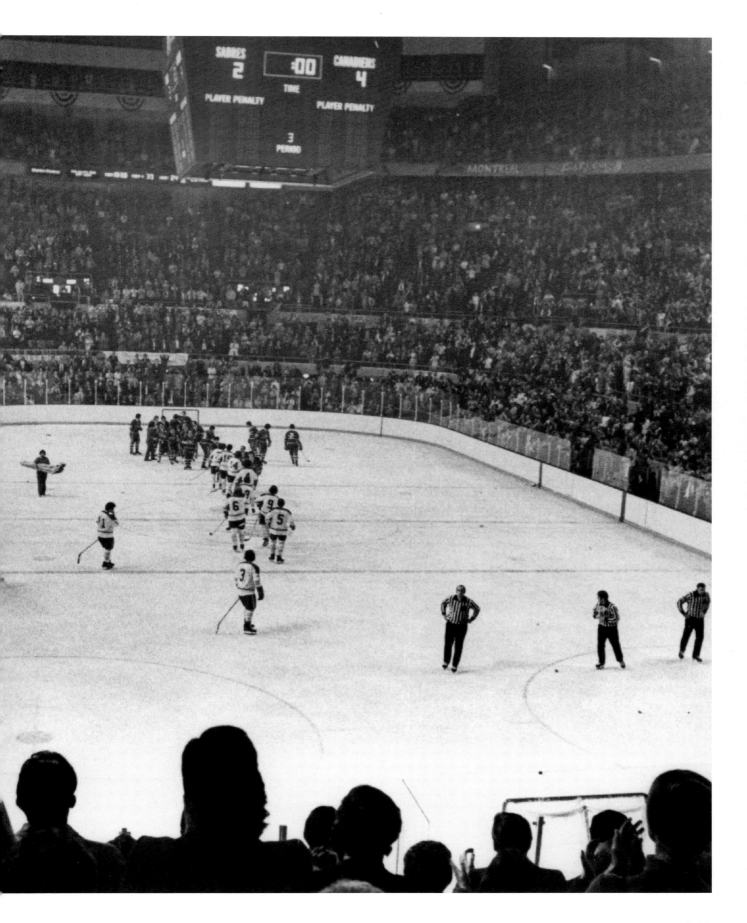

With pen in hand, Punch Imlach signs on to become the Sabres' first coach and general manager. He is joined, from left, by Seymour Knox III, David Forman and Northrup Knox.

A Franchise is Born

On Thursday, January 8, 1970, Punch Imlach – who earlier that week had officially become a former employee of the Toronto Maple Leafs – hopped into a chintzy rental car and drove from Toronto to Buffalo for the purpose of agreeing to become the first coach and general manager of the new National Hockey League franchise that had been awarded to Buffalo.

In his book, *Heaven and Hell in the NHL*, Imlach recalled that he stopped to get gas that day and the attendant came up to the window, shook his head as he checked out Imlach's subservient vehicle, and said, "I guess things aren't quite the same now that you're not with the Leafs."

Imlach had forged a legendary career with Toronto, having guided one of the most storied franchises in NHL history to the playoffs in 10 of his 11 seasons there, in the process winning four Stanley Cup championships in the 1960s. He was one of the most popular sports figures in Canada, let alone Toronto, but on April 6, 1969, moments after the Boston Bruins had completed an easy four-game quarterfinal playoff sweep of the Leafs, team president Stafford Smythe pulled Imlach into an office at Maple Leaf Gardens and said, "Well, that's it. You're through. I want to run the club."

Eight months later, lawyers for Imlach and the team came to an agreement on a settlement for the remaining year left on his contract, so on January 5, 1970, Imlach picked up his compensation check at the Gardens and returned his fancy company car, a big, classy Oldsmobile that he had cherished. This is why he was driving a second-rate rental car on that trip to Buffalo.

As he pulled out of the gas station that day, the attendant's words burned in his ears. Whether he liked it or not, though, the symbolism was unmistakeable considering the step he was about to take, going from the glamorous, tradition-rich Leafs to the infantile, sure-to-be-laughable and as-yet-unnamed Buffalo team.

Upon arriving in Buffalo, Imlach perused the proposal tabled by the team's owners, brothers Seymour III and Northrup Knox, concluded that everything appeared to be in order, and said he would agree to the terms if

From left, Northrup Knox, Punch Imlach and Seymour Knox III display the Sabres' home and away jerseys before the inaugural 1970-71 season.

they granted him one additional request: He wanted as his company car, "the biggest and brightest Cadillac Eldorado in town." The Knoxes agreed, a week later Imlach signed the papers, and so began his quest to not only prove that Stafford Smythe was a buffoon who had made a grievous mistake firing him, but to build an exciting, winning hockey team in Buffalo.

"When we conducted meetings and interviews with the candidates we had lined up, Punch stood out like a bright light," the late Seymour H. Knox III told Wayne Redshaw, one of the contributing writers for the book, *Sabres - 26 Seasons in Buffalo's Memorial Auditorium.*

"He liked the challenge our franchise presented. He certainly had everything we wanted in a general manager: stature and credibility within hockey circles, a background of being successful, and a business awareness that was truly a revelation to some of the members of our board. He was a guy who could do it all, and on top of that, he was brash, topical, entertaining, and exactly the kind of personality we needed to sell NHL hockey in Buffalo."

Meehan, who became one of the first Sabres when Imlach selected him in the 1970 expansion draft, agreed.

"I think great stability is what comes to mind when I think of Punch," Meehan said. "He brought to the organization a reputation as a winner from Toronto, and he was a winner at the minor pro level in Quebec City. He was a steely, hard-working, aggressive, no-nonsense leader that this young team needed. I can't imagine anyone else being more perfect for this job.

"His departure from Toronto was not entirely justified. He'd won four Stanley Cups, he'd built a dynasty in Toronto, and I don't know what happened there, but in those situations in today's hockey, four Stanley Cups would have kept him there."

Imlach, bursting with confidence, and, some would say, arrogance, stood in front of the media at the press conference announcing his hiring and said, "Running the Buffalo hockey club will be the toughest job in hockey. The tougher it is, the better I like it. This is a job of building from the bottom up. I've done it before and I can do it again."

The first step in the building process was bringing aboard John Andersen to direct the scouting department. Knowing how important the June 1970 amateur and expansion drafts – and the amateur drafts over the next few years – were going to be to the future success of the club, Imlach knew constructing a competent scouting department was vital. Andersen had worked with Imlach in Toronto and was a trusted friend and respected evaluator of hockey talent. With the permission of the Knoxes, Imlach hired more scouts than a team would normally need so that no stone would be left unturned in the search for viable players. Imlach hired Doug Minor to scout the West Coast, Bucky Kane to handle the Boston area, Jim Cherry and Roy Cast to scour Ontario, Mike Racicot and Al Millar for Quebec and Montreal, Len Poore to cover the Maritimes and Paul Roach for Windsor.

With his scouting staff organized, David Forman already on the job handling business affairs, and the nickname

David Forman (left) and John Andersen (above) were two of the first men hired to work in the front office. Forman handled the team's business affairs, and Andersen directed the scouting department.

"Sabres" selected from a list of 1,047 suggested by fans during a contest, Imlach fit the final piece of the front office puzzle in place when he asked Fred Hunt to be his assistant general manager. Hunt had been the general manager of the Buffalo Bisons of the American Hockey League before they were disbanded to make room for the Sabres. He was a popular figure in Buffalo who had wide-ranging connections in the city, and Imlach – who understood that Hunt was a bit perturbed that he hadn't been chosen general manager of the Sabres given his tenure with the Bisons – was thrilled that Hunt agreed to accept his offer because he knew Hunt would be an invaluable employee.

With the infrastructure set, Imlach began the tedious task of finding prospects to fill the roster. The NHL made it very difficult for Buffalo and fellow expansionist Vancouver to stock their rosters. The two new teams were going to have the first two picks in the amateur draft, with the selection order to be determined by the spin of a wheel that had been specially designed for this occasion.

But for the expansion draft, the league was allowing each of the existing 12 teams to protect 15 skaters and two goalies, plus all of their first-year players, meaning – as far as Imlach was concerned – veritable dog scraps would be left for the Sabres and Canucks. To make matters worse, once an established team lost a player in the draft, it was allowed to protect an additional player. For instance, at worst, a team would lose its 16th-best skater, and then it would be allowed to protect its 17th-best, so the next player available would be the 18th-best player on that team, and so on. Once a team lost three players, including goalies, its roster could no longer be invaded.

After serving as general manager of the Buffalo Bisons' American Hockey League team, Fred Hunt was hired by the Sabres to be Punch Imlach's assistant general manager.

Facing these restrictive rules, Imlach knew he wouldn't get much talent from the expansion draft, and his philosophy all along was to use the expansion draft solely as a means to fill out the roster, then take steps through trades to improve the team. It was the amateur draft where Imlach was going to get the player he could build the franchise around. That player was Montreal Junior Canadiens sensation Gilbert Perreault, far and away the best player available. The problem was, in order to get first crack at Perreault, the Sabres had to be lucky enough to be awarded the first pick in the amateur draft.

On June 9, 1970, the ballroom of the Queen Elizabeth Hotel in Montreal was filled to capacity to witness the two historic spins of the wheel that would determine which team – Buffalo or Vancouver – would get to choose first in both the expansion and amateur drafts. Imlach won a coin toss for the right to choose which numbers on the wheel he wanted. The wheel was numbered 1 thru 13, with seven considered neutral and cause for a re-spin. Imlach chose the high numbers, 8 thru 13. It was the beginning of a very fortuitous day. The first spin was for the first choice in the expansion draft, and when the wheel stopped on No. 8, the Sabres were winners. Imlach smiled, but to be honest, it was a hollow victory. The next spin, the Perreault spin, was the one that very likely would determine the course the team would take for at least the next decade.

NHL president Clarence Campbell spun the wheel, and for the tortuous seconds that it was spinning, the members of the Sabres and Canucks delegations held their collective breath. Finally, the wheel came to a stop, and Campbell mistakenly thought the lucky number had been 1. He bellowed, "Number one. Vancouver wins first choice in the amateur draft." The announcement touched off a celebration at the Canucks table, but Imlach and Sabres' officials immediately leaped out of their seats yelling, "Eleven, eleven!" The hand on the wheel had partially obliterated the 11 and all Campbell saw was a solitary 1. Quickly, Campbell said, "There has been a mistake (although he didn't say it had been his mistake). The winning number is 11." With that, the Vancouver group grew glum while the Buffalo contingent rejoiced.

Thanks to a lucky spin of the wheel, the Sabres were awarded the first pick in the 1970 amateur draft and they used it to select Montreal Junior Canadiens center Gilbert Perreault.

After the wheel of fortune capades, Imlach selected Kevin O'Shea, Cliff Schmautz, Brian McDonald and Billy Inglis in the inter-league draft, and claimed goalie Joe Daley off the waiver wire from Pittsburgh. They were the first five players to be called Sabres.

The next day, June 10, Imlach continued to pad the roster by laboriously choosing players in the expansion draft, and while the talent pool was decidedly weak, he did manage to harness a few serviceable bodies. The first one was Detroit goalie Roger Crozier, who had been the NHL rookie of the year in 1965 and the Conn Smythe trophy winner as MVP of the 1966 playoffs. Red Wings general manager Sid Abel had checked the protected lists of the existing teams, and he noticed that the Bruins had left promising right wing Tom Webster off their list. Detroit wanted Webster, so Abel told Imlach if he selected Webster first, Abel would trade Crozier for Webster. Imlach was thrilled because he would get a quality goaltender, the most important building block for any team.

Boston GM Milt Schmidt, not knowing Imlach had already cut a deal with Abel, asked Imlach to lay off Webster and choose Garnet Bailey, because he wanted to trade Webster to Detroit for Crozier. Imlach never said yes, but Schmidt walked away thinking the Sabres GM had agreed to his request. Naturally, Schmidt erupted in a fit of anger when Imlach plucked Webster and immediately shipped him to Detroit. The first seed of the heated Sabres-Bruins rivalry was planted that day.

NHL veteran Floyd Smith joined the Sabres for their inaugural season and was named the team's first captain. He retired in 1971, became an assistant coach under Punch Imlach, and in 1974, was named head coach of the team. That season, he led the Sabres to their only appearance in the Stanley Cup Finals.

Imlach picked up a second veteran goalie when the Chicago Blackhawks gave him Dave Dryden for agreeing not to select defenseman Jerry Korab. Other decent veterans procured included Meehan, Don Marshall, Phil Goyette and Reg Fleming. The rest of the selections were: Chris Evans, Paul Terbenche, Craig Cameron, Skip Krake, Mike McMahon, Jean-Guy Legace, Francois Lacombe, Jim Watson, Tracy Pratt, Al Hamilton, Brian Perry, Howie Menard, Rocky Farr, Doug Barrie and Gary Edwards.

The following day, June 11, Imlach proudly kicked off the amateur draft by announcing the Sabres were taking Perreault with the first pick. He made eight other choices, and three – Butch Deadmarsh, Randy Wyrozub and Doug Rombough – eventually played for Buffalo.

Just before training camp started in September, Floyd Smith was purchased from Toronto and he wound up being named the Sabres' first captain. And a week before the first regular-season began, Imlach dealt Cameron to St. Louis for Ron Anderson. Everything was in place. Now it was time to go play hockey.

Can Anybody Around Here Play This Game?

In that first season, Imlach knew winning was going to be as rare an occurrence as a sunny, wind-free January day on the Niagara Frontier. He admitted to spending much of his time pacing behind the Buffalo bench rolling his eyes and muttering, "Unbelievable." Quite frankly, after more than a decade in Toronto coaching one of hockey's best teams, Imlach felt like he was running a squirt team in Buffalo, so gruesome were the Sabres in their first couple of months of existence.

But they weren't bad on the evening of October 10, 1970, when they made their regular-season NHL debut at the Pittsburgh Civic Arena and defeated the Penguins, 2-1.

"I remember we played a pretty good game," Meehan said of that historic night. "My biggest memory of Pittsburgh was the size of the ice. It was bigger than most rinks. I was a good skater, I liked to have a lot of room to manuever with the puck, so it was great to play in Pittsburgh. But mostly I just remember the momentous feeling of being part of a new franchise. It was quite a thrilling experience.

"We had played Pittsburgh three times in the preseason, and we'd won a couple of those games, so we went into that game with sort of an expectation that we could do pretty well, so it wasn't as scary as it might have been had we played the Rangers or the Canadiens."

Well, Meehan and his teammates didn't have much time to savor that victory because, as fate would have it, their next two opponents were indeed those Rangers and those Canadiens. In New York's Madison Square Garden, reality set in faster than a Perreault rush up ice as the Sabres were humbled by the Rangers in a 3-0 loss.

If possible, it was far worse the next night when the Sabres returned to Buffalo to play their first regular-season game at the Aud. Montreal rained 53 shots on Crozier and buzzed around the ice in such a dominating manner that the Sabres rarely had possession of the puck. It looked like the Harlem Globetrotters against the Washington Generals, and had it not been for

Roger Crozier was a busy man in goal for the Sabres during their first two seasons as the team played terrible defense in front of him.

Crozier's acrobatic brilliance, the score would have been far worse than the 3-0 final.

Afterward, Imlach characterized his team perfectly when he said, "We don't move the puck fast enough, we don't shoot fast enough and we don't skate fast enough. Our guys don't quit, but they don't accomplish much."

At the conclusion of the June drafts, Imlach had told reporters, "This is only the beginning. Now we'll try to improve on what we have. We'll be making deals from now, 24 hours a day, seven days a week, 52 weeks a year."

He wasn't kidding. Imlach worked the waiver wire feverishly and he spent more time on the telephone than an AT&T operator. For instance, within a three-day period in early November, he picked up Steve Atkinson, Paul Andrea and Bobby Baun, then traded Baun to St. Louis for Jean-Guy Talbot and Larry Keenan. A few weeks later, he dealt Mike McMahon to Los Angeles for Dick Duff and his old buddy from Toronto, Eddie Shack.

There were good nights – most notably a 7-2 shellacking of Toronto in Imlach's first visit to the Gardens since his firing – and plenty of bad nights such as a 7-2 loss to expansion brethren Vancouver, an 11-2 hammering via Montreal, and an 8-2 rout by Boston in which the Bruins fired 72 shots at Daley, still a Sabres futility record.

Left: Eddie Shack, shown here battling Garry Unger, was a free spirit who provided Sabres fans with plenty of entertainment in the year and a half he spent in Buffalo.

Below: Considering the number of shots goalie Joe Daley faced in Buffalo's first NHL season, he was a brave man to play without a mask. Daley was traded before the 1971-72 season for Don Luce and Mike Robitaille.

Gerry Meehan's hockey career was in limbo and he was considering quitting when the Sabres selected him in the 1970 expansion draft. He captained the 1972-73 team.

Regardless, the city was in love with its new hockey club and the Aud was packed on a nightly basis. The Knoxes knew enough to be patient and they left Imlach and his staff alone, and after a few months, the team began to make progress.

When the new year rang in, Buffalo had just seven victories, but in January of 1971, the team won six times. That's because the roster wasn't quite as bad as Imlach had made it out to be early in the year, Meehan said.

"That was the second expansion," Meehan reasoned. "It had gone from six to 12 teams and now it was going to 14, and there were a lot of good hockey players out there. We had players on that first team who had had good, long careers, nine, 10, 11, 12 years in the league. It wasn't that we had dogs out there. The dilution of the talent hadn't really started. You have to consider the number of high-caliber players who played in the American League for years before the 1967 expansion. They probably, in today's hockey, would have been stars, and now they were getting a chance to play in the NHL.

"It wasn't as though we weren't good players, we were some high-level players. When you had six teams employing about 20 players each, that was only 120 players in the league. Add six teams, and that's 240, and add two more teams and 40 more players, that's 280 of the top hockey players in the world. That's not exactly chopped liver, that's pretty good talent."

After their productive January, another slump ensued as they went 2-10-1 over a 13-game stretch. But on February 28, a 5-2 victory over Minnesota kicked off an 8-3-4 run over the last 15 games which propelled the Sabres to a surprising sixth-place finish in the eight-team Eastern Division. With a final record of 24-39-15 and 63 points, not only had the Sabres beaten out Vancouver (24-46-8, 56 points), but they outdistanced an original six team, Detroit (22-45-11, 55 points). And in the Western Division, Los Angeles could only match Buffalo's point production, while Pittsburgh (62) and California (45) ranked below the Sabres.

"The games were tough and the nights were long, but there was a lot of satisfaction in bringing a franchise into the league and being reasonably successful right away," Roger Crozier was quoted as saying in the Sabres' 20th anniversary history book, *Celebrate the Tradition*, written by Budd Bailey. "It wasn't easy, but we weren't as low as a lot of expansion clubs."

Of course, none of the expansion clubs – Vancouver, plus the six who joined the NHL in 1967 – had Perreault.

Imlach wrote in *Heaven and Hell in the NHL* that during the second game of the season, that 3-0 defeat in New York, he remembered standing behind the bench and thinking not one of his players could make New York's team. Well, that was a bit of an exaggeration because he forgot about a certain guy wearing a No. 11 jersey, who, according to Meehan, "would have done just fine on that Rangers team."

"I knew it was time to hang up my skates the first time I saw Gilbert Perreault play," Don Marshall told sportswriter Randy Schultz when he was being interviewed for *Sabres – 26 Seasons in Buffalo's Memorial Auditorium*. "He wasn't the second coming of Jean Beliveau, who I played with for several seasons in Montreal. He was the first coming of Gilbert Perreault. The young man was a hell of a hockey player, and I believe this is where the genius of Imlach came into the picture. Punch never told Gilbert how to play. You don't tell players of his caliber what to do."

The flashy French Canadian was everything he had been advertised to be. He set a league rookie record with 38 goals, finished with 74 points, and provided the fans with an interesting exercise program at the Aud, what with all the jumping up and down they were doing.

"This was a new team, a new franchise, and the public – I don't know how many years they had waited to get an NHL team – they were great fans, and still are," Perreault said. "They were so involved with the team. It was new for them, it was new for us, and it was just great to see that."

Gilbert Perreault was everything the Sabres' front office expected in 1970-71 as he scored 38 goals to set an NHL rookie scoring record.

The St. Louis Blues figured out that tackling Rick Martin was a good way to slow down the high-scoring left winger.

The Sophomore Jinx 3

Perreault had excelled as a rookie despite having to play with a number of different wingers, none of whom were capable of keeping up with him. When Shack was acquired, Imlach tried him with Perreault, leading Shack to say, "Trying to follow his moves, I even deked myself. Trying to play with him, I was like a calf slipping in its own manure."

So in the amateur draft of 1971, Imlach's primary goal was to find a sniper, someone who could take some of the offensive burden off Perreault's shoulders. With the fifth choice in the first round, Imlach knew he'd never get Guy Lafleur, a sure-fire superstar who had scored 130 goals and 209 points in his final junior season with the Quebec Ramparts of the Quebec Major Junior Hockey League. The California Golden Seals had finished with the worst record in the NHL, but they had traded what turned out to be the No. 1 overall choice in the draft to Montreal, so Lafleur went to the Canadiens.

Detroit used the second pick to take Marcel Dionne, and then the Sabres got lucky because left winger Rick Martin should have been the third pick. Martin had scored an Ontario Hockey Association record 71 goals the previous year as a member of the Junior Canadiens, but for some reason, Vancouver opted for Martin's Junior Canadiens teammate Jocelyn Guevremont, and then St. Louis inexplicably chose Gene Carr, leaving Imlach to happily grab Martin.

Martin and Perreault had been teammates with the Junior Canadiens, and Perreault had lived with Martin's family during the 1969-70 season, but the two never played on the same line together as juniors. Perreault centered a line that included future Canadiens Rejean Houle and Marc Tardif, while Martin teamed with Bobby Lalonde and future Sabre teammate Norm Gratton on the second unit for the Memorial Cup winners.

"That summer before the draft, I had a chance to talk to Gilbert, and he said, 'If you get drafted by Buffalo, you'll love it, you'll probably make the team right away' and he was right," Martin said. "I didn't care where I

Right: Rick Martin was Buffalo's first-round draft choice in 1971 and he went on to score 44 goals in 1971-72, breaking Gilbert Perreault's NHL rookie scoring record.

Below: Craig Ramsay was the Sabres' second-round draft choice after Martin in 1971, and though he started his rookie season with the farm team in Cincinnati, he was promoted to Buffalo by November.

played. A lot of guys wanted to play for Montreal, but I didn't care. I just wanted to be drafted, and I knew I'd have a better chance of making it with an expansion team."

In the second round of the draft, Imlach wanted to pick defenseman Bill Hajt, while John Andersen preferred Craig Ramsay. With Martin in the fold, Imlach planned to concentrate on defense, because the Sabres couldn't continue to allow their goalies to get shell-shocked every night. Crozier, Daley and Dryden had faced 2,800 shots in 1970-71, still a Sabres single-season record even though the NHL schedule has been expanded. But Andersen was adamant about Ramsay, arguing that he was the best player available on the board at that time. Imlach had hired Andersen for a reason, and this was it, so the general manager deferred to the scouting director and selected Ramsay. Fourteen picks later, in the third round, Hajt was still available and Imlach got him, too. The other three players Imlach chose in that draft never played for the Sabres, but Martin, Ramsay and Hajt went on to appear in a combined 2,605 games for Buffalo.

"If anybody else ever got three players of that quality in three picks, I haven't heard of it," Imlach said.

Two weeks before the draft, Imlach had made two other key additions to the team, beating the trading deadline by five minutes when he sent Daley to Detroit in exchange for checking center Don Luce and defenseman Mike Robitaille.

"I remember Punch calling me at my summer home in Canada, and I just about jumped through the roof I was so happy because I didn't like playing in Detroit," Robitaille said. "I wasn't getting much ice time there, and I hadn't gotten much ice time when I was with the Rangers, either, so this was my first chance to be a regular in the National Hockey League."

Luce had also played sparingly for the Red Wings and Rangers, and like Robitaille, was thrilled to be coming to a young team like Buffalo because he knew he would get a regular shift.

"I was happy to get to a team where I felt I would get a chance to play," Luce said. "Punch was gathering players that he felt had ability, players who were on the edge of making the NHL. Back then, players had to play in the minors before they got a shot at the NHL, but he knew two years in the draft wasn't going to be enough. Punch had to wheel and deal, and he was very good at that."

Martin was an instant hit, and Luce and Robitaille certainly improved the club, but it became apparent early in the season that some of the veterans from the previous year weren't going to be very productive. Don Marshall was already gone, lost in the intra-league draft

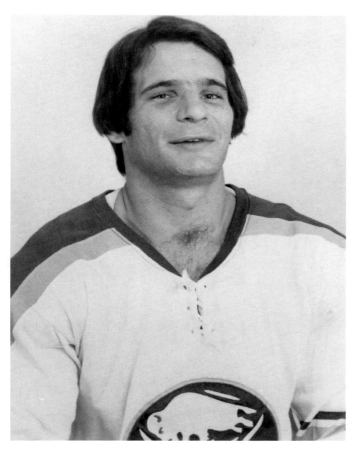

Don Luce (above) and Mike Robitaille (left) both came to the Sabres from the Detroit Red Wings in a trade for goalie Joe Daley in May of 1972.

to the Leafs. Floyd Smith was 36, and six games into the season, Imlach approached Smith and basically told him it was time to retire. Rather than just release Smith, a friend who had also played two years for him in Toronto, Imlach offered Smith a chance to start his inevitable coaching career by becoming Imlach's assistant. Smith agreed, and hung up his skates. Dick Duff retired after eight games, and Phil Goyette and Eddie Shack weren't scoring nearly enough goals to warrant Imlach keeping them around.

The Sabres had started their own minor league affiliate in Cincinnati with Imlach's most loyal friend, Joe Crozier, coaching the team. The Swords got off to a good start and were winning regularly in the American Hockey League, so clearly, the Sabres had some prospects on the farm. Rather than break that team up, Imlach let them play together and accrue valuable game experience. However, when Duff retired, he did pluck Ramsay off the Cincinnati roster, and like Martin, Ramsay proved right away he was going to have a great future in the NHL.

Imlach acquired Larry Mickey in a trade for Larry Keenan midway through November, and sent Doug Barrie and Mike Keeler to Los Angeles for Mike Byers and Larry Hillman in mid-December. Still, the team was struggling terribly and, following an 8-1 rout at the hands of the Leafs on December 18 in Toronto, the Sabres stood 6-21-6.

Imlach was frustrated by the team's inability to continue the upward swing it had enjoyed at the end of its first year. He was putting in substantially long hours trying to

Above: Joe Crozier had been associated with Punch Imlach since the early 1950s, and Imlach hired Crozier to be the head coach of the Cincinnati farm team in 1971. When Imlach suffered a heart attack in January of 1972, Crozier was named coach of the Sabres.

Right: Larry Mickey was a journeyman veteran who was acquired in a trade during the 1971-72 season, and he was a steadying influence for the youthful Sabres.

juggle coaching with general managing, and on the afternoon of January 7, 1972, it all caught up to him. He and Smith were sitting in his office and Imlach was talking to Joe Crozier on the telephone when he began to feel pains in his chest. He gave the phone to Smith, but did not call his doctor because the pain subsided within a couple of minutes.

A few hours later, Imlach was again talking to Crozier when the pain returned, and this time it did not go away. The 54-year-old Imlach suffered a massive heart attack, and that day marked the end of his coaching career in Buffalo.

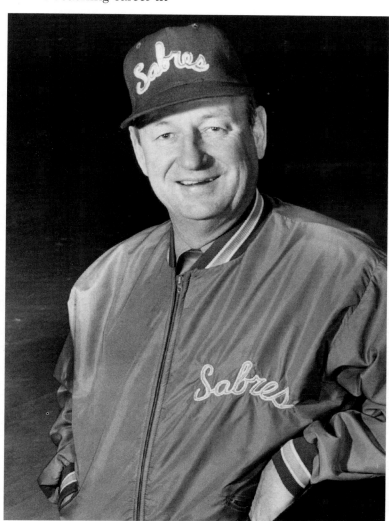

"There was nothing I could do, I was away in Cincinnati, and I couldn't help him," Crozier said, recalling that awful day when he thought he was going to lose his best friend. "He meant so much to me, I was just praying and hoping everything would work out for him. It was very scary, very upsetting."

Imlach spent the next 25 days in Deaconess Hospital in Buffalo, including 12 days in the intensive care unit, and after returning to his home in Toronto to recuperate, he only saw the team play one more game that year, the season finale at the Aud on April 2 against Philadelphia. On that night, Meehan gave Imlach quite a thrill, scoring a goal with four seconds left to play that in addition to producing a 4-3 victory, eliminated the Flyers from the playoff race.

"Obviously we were concerned, and I think we were surprised, we had a sense that the invincible person was not invincible," Meehan said recalling the atmosphere around the locker room upon learning Imlach had fallen ill. "I just remember that in hockey, regardless of whether someone gets ill, there's a death in the family, your wife has a baby, your coach gets sick, you go play. And that's what we did, we went and played."

Punch Imlach's coaching career came to an end when he suffered a heart attack. He continued as the Sabres general manager until 1978. (Photo courtesy of Ron Moscati)

Within hours after Imlach had been stabilized following his heart attack, he sent word to the Knoxes through his wife, Dodo, that although Smith was technically his assistant coach and he ran most of the practices, he felt Joe Crozier should be brought to Buffalo to coach the Sabres, Smith should go to Cincinnati, and Fred Hunt should be made acting general manager.

Two nights after Imlach was stricken, Smith coached the team to a 2-1 loss against Toronto because there wasn't time to get Crozier to Buffalo, but Crozier was behind the bench on January 13, making his NHL coaching debut in a 5-2 loss to the Rangers.

PROFILE - Joe Crozier

Crozier and Imlach had a special friendship that to this point had spanned more than 20 years, dating to 1951 when Crozier and future Hall of Famer and Canadian icon Jean Beliveau teamed together on the power play unit for Imlach's Quebec Aces, the senior team in the Quebec League with which he began his coaching and management career.

Crozier remained with the Aces as a player for a few years, and then his duties increased exponentially when he, Imlach and a couple of other investors bought the team. For a short time, Crozier was a player, coach, general manager and owner because Imlach had left in 1957 to become coach of the Springfield Indians, Boston's farm club in the American Hockey League.

Imlach spent one season in Springfield, taking the Indians to the Calder Cup finals where they lost to Hershey, before he was hired by the Maple Leafs as general manager in 1958. A year later, Crozier sold his shares in the Quebec team and Imlach convinced him to go to Rochester – Toronto's farm club in the AHL – as a player. By this time, Imlach had also assumed the Leafs' coaching duties. Late in the 1959-60 season he called Crozier up to the Leafs, and at the age of 31, Crozier played the only five NHL games of his career.

Crozier returned to Rochester for one more season, scoring 14 points in 35 games, then retired as a player in the spring of 1961. Knowing his future was in hockey as a coach, general manager, or both, he went to Charlotte of the Southern League "to learn the business." Two years hence, suitably trained, Imlach called Crozier and asked him to come back north and coach Rochester in the AHL.

With players like Al Arbour, Larry

Hillman, Bronco Horvath, Dick Gamble, Don Cherry and Gerry Cheevers, Crozier guided the Americans to the AHL's Calder Cup championship in 1965, then repeated the feat in 1966 even though Cheevers had graduated to the Boston Bruins.

"I felt I was one of the better coaches because I had a great teacher," Crozier said of Imlach. "He was the best coach

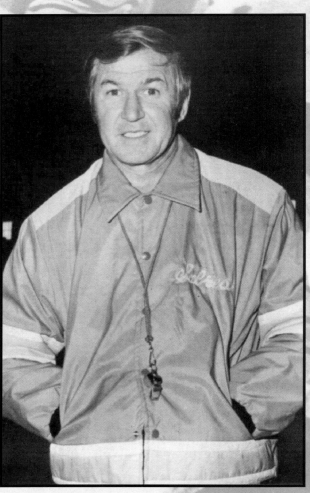

and general manager that ever existed. He had brought me along, helped me in a lot of ways."

Crozier's Americans lost to Pittsburgh in the 1967 finals, then won the Calder Cup again in 1968. His three Cups in four years made Crozier a hot property and the Western League's Vancouver

Canucks pried him away for the 1968-69 season. Vancouver, like Buffalo, had been spurned in the 1967 NHL expansion, but it was a mortal lock that Vancouver was to be part of the next expansion in 1970. The minor league Canucks were being groomed to go into the NHL, and the thinking was to put Crozier in place now as coach, and when the team was admitted to the NHL, it would already have a key position filled.

Crozier had a different plan. He, Imlach and renowned hockey broadcaster Foster Hewitt had bought shares in the Canucks a few years earlier, and they were hoping to purchase the franchise when Vancouver entered the NHL. Imlach went to his grave believing that Stafford Smythe got wind of his plan, convinced the NHL there was a conflict of interest, and that prompted the NHL to seek other ownership groups for the Canucks. Ultimately, the league settled on a Minneapolis-based company called Medicor.

Knowing Crozier's intentions, Medicor's Tom Scallen fired Crozier midway through the 1968-69 season, even though Crozier had the Canucks so far ahead in their division, they could have quit playing right then and still made the playoffs. In fact, that Vancouver club, playing Crozier's system, went on to win the league championship, in effect giving Crozier four championships in five years.

After Imlach was fired by the Leafs, and before he had begun speaking to the Knoxes about the Buffalo job, Imlach was offered Vancouver's general manager position by Scallen. Imlach told Scallen he would take the job only if he could hire Crozier as coach, and when Scallen refused, Imlach told him "no deal."

A few weeks later, Imlach was being introduced as coach and general manager in Buffalo, and Crozier – after spending time cleaning up his affairs in Vancouver and serving part-time as a sportscaster – would join the organization a year later as coach of the farm team in Cincinnati.

"To me, this is a mission of help for the best friend I have in the world," Crozier said just before his debut against the Rangers. "I've waited a long time to make it to the National Hockey League, but believe me, I'd rather never have made it than do it

under these circumstances with Punch sick."

Despite his stated life-long goal of coaching an NHL team, when Seymour Knox informed Crozier he was being promoted to the big club, Crozier wasn't exactly elated. His Cincinnati club – led by future Sabres Tracy Pratt, Butch Deadmarsh, John Gould, Hugh Harris and Rick Dudley – was hovering around the .500 mark at the time of Crozier's departure, but he knew the team had vast potential, and he was right. Cincinnati wound up reaching the Calder Cup semifinals in 1972

before losing to Baltimore, and in 1972-73, the Swords had a record of 54-17-5 and won the Calder Cup. The 54 victories were an AHL record that stood until 1993 when Binghamton won 57 games.

"I had a powerhouse in Cincinnati, a team that I thought I could win another championship with," Crozier said. "Coming up here, it wasn't a very good team, so there was a little hesitation on my part. But because of Punch's heart attack, I had to come. I was the best man in the organization, he chose me to do the job, and I came up to do it."

Just because Imlach wasn't going to be at the Aud didn't mean he was going to take his finger off the Sabres' pulse. A week after his heart attack, he was lying in his hospital bed when John Andersen told Dodo to tell the boss that a player named Jim Lorentz was available if the Sabres were willing to give the Rangers a second-round pick in the next amateur draft. Imlach gave the go-ahead, and Lorentz joined the team.

And less than two months later, while resting in his Toronto home, he pulled the trigger on perhaps the most important trade the Sabres made in their first decade of existence. On March 4, Imlach dealt the ever-popular Shack to Pittsburgh for right winger Rene Robert, the player who would eventually join forces with the already dangerous duo of Perreault and Martin to form the fabled French Connection line.

By trading Shack, the Sabres unloaded one of the most comical characters to ever skate in the NHL, a man who

Above: Jim Lorentz came to the Sabres in a trade from the New York Rangers. He had spent the past few years bouncing around from Boston to St. Louis to New York, unable to get a regular shift. The trade to Buffalo jump-started his career.

Right: Acquiring Rene Robert was one of the most important moves Punch Imlach made because he was the perfect right winger to fit with Gilbert Perreault and Rick Martin. Robert joined the Sabres in March of 1972, played a few games with Perreault and Martin and the trio clicked immediately. The following year, The French Connection was born.

Left: Eddie Shack packed his bag after learning that the Sabres had traded him to Pittsburgh in exchange for Rene Robert.

Below: The Sabres used their second pick in the 1972 amateur draft to select Larry Carriere, a rugged stay-at-home defenseman.

Imlach used to call Eddie the Entertainer. He played an invaluable role in Buffalo because he kept his young teammates loose and upbeat in the face of their incessant losing, and he kept the fans laughing. However, Imlach knew that Shack's personality also illuminated the bumbling nature of his team, and the time had come to clarify for the fans the difference between being entertained at a hockey game, and witnessing entertaining hockey.

The day after the Robert deal, Imlach sold Phil Goyette to the Rangers, and traded Chris Evans to St. Louis for a second-round pick in the 1972 amateur draft which he wound up using to select defenseman Larry Carriere.

The Sabres lost their first three games following the Robert transaction, but they went 3-2-4 the rest of the way and that little surge enabled them to avoid the Eastern Division cellar. With a 16-43-19 record for 51 points, they again finished ahead of Vancouver (20-50-8, 48 points), but the only other team they outdistanced was Los Angeles (49 points). Buffalo had dropped 12 points in the standings from the previous year, but with all the roster turnover, the exporting of aging veterans and the importing of young, up-and-coming players, Imlach was convinced this step back was the prelude to many steps forward in the coming years.

"I think we had a group of guys who really wanted to prove that we were legitimate NHL players," Lorentz said. "When you're young, you need that confidence because you don't know if you're good enough to play in the league. That's one of the things we started to find out (at the end of the 1972 season), that a lot of us could develop into pretty good NHL players."

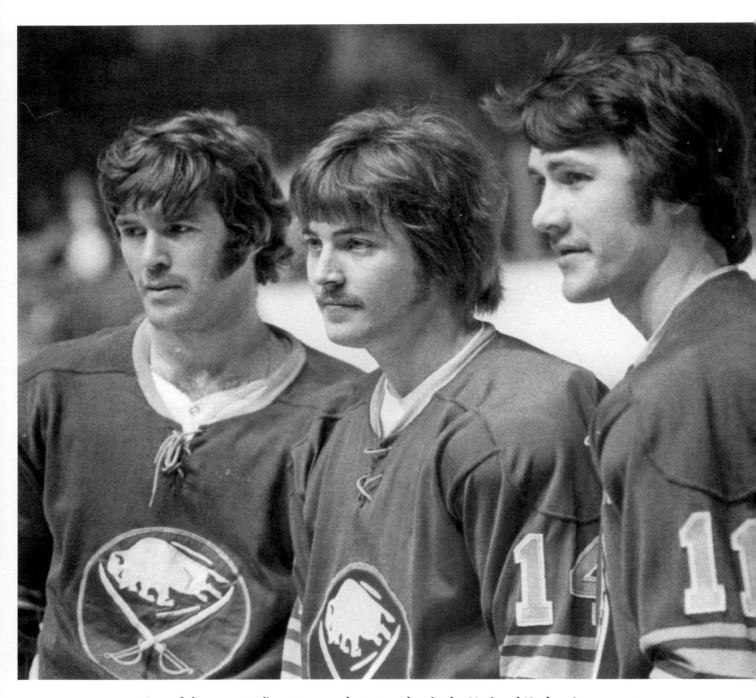

One of the greatest lines to ever skate together in the National Hockey League, The French Connection: From left, Rick Martin, Rene Robert and Gilbert Perreault. (Photo courtesy of Ron Moscati)

Looking Pretty
Good on Paper

Imlach bounced back nicely from his heart attack and he was hard at work during the spring of 1972 looking for ways to continue improving the club. The first step he needed to take was to come to the realization that continuing in his dual role as coach and general manager was no longer the prudent thing to do. So on May 20, 1972, the Sabres announced that Joe Crozier would take over as coach, with Imlach concentrating solely on general manager duties, and Floyd Smith would remain in Cincinnati as coach and general manager of the Swords.

"The doctors tell me I'm all clear to go back to work, with a very few minor restrictions," Imlach said. "And I made my decision to give up coaching based on their recommendations, the feelings of my family, and my own personal attitude. I'll miss coaching because I've always loved it, but the time has come that it's going to have to be one or the other."

With his personal situation cleared up, Imlach began sizing up the Sabres roster, and this is what he was confronted with: He had a few outstanding offensive players (Perreault, Martin and Robert), a couple of demonic defensive forwards (Luce and Ramsay), some complementary two-way forwards (Meehan and Lorentz), pretty good goaltending in Roger Crozier and Dave Dryden, and a weak, inexperienced group of defensemen.

The Perreault-Martin-Robert line had looked very promising at the end of 1971-72, and with a full training camp together under the tutelage of Joe Crozier, Imlach fully expected that unit to be a dynamic offensive force in 1972-73.

"We finished that 1971-72 season pretty strong, scoring a lot of goals and getting a lot of points," Martin said. "When we went into training camp the following year, it was just a matter of building on that because it was obvious we had a pretty good mesh."

"We all knew that we had a natural line with Perreault and Martin, and things really came together when Robert joined the team," Joe Crozier said. "The team hadn't played very well (in 1971-72), but I knew Perreault and Martin could play, and when Robert came, I knew he was going to be the key to that line. He'd be the high guy, and he had a good shot. He had a tough job because I put him out there with two tough guys to play with. One guy (Perreault) barreled down the ice with the puck, and the other guy could really fire it, so where do you fit this fella in? Well, he fit in just right. I put them together and things really started to take off."

Imlach also knew he had a potentially superb checking line with the combination of Luce and Ramsay. Luce had been a wonderful pickup the previous year and was the anchor of the defensive line, in addition to being a master penalty killer. He played in all 78 games, and despite matching up against the opposition's highest scoring lines every night, he was only a minus 18. By comparison, Perreault was minus 40 and Martin minus 38.

Ramsay was even more impressive, finishing at plus 5 in 57 games. When Ramsay was called up from Cincinnati, he was paired with Luce from the start, and they instantly became a pesky pair that frustrated the opposition.

"It was one of those things where we had a feeling right away what the other guy was going to do, a sixth sense or whatever you want to call it," Luce said. "It was easy to play with Craig, and it just sort of came together. Looking back, you wouldn't say it came together very fast, but actually, it did."

Said Ramsay, "Yeah, I thought there was something there right away. We fed off each other, and we believed in us, we believed in what we

Craig Ramsay (above) and Don Luce (right) began playing together on the same line during the 1971-72 season, and their checking and penalty-killing skills meshed perfectly. (Photos courtesy of Ron Moscati)

were doing, we believed in our value and our contributions to the team. I think having all the focus on The French Connection, we didn't allow that to dishearten us, we tried to make it another focus to make us play better. If they had a good shift, we tried to go out and have a good shift on top of them.

"In games that weren't going well, we would try to go out and dominate territorial play, make the other team play in their own end, and then The French Connection would come out behind us with a faceoff in the offensive zone, and they had the skill to make something happen. We tried to be a good second line. We were certainly different, but we had our roles and we believed in what we were doing."

What made Luce and Ramsay special is that not only could they routinely shut down the snipers they were skating against, but they could also turn around and go play offense. When they gained possession of the puck, they didn't just dump it in and head to the bench, they tried to attack.

"I had played against Donnie in junior when I was with Peterborough and he was with Kitchener," Ramsay said. "He was a big strong guy, he had some offense to him, and he wanted to play the game the way I did. His idea of a checking line was not to just follow people around the ice. He was very insistent on trying to score goals. He went to the net hard, he stood around the front of the net. There wasn't a ton of offense right away, but as far as being able to go out and play against good lines and not get scored on, we were pretty good.

"Donnie had a lot of confidence in his ability to perform. He was not afraid to play against Phil Esposito, Jean Ratelle or any of those players. Nothing fazed Donnie, he just played his game. So it was real good for me to play with a guy who had some experience, had the confidence to play, and had an idea of the same style that I liked."

Luce elaborated on those points.

"I enjoyed the checking aspect, but I looked at it a little differently than just being a checker," Luce said. "Coming from juniors when I was a scorer, I looked at playing on the checking line as a way to take advantage of a situation offensively. We were playing against the other team's top scorers, and usually the top scorers don't worry too much about defense. They're a little more lax in their own end, and most of the time, they weren't very good defensively. So you could take advantage of that by playing a strong checking game in your end, and taking the puck from them. We could bottle them up in their own end, and that would frustrate them because they didn't want to be in their end, they wanted to be in your end. I looked at our line as a two-way line that could score goals as well as stop them."

Luce and Ramsay combined for 17 goals in their first year together, and both players felt their scoring totals were only going to increase, especially with the addition of Larry Mickey, who was perhaps the consummate defensive forward because he rarely looked to play offense. With Mickey staying high and protecting against breakouts, it would allow Luce and Ramsay to force the issue on offense when they got the chance.

The other line, with Meehan and Lorentz as the mainstays, gave the Sabres great versatility. Meehan and Lorentz were good enough on offense to play the second half of power play situations, and they were steady enough on defense that they weren't a liability, as the Perreault line often was. Also, Lorentz could play all three forward positions if needed.

Meehan's goal production had dipped from 24 in 1970-71 to 19 in 1971-72, but Lorentz had pumped in 10 goals in the 35 games he played after coming over from the Rangers. It was expected that Meehan would benefit from a full year playing with Lorentz, especially if Crozier could find someone to play right wing with them.

"I really enjoyed playing with Gerry, he was a very intelligent player, very good with the puck, very good defensively," Lorentz said. "I was more of a corner guy, an in-front-of-the-net player, so our combination worked very successfully. We could read off each other very well. I was a natural center-man, but I became adept at playing both wings."

"We used to refer to Jim as the spade man because he was very good at digging pucks out of corners, and what he really excelled at was finding the open man with the puck coming out of traffic," Meehan said. "Jim was a heady, pretty alert guy with the puck. He could steal the puck, he knew how to get in and forecheck, and we developed a pretty good chemistry. I'd move it to him, he'd find a way to get it back to me in the slot and I'd trigger it."

Gerry Meehan (above) had suffered through a disappointing season in 1971-72, but when Jim Lorentz (right) joined the Sabres and was put on Meehan's line, Meehan's scoring problems were solved and he had a huge 1972-73 season.

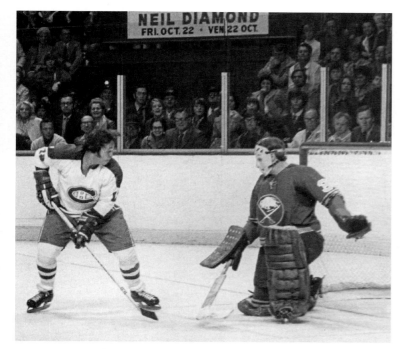

In goal, Roger Crozier had stayed healthy throughout 1971-72 and played in 63 games, posting a respectable 3.51 goals-against average. And his backup, Dryden, was a proven NHL goalie who could step in and perform admirably when called upon.

"Roger was one of the best in the business, but when we had back-to-back games, he couldn't do it very often," Joe Crozier said. "He was very quick and he could come up with the big game for you, but Roger wasn't always well (health-wise) for us. A lot of nights I'd have to wait until after the pre-game warmup to see if he was OK, or would I have to go with Dryden.

"He was a small man and fatigue would set in, so we'd have to go with Dave, and Dave would play well for us. You could use him anytime and he'd work as hard as he could for you. In practice, he'd be the last guy on the ice. Everyone would be shooting at him and he'd stay out there until the last guy was done."

On defense, the Sabres had problems. Larry Hillman was the only solid, reliable veteran defenseman the team had at the end of the 1971-72 season. Robitaille had played well for Buffalo, but he participated in just 31 games due to a shoulder operation and later, a knee injury. Tracy Pratt was on the ice for only 27 games, splitting time between the parent club and Cincinnati. Bill Hajt had sat out the previous year because he wanted to finish college, plus get married, and wasn't prepared to commit to pro hockey. Although he was ready to play again, he wasn't going to be ready for the NHL this year. And Al Hamilton, Chris Evans, Doug Barrie and Jim Watson had either been traded away or left the organization in the offseason.

So it was plainly simple that Imlach had to shore up his back line. He implemented a two-pronged attack to accomplish this goal: Use his first couple of draft picks on defensemen, and lure 42-year-old veteran Tim Horton out of retirement to teach the kids how to play.

PROFILE - Tim Horton

The majority of the players on the Sabres' roster either hadn't been born yet, or were barely eating solid foods, when Horton played his first NHL game with the Toronto Maple Leafs in 1950. He played only that one game in 1950, then was sent back to the Leafs' AHL farm club in Pittsburgh where he spent the next two seasons helping the Hornets reach the Calder Cup finals both years, winning the title under coach King Clancy in 1952.

In 1952-53, Horton made the Leafs out of training camp, and over the next 19 years was Toronto's premier defenseman, carving out a fabled career that produced four Stanley Cup championship rings and six All-Star selections including three times on the first team.

He had played for Imlach all 11 years Punch labored in Toronto, and it was during that time that Horton kissed the Stanley Cup four times.

After Imlach was fired, Horton was traded to the Rangers late in the 1969-70 season and stayed in New York through the end of the 1970-71 season. He came out of retirement to play for Pittsburgh during 1971-72, and though he was limited to 44 games because of a broken ankle, he returned in time to help guide the Penguins into the playoffs for just the second time in their history. He was planning on retiring again when Imlach called to persuade him to come to Buffalo. Imlach said Horton once told him he was never paid

a decent salary until he started retiring every year, and it took $100,000 to convince Horton to join the Sabres. There wasn't a person in the organization who would tell you he wasn't worth every single penny.

"Tim was extremely important to the growth of that team," said Luce. "I had played with Tim in New York before I came to Buffalo, so I knew Tim coming in. He added to the whole team, not just to the defensemen who he took under his wing and taught so many things. He was such a force back there, such a steadying influence. He knew how to ride the low times and how to take advantage of the high times. He kept everyone in a mode of confidence. With his experience back there, when you were on the ice with Tim, you knew that if you screwed up, he's probably going to stop them for you and cover up your mistake. He made the forwards think that we could take more chances, and when you do that and it works out, you gain more confidence and you're willing to take more chances."

Ed Westfall spent the first 11 years of his career with the Boston Bruins and he knew all too well how good Horton was. The year Horton joined the Sabres, Westfall moved to the expansion New York Islanders and became that team's first captain. He remembered thinking that Buffalo's signing of Horton was going to be a key move.

"When Tim Horton came over, he brought a lot of stability to them," said Westfall, who now is an analyst on Islanders television broadcasts. "Imlach was running the show, and I remember thinking when they got Tim Horton, 'Can you imagine all these young guys all of a sudden playing on the same team with a guy who already

Photo courtesy of Ron Moscati

has such a tremendous history.' He could still play fairly well then, and he had a great work ethic. No one ever outworked him, so for those young players to see what kind of a work ethic he had at the end of his career, that was going to be important. He made everybody a little better. He was such a visible person with all his great years with Toronto. When they made that move, I knew they'd be a better team."

Horton was voted the Sabres' most valuable player in 1972-73 as he single-handedly solidified Buffalo's defensive corps.

"Tim was the greatest as far as I'm concerned," Joe Crozier said. "I've never met another individual like him with his dedication, and the way he helped the kids. He was 42 years old, yet he was first in everything we ever did. If we were running, he was the first guy there and the first guy back, same thing if we were doing sprints on the ice. The guy was unbelievable. And he meant so much to the kids on the back end, like Robitaille and Schoenfeld and Carriere. It took so much off of me because he did so much for them."

Imlach talked him out of retiring again after the 1972-73 season, bumped his salary to almost $150,000 for 1973-74, and also granted Horton's request of a Ford Pantera, a hot new sports car that Horton – an automotive enthusiast – had to have.

It was in that Pantera that Horton's life came to a tragic and violent end.

The Sabres were playing the Leafs in Toronto on Wednesday night, February 20, 1974. Two days earlier, Horton had suffered a fractured jaw in practice, and the pain was bad enough that Horton begged out of practice Tuesday and drove to his home in Oakville, Ont. He owned a growing chain of donut shops in southern Ontario and Western New York called Tim Horton's Donuts, and he was going to tend to some business, then meet the team in Toronto on Wednesday for the game.

When he arrived at Maple Leaf Gardens, doctors informed him of the fracture, then refused to inject a pain-killer because they didn't think a 44-

year-old man should be taking that type of shot. Despite great pain, Horton dressed anyway, and through the first two periods was one of the best players on the ice. However, he was unable to continue in the third period, and the Sabres ultimately lost, 4-2. Although he missed most of the final 20 minutes, Horton was still named one of the three stars in the game.

The team bused back to Buffalo, but Horton had his beloved Pantera, so he was going to drive back on his own. At approximately 4:30 a.m. on Thursday, February 21, Horton was speeding down the Queen Elizabeth Way when he lost control of his vehicle just outside of St. Catharines, Ontario. Horton was not wearing a seatbelt, and when the car flipped over, he was ejected. Police reasoned that the car – which ended up tumbling through the median and stopping in the opposite lanes – probably rolled onto Horton's body, breaking his neck and killing him.

In Horton's wallet was Joe Crozier's phone number, so Crozier was the first to learn of the accident.

"When they called me to come down and identify the body, I couldn't believe that this could ever take place," Crozier recalled. "When I lost Tim Horton, damn it, I lost my heart."

While the entire team was saddened by the death of its leader, it was the young defensemen who Horton had tutored who were particularly devastated.

"I think of Timmy every day of my life," Robitaille said. "He has never left my mind. He made the biggest impact in my life of anyone I've ever been involved with in hockey. He never taught me a damn thing verbally about hockey, but I learned things from watching him. I learned how to play angles, putting players at bad angles so when they shoot they can't score. I didn't know any of that stuff early in my career.

"I became an experienced player because of Tim, he was everything to me, my mentor, my hero. I idolized him. I used to stand at the blue line during warmups the way Tim did. He would

stand there and take his one foot and bring the heel of his skate up, so I did the same thing just because Tim did.

"I'll never forget the first game we played after he died (that same night, February 21 at the Aud against the Atlanta Flames). It was an awful night to walk in and see his locker stall empty. You had a feeling like he was a safety net for all of us. When he walked in the dressing room everything was OK, Timmy's here. When he wasn't there, we were a little helter skelter, you felt things could fall apart. He was the glue, just his presence, his past experience, and being the person that he was."

Carriere was 22 years younger than Horton and one of those players who hadn't been born when Horton broke into the NHL. He occasionally roomed on the road with Horton, and it was like being at home in his native Montreal because Horton was the same age as Carriere's father.

"At that age you're so impressionable off the ice, everything would happen so fast, but he was like a built-in father figure," Carriere said. "I had the utmost respect for how he still played the game, even after 20 years of playing. I used to be so impressed with him and the Leafs defensive corps on those teams from the 60s when they won all those Cups.

"He was the ultimate professional, and that helped the development of Schony and myself. He showed us the work ethic that was needed to not only play at this level, but stay at this level. I can remember going into some of the tough buildings like Philly, Boston and Montreal, and you look over and you think, 'This guy has been through 20 years of this.'

"It gives you a very reassuring attitude towards some of the tougher games. Montreal would be coming at us 100 miles per hour, but he'd calm us down. Tim was our leader, he was there for us all the time. If we had any concerns on the ice or off, anything, Tim made it easier for us."

Perhaps the saddest night in the history of the Sabres' franchise, February 21, 1974. Early that morning, defenseman Tim Horton was killed in an automobile crash. That night, the Sabres had to play the Atlanta Flames at the Aud and before the game, the team stood at the blue line and honored Horton with a moment of silence.

Imlach knew this was the type of effect Horton would have on the team, so when the Penguins left him unprotected in the intra-league draft on June 5, 1972, Imlach claimed him, figuring he'd be able to talk Horton into playing.

A few days later, Imlach used the fifth overall pick in the first round of the amateur draft to select Jim Schoenfeld, a hulking defenseman from the Niagara Falls Flyers, and used the second-round choice he had obtained in the Chris Evans trade a few months earlier to pick Carriere No. 25 overall out of Montreal's Loyola University.

When the draft proceedings concluded in Montreal, Imlach flew back to Buffalo feeling like he had really improved the Sabres. Within a matter of weeks, his enthusiasm was severely tempered by the reality that the fledgling World Hockey Association was going to make his and every other general manager's life a living hell.

Just as he had done when he created the American Basketball Association to provide competition and headaches for the established National Basketball Association, California businessman Gary Davidson founded the WHA for the same reason, and the rebel league's effect on the NHL nearly drove Imlach out of hockey in the turbulent summer of 1972.

The WHA debuted with 12 teams, including franchises in major media markets such as New York, Los Angeles, Philadelphia, Chicago and Houston. Its owners had pockets deeper than the Atlantic Ocean, and they began offering star NHL players huge contracts in an effort to lure them to the new frontier. Some took the bait, most notably Bobby Hull, who bolted from the Chicago Blackhawks to sign a landmark $2.75 million deal to coach and play for the Winnipeg Jets, including a $1 million upfront bonus.

Boston's Derek Sanderson, John McKenzie, Ted Green and Gerry Cheevers, Montreal's J.C. Tremblay, Philadelphia's Bernie Parent and Toronto's Dave Keon were other name players who abandoned the NHL, and in 1973, the great Gordie Howe left Detroit to join his two sons, Mark and Marty, with the Houston Aeros.

The purge did not stop there, though. Because they needed to bolster their rosters, the WHA owners also lobbed lavish offers at rookies and mediocre NHL players, and not surprisingly, many of those players jumped at the money. And why not? At this time, professional athletes were not making the staggering sums they make today, and NHL payrolls were by far the lowest of the four major team sports.

"When the WHA came along, it had the effect of doubling and tripling salaries," said Meehan, who because of the rival league received a salary in 1972-73 that was more than triple what he had made in 1971-72. "The year before, I was making about $20,000, so the New England team in the WHA approached me with a three-year contract at $75,000 per season.

"I drove down from Toronto one summer day and I told Punch, I've got this offer from New England for $75,000 a year for three years. He came in the room, put the numbers on the table, and it was for somewhere in the neighborhood of $70,000, $75,000 and $90,000 for three years. He said, 'Gerry, we know you were an important part of our team last year and we're counting on you to be that way this coming year. I'm making you this offer on one condition – it stays open for your acceptance for one hour.' He matched their offer, and went a little better. But I think Punch knew that I wasn't doing any negotiating because I wanted to stay here, my family was happy here. I had no intention of leaving Buffalo, especially if Buffalo's offer was anywhere near the level that New England offered me."

While Meehan stayed, a number of players in the Sabres organization took the leap, including Al Hamilton, Jim Watson, Paul Andrea, Steve Cuddie, George Morrison, Jim McMasters, Gilles Gratton, Mike Byers and Danny Lawson. What the WHA did was tear apart the depth of NHL teams, and in the case of a new organization such as Buffalo's, the WHA

Defenseman Jim Schoenfeld, shown in the uniform of his Niagara Falls junior team, was the Sabres' first-round choice in the 1972 amateur draft.

defections created serious gaps on the roster, not only in Buffalo, but in Cincinnati. Equally frustrating for Imlach was the fact that because the WHA had driven up salaries, players in Cincinnati had to be paid far more than they were worth just to keep them in the system.

"I know looking back and reflecting on what I've heard, Punch felt betrayed in many ways by the business of hockey and by the players who he basically had rescued from oblivion in the minors," Meehan said. "I think he felt a little bit resentful, not so much toward the players themselves, but to the system. He was always sort of a paternalistic kind of guy, even though he had this gruff exterior. I think the business of hockey changed dramatically for all of those (general managers and coaches) that summer, and having been a general manager, I can relate to that, and I know I suffered the same frustrations over the years, seeing costs going beyond your ability to control them, and your only response is to either move the player, or pay the exaggerated price."

Like Meehan, Joe Crozier benefited greatly from the WHA because in 1974, he was offered a substantial pay raise by the Vancouver Blazers to leave Buffalo and come coach their team, and he took it. But he was no fan of the rebel league that first year.

"I knocked it when it first started, but I ended up joining the WHA in 1974," Crozier said. "It was a good thing for other players to play in a high-level league who weren't going to get an opportunity to play in the NHL. But what I didn't like is they were taking some of the good kids out of the NHL, and then they took some superstars for drawing power. In the end it really didn't work because outside of a couple of teams, they didn't draw very well.

"Every general manager had a tough time because they were afraid they were going to lose guys to the WHA. They were throwing money around like it was going out of style. It was a rough time for them all and I know Punch went through a tough time."

So tough that Imlach thought about the aggravation of having to fight for the services of players, factored in his heart attack, and came to the conclusion that maybe it was time to get out of hockey and move on to new challenges in his life. He actually went so far as to type a letter of resignation that he was going to hand-deliver to the Knoxes in July. He never did let his bosses see that letter. Instead, as he had done all his life, he rolled up his sleeves, put up his dukes, and came out of almost every distasteful negotiation unbloodied. Imlach signed or re-signed every player he felt was an integral part of the organization, and when it was time for the club to go to training camp, there weren't any distractions.

The Crow Cracks the Whip in Training Camp

Horton hated practice, just flat out despised it. In his last years in Toronto, and then when he played with the Rangers and Penguins, Horton would make sure he didn't sign his new contract until late in training camp; therefore, he'd miss the drudgery of practicing. He was fond of saying, "What I get paid for is the practices. I would play the games for free because they're fun, they make it all worthwhile. It would be nice to go to sleep and wake up ready for the season."

However, Horton shocked Imlach by signing his new deal with Buffalo almost a week before veterans were scheduled to report to the Sabres' training camp. Had Horton known what he was in for at Camp Crozier, he likely would have stuck to his old policy.

Thirty-five players, mostly rookies and minor leaguers, checked in at the Garden City Arena in St. Catharines, Ontario, on the morning of Wednesday, September 6. This was Crozier's first day of training camp as an NHL coach, and as the players dressed in the malodorous, cramped locker room, Crozier was already skating around on the ice, a lion waiting to feast on the Christians, Andy Cipowicz preparing to shake down a suspect.

Crozier knew he had a monumental chore in front of him, trying to mold a collection of predominantly young, inexperienced players into a competitive club that could possibly challenge for a berth in the playoffs, and he knew the only way to achieve that objective was through hard work. Little did those players know that the moment they filed onto the ice that morning, they were beginning a month-long ordeal in which they would work about as vigorously as the dogs in the Iditarod.

In that first week before the veterans arrived, Crozier put the kids through two practices every day, and when Horton and the veterans checked in, the work increased as some of the practices were replaced by hard-driving scrimmages. The only break the players were given from this rigid program were on days when there was an exhibition game to be played. Crozier demanded maximum effort, and if the players didn't give it to him, he made it clear that they wouldn't be with the team.

Joe Crozier was the perfect coach for the youthful Sabres because he taught them fundamentals.

"He wanted one thing from a player, and that was for you to give everything you had on the ice, and if you didn't do that, you were in trouble with him," said Lorentz. "That's what I respected most about Joe. I thought he was a great coach for that particular team because we needed discipline, and he gave us that discipline. That was important. We needed direction and he gave us direction."

And it didn't matter if the player was Pratt or Perreault, Harris or Horton, Crozier was tough on everyone.

"We always worked hard because that was our job," said Perreault. "Joe didn't like to lose so everytime we had a little bit of a struggle, Joe was there to really give it to us with hard practices. Every coach, that's his job, to do that to keep pressure on the players and make you realize you have to work hard to be a winner."

Crozier's methods were unorthodox at times, but he usually produced results.

Martin had a habit of shifting only one way when he was breaking in on goal from his left wing position, so Crozier moved him to right wing during various scrimmages, therefore making him diversify his moves. "He was young and feisty, and he didn't want to be told sometimes, but he listened,"

Crozier said of Martin.

On some days, Crozier would furrow a multitude of eyebrows by moving Perreault back to defense for a couple of shifts, just to broaden his horizons. "Gil can play other positions, and it doesn't do him any harm to play other positions," Crozier said at the time. "If I use him on the power play, he can finish that shift on defense and then play his regular shift. He would make a fine defenseman, but no, I have no plans on switching him."

Carriere remembers Crozier threatening to send him to tap dance lessons to improve his turning. "He told me my left foot wasn't going as good as my right foot when I was turning, so he says, 'I want you to go take tap dance lessons,'" Carriere said. "I'm thinking, 'Tap dance lessons? I don't think so.' He knew I wasn't too excited about that, and he said we'd talk about it later, but then he kind of forgot about that."

Laugh if you want, but Crozier still believes in that method. "Eddie Shore used to give all his guys tap dance lessons to help with their quickness and agility," Crozier said.

"I'll tell you what, he was the only coach who taught me tricks that I could use in games," Martin said. "Little stuff like how to use your legs, how to hold a guy without getting caught, how to tie a guy up, how to attack a certain player. He was very good at spotting little nuances in the game, little fine points."

"My strength was teaching and motivation in the locker room," Crozier said. "There were so many things I taught them, they probably got sick and tired of listening to me, but I had to give it to them if they were going to improve. This was a young team, and I had to coach them.

"I showed them where they should be on the ice, I actually marked the ice with red paint to show them where they were supposed to be. I showed them where to go when they were killing penalties, I taught them off the faceoff, how to play in their own end. I spent so much time teaching, but I knew that's what I had to do because I knew what would happen if I didn't. We were an expansion team, this was the NHL, you've got to work. I bore down on those fellas.

"I believed in teaching in any hockey I ever coached. I always looked at coaches and thought there was more than just skating and shooting. I've always thought you could teach players how to play and how to play better. That was my theory, that they would get better, and that's exactly what happened."

That was especially true of the rookies such as Schoenfeld and Carriere. Crozier knew the key to any success this team might have was going to hinge on its defensive play, a scary proposition considering two of the regulars were going to be those rookies. So he paid special attention to them during camp, properly schooling them in the fundamentals and making sure they understood their roles in every possible situation.

"Joe used to take the young guys down to one end of the rink and work with us," Carriere said. "He was always reassuring us that we were doing well, and that gave us the confidence we needed. Joe went out of his way to spend time with the young people, especially Schony and myself."

"I remember Larry and I sort of as a twosome because we got a lot of instruction from Joe," Schoenfeld said. "We were gung-ho guys trying to make our way into the league, and he'd take us both aside and teach us. I thought Joe was real good for us as young players coming into the league.

"I think he did two things – he gave us very sound instruction and special attention, and the second thing, he was a good coach in that he recognized that a great part of the teaching process was having a player become a mentor, and that's where Timmy came into it."

Everyone who played for Crozier has a story to tell, but there are two that seem to rank among the most popular.

One was the time at the Aud when he sent Perreault, the best skater on the team, out for the pre-game skate all by himself, while he made the rest of the team watch him on the television monitors in the locker room.

"That was back when they were first starting to use TVs so the coaches could watch tapes between periods and tell the players what was going on," Luce said. "We hadn't played well the night before (in a 1-1 tie with the woefully inept expansion New York Islanders), and Joe felt the team wasn't skating very well. We're in the locker room, getting dressed for the warmup, Joe comes in, and now we're not going out for the warmup. Everyone was like 'What the hell's going on here.' What he did was send Gilbert out to skate alone.

"Joe's telling us 'Now watch Gilbert skate.' Gilbert's out there skating around and Joe says 'Skate like that, skate like Gilbert, hard and fast.' So we're all watching, and you could see Gilbert looking around, not sure what's going on. The other team is looking at him, we still haven't come out, and he's wondering what he should do. Meanwhile, we're in the locker room kind of chuckling to ourselves."

"That was a little embarrassing," Perreault said. "But everybody was laughing about it, I guess, because it was so funny. Joe had his own style, but we always got along very well with him. Sometimes he was tough on the players, but that's the way it has to be. If you don't perform, that's why you have a coach. He's there to get the best out of you."

Then there was the time in Vancouver when Crozier, sensing his team was lifeless, tried to light their fire by lacing up his skates and joining them for the pregame warmup.

"Joe had long ties to Vancouver that went back to the days with Punch when they owned that team, and he hated to lose in Vancouver," Lorentz recalled. "We were at the end of a road trip, we hadn't done well, and he was looking for something to get us going. We were sitting there in the dressing room before the pregame skate and Crow brought a chair into the middle of the room, started taking off his suit, his tie, his shirt, and he put on this old red sweatsuit that he used to skate around with, and he put his skates on. We had no idea what he was doing. I'm sure this is the first time in the history of the NHL a coach had ever done this, but he came out with us for the pregame skate. Don Lever (now a Sabres assistant coach) was playing for the Canucks and they didn't have any idea what was going on. Joe wanted to win, and you can never knock that."

Robitaille remembered the night just as vividly. "That was unbelievable," he said. "He had that red sweatsuit on, and I couldn't believe it. We're out

there skating and all of a sudden, zoom, this red flash goes by us.

"With Joe, you were always thinking, 'What's next?' He was a very good psychologist, he worked on you, pretty well controlled your emotions. He could bring you right up to where there was fire coming out of your eyes. There would be times when you'd come off the ice thinking you had a great game, then he tells you you didn't have a great game, so you're down on yourself. Then the next day you don't think he's ever going to play you again and all of a sudden he says, 'I can't win this game without you, you have to play 25 minutes.'

"He always kept you off-balance, there was no time that you ever felt comfortable. You were on the edge, you were always pushing the envelope right to the edge. We were set to play when we went out the door with him, I can tell you that much."

Lorentz said it's a shame that Crozier never received the proper credit he deserved for the Sabres' run to the Stanley Cup Finals in 1975, their only trip to the NHL championship series. Floyd Smith was coaching the team by then, but Lorentz said, "I think it was the seeds that Joe sowed that really took over in 1974-75 when we went to the Finals. There were a lot of players who played for him that were still on that team. We made the playoffs that year (1972-73), but (playing for Crozier) really reaped benefits a couple years down the road because he's the guy who really taught us how to play."

Not only was Crozier's style a drastic change from the first two years, but the players who were being put through the grind were markedly different, too. After participating in his first day of camp, Meehan was struck by the fact that only five original Sabres were left from the team's inaugural 1970 season – himself, Perreault, Roger Crozier, Dryden and Pratt. "It's funny, I look around and there's no Phil Goyette, no Reg Fleming, no Eddie Shack. This is a different training camp from the other years. We've had quite a turnover since the club started two short years ago."

And according to Imlach, the architect of that turnover, they were certainly changes for the better. After watching practice one afternoon, Imlach said, "Our rookies seem to get better each year. Some of these rookies are superior to the guys we had playing when we started the hockey season two years ago."

Clearly the competition for jobs was keener. In the first two training camps, the roster was pretty much set midway through September because there wasn't a lot of talent to choose from, and the majority of the spots on the depth chart were held by veterans. But with Imlach obtaining younger players through trades the previous year, and then adding the draft picks into the mix, he and Crozier were going to have some tough choices to make.

"Our club didn't play very well last year," Crozier said early in camp. "We were a seventh-place club, so not everyone is assured of a job. I've told these guys the door is open for guys who work hard and show us something. There could be six or seven changes in this hockey club."

Crozier's fondness for scrimmaging would therefore be a useful tool because while drills helped fine-tune the players' skills, game situations via scrimmaging allowed Crozier and Imlach to evaluate vital intangibles such as instincts and timing.

"I'm scrimmaging them more because we have a young club and I can show them their mistakes right there when they make them in a game condition," Crozier said.

It was an approach that Meehan definitely approved of.

"You learn how to play hockey by playing hockey, and that's what we did with Joe," Meehan said. "Skating between pylons and doing all these drills, if they're not related to how you play the game, then they're really just skill development, they're not hockey game development skills.

"Scrimmaging was important to see how players handled their assignments in a game setting, and also how they matched up one-on-one against someone in a competitive atmosphere. It's like telling a kid to skate around a pylon and shoot a puck at an empty net; he'll do it skillfully, but if you put him up against somebody else in a game situation, he'll do it much more aggressively and intensely."

In the early stages of camp, the primary goal was to get the defensive unit in order, and get the pairings figured out. Horton and Hillman were locks to make the team, but the remaining four or five back line slots were up for grabs and Crozier had to choose between Schoenfeld, Carriere, Robitaille, Pratt, Hajt, Paul Terbenche, Ray McKay and Jack Taggart.

One of the first things the coach did when the veterans came in was to put Schoenfeld together with Horton, and Carriere with Hillman. Crozier wanted the two aging veterans to take the rookie draft picks under their wings and teach them the ropes. The other defensemen switched off regularly, always playing with a different partner as Crozier tried to find the proper combinations.

After his first day working with Horton, Schoenfeld said, "Horton can teach me a lot. He could play the game standing still and still be better than most. He's got a lot upstairs."

Crozier's next priority was finding a couple of right wingers, one to play with Luce and Ramsay, another to play with Meehan and Lorentz. The right wing candidates were Rick Dudley, Larry Mickey, Jim Nichols and Ron Busniuk, and in the first few days, Dudley took the initiative and caught Crozier's eye.

"This year Dudley seems to know where the goal is," said Crozier, his coach for part of the previous year in Cincinnati when Dudley had struggled with his shooting. "He's going up and down his wing, working very hard. If I had to pick somebody right now for the right side, it would be Dudley."

With Perreault and Martin absent for the first three weeks of camp because they were members of the Team Canada squad that was opposing the Soviet Union in the historic eight-game challenge series, Crozier continually tinkered with his forward lines. During one stretch of six scrimmages spanning three days, a unit consisting of Meehan, Ramsay and Nichols scored 18 of their team's 26 goals. Nichols, the right wing on that line who had scored 25 goals in Cincinnati the year before, thus replaced Dudley in Crozier's ever-changing penthouse.

Crozier received great news on September 20 when he learned that Perreault and Martin, along with Vancouver's Jocelyn Guevremont and Vic Hadfield of the Rangers, had decided to quit Team Canada because Harry Sinden, the Boston Bruins coach who was running the all-star team, was

To Joe Crozier, physical training was every bit as important as on-ice instruction, so he put the players through a rigorous training camp. Here Don Luce is out in front of his teammates on their daily jog.

not using them. In the case of the two Buffalo stars, it was because Sinden felt they were too young and lacked the necessary big-game experience.

Perreault had played sparingly during the four games that were contested in Canada, while Martin never dressed. When the team went to Sweden to play a couple of exhibitions before the series resumed in Moscow, Martin finally got a chance, but like Perreault, was not a key component of the team. Upon arriving in Moscow and learning that they weren't in Sinden's plans for the final four games, the players decided to come home and join their teammates in preparing for the regular season.

In the exhibition opener in St. Catharines, the Sabres edged California, 3-2, as Luce scored twice within three minutes in the third period, but the next night, they bused to Peterborough, Ontario, and lost to the expansion New York Islanders, 2-1. The Sabres thus became the first team to lose to the Islanders, who had started 0-2-1 in their first three preseason games under coach Phil Goyette, the ex-Sabre.

Crozier was not pleased with that effort, and although the team arrived back in St. Catharines at 2:30 a.m., he had the club back on the ice for practice less than eight hours later.

On September 24, Buffalo beat the Penguins, 3-1, and after the game, Perreault, fresh off a 15-hour flight from Moscow, went strolling into Crozier's office at Garden City Arena and asked what time practice was the next day.

"When Gil walked through the door I felt like I had a new lease on life," Crozier said. "You can see he wants to play."

A couple of days later, Martin arrived in St. Catharines ready to practice, and he and Perreault answered questions about what was being wrongly perceived as their defection from Team Canada.

"Some newspapers said we quit the team because we were dissatisfied with the way things were run," Perreault said. "That's not true. We left because we wanted to get back to our teams to get ready for the season. We weren't playing much, so it wouldn't hurt Team Canada. I didn't play much, but I thought when I did play, I played pretty well. They had a lot of good players, big names. They couldn't use everybody."

Said Martin, "I wanted to pick up my timing and competitive edge. I have no complaints concerning Team Canada. I'm in good shape from practicing with the team, but mentally I need the work that comes from actual games. That's why I came home."

After a disappointing 3-3 tie against California in Oshawa, Ontario, in which Rocky Farr let in the tying goal with 16 seconds left to play, Perreault and Martin made their debuts the following night in a 1-0 victory over Chicago at the Aud. Dudley joined them on their line, but the trio did nothing, and Luce scored the only goal of the game.

To this point, the Buffalo defense had allowed only eight goals in five games, and Crozier pointed to the play of Carriere as one of the reasons. "If Carriere continues playing as he has been, he will be a regular on my hockey club," said Crozier. "He moves the puck right away, doesn't hesitate. Play like that and you get your club out of a lot of trouble in your end."

While Crozier and Imlach were quietly thinking to themselves that this team looked much improved and could very well become a playoff contender if everything fell into place during the season, Pittsburgh general manager Jack Riley became the first person outside of Buffalo to dare think that the Sabres were making strides. Riley watched his Penguins play the Sabres to a 2-2 tie in Brantford, Ontario, and afterwards said, "Buffalo is going to make the playoffs. I really think so. The Sabres now have Tim Horton, a good draft choice in Schoenfeld, have the good goaltending, and their young forwards are going to score more than they did last year."

The exhibition season drew to a close with unique home-and-home doubleheaders on back-to-back nights against the Philadelphia Flyers. In the preliminaries, Buffalo's farm club, Cincinnati, played Philadelphia's farm club, Richmond. It was a good weekend for the Sabres organization as the Sabres lost, 1-0, in Buffalo, then returned the favor with a solid 5-3 victory at the Spectrum as Harris made his bid to make the team with two goals and two assists. Meanwhile, Cincinnati won 3-1 and tied 4-4.

When training camp was over, Crozier kept 22 players in Buffalo and farmed the rest out to Cincinnati, including the fast-finishing Harris. Carriere, Robitaille, Pratt, Hillman, Horton, Schoenfeld, McKay and Terbenche made the team on defense, the centers were Perreault, Luce, Meehan and Lorentz (though he would be moved to wing), the left wings were Martin, Ramsay, Butch Deadmarsh and Randy Wyrozub, the right wings were Robert, Mickey, Dudley and Steve Atkinson, and the goalies were Crozier and Dryden.

"This has been the best training camp I've had in all the time I've been coaching," Crozier said in Philadelphia. "Everybody worked and the results showed tonight."

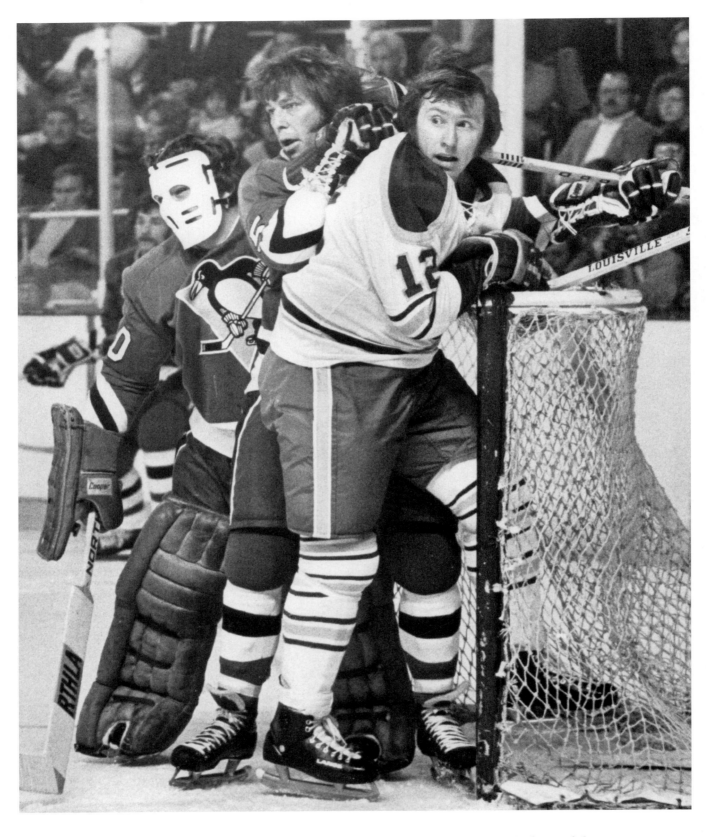

Larry Mickey certainly wasn't a glamour guy. His job was to mix it up in front of the net and he did it very well, as the Pittsburgh Penguins found out in this game.

October: They Might Never Lose

In the October 9, 1972, issue of *Sports Illustrated*, Mark Mulvoy, who would go on to become that magazine's managing editor but was then its hockey writer, had this to say about the Sabres: "It will be a short season for the Vancouver Canucks, Buffalo Sabres and New York Islanders since all three teams can expect to be out of the playoff race by about November 1."

Considering the Sabres' performance the season before, the fact that defending Stanley Cup champion Boston, perennial powerhouse Montreal, the talented New York Rangers, and other established original six teams such as Detroit and Toronto also resided in the Eastern Division, you could not berate Mulvoy for making the assumption that the Sabres stood no chance of breaking into the top four and earning a playoff berth in this, just their third season of existence.

Yes, the NHL had expanded again by two teams, adding the Atlanta Flames and the New York Islanders, and that meant 11 games against very weak competition, a definite benefit for the Sabres. Nonetheless, as Dick Johnston, the optimistic Sabres beat writer for the *Buffalo News*, pointed out in picking the team to finish fifth, making the playoffs would still "probably be a little too much to expect."

However, there was no way to gauge the impact Joe Crozier was going to have on the team; no way to tell how important Robert was going to be to Perreault and Martin; no way to comprehend the influence Horton was going to have on the young defensive corps; no way to foretell what a superb defensive and penalty-killing forward pairing Luce and Ramsay were going to be; no way to know career journeyman Dryden was going to have his finest season ever, taking the heat off Roger Crozier with sterling relief performances. The Sabres were a great mystery, and Mulvoy, Johnston and many of the other hockey experts who expected very little from Buffalo couldn't possibly have predicted this team would suddenly become a contender.

Or could they?

"Looking at the kind of players Punch had assembled, recognizing

Perreault, Martin and Robert were on the verge of exploding offensively, looking at the addition of players like Jim Schoenfeld and Craig Ramsay, Don Luce having come into the organization the year before, to me there was no question the team had the capability to do what it did," said Meehan.

"When you build a hockey team, you build it in components. Many of the media or non-hockey people who were outside the workings of the team may not understand how important components are to a team. And look at the components that Punch began to assemble in the first two years. When you put a Don Luce and Craig Ramsay onto a team that already has Perreault and Martin, that's a powerful offensive-defensive combination. When you talk about a second line that could produce 70-75 goals and close to 200 points, that's an awful lot of points for a second line. And adding a young, aggressive defenseman like Jim Schoenfeld to the mix, who in those days kept everyone in the league on their toes, I don't think it was fair to say that team wasn't going to be competitive."

Ramsay also felt coming out of camp that this team was going to surprise a lot of people.

"We looked around at our team that year and we were young, we got around the ice well, we could battle, we had size and speed," Ramsay said. "We thought, 'What don't we have?' We liked our team, we believed in where we were going with that team. Right away that year we found out we could score goals when we had to, we could hold a lead, we could kill penalties, we had a good power play. Hey, it looked pretty good."

Joe Crozier respected the writers' opinions, but like Meehan and Ramsay, he courteously disagreed with their evaluations.

"I'm optimistic," he said on the eve of the season opener against Atlanta. "We're stronger than last year, and our goal is fourth place. Our defense has improved, but I'll have to see how the season progresses before I know how much. I will say our defense is more mobile and tougher. I think this is going to be a very entertaining year."

The Sabres had allowed 289 goals the year before. Only Los Angeles (305) and Vancouver (297) were more generous to opposing offenses. Joe Crozier, as he had been preaching since the day training camp opened, continued to point to defense as the element that would make or break the season.

"We have to cut down those goals against by 100," Crozier said. Realizing a reduction of 100 would bring that total down to 189, and that only one team had beaten that figure the previous season (Chicago with 166), Crozier amended his statement by saying, "Well, maybe we could settle to holding them below 200. That could be enough. Look at the clubs that made the playoffs last year, look at what they did in this department – Chicago 166, Minnesota 191, New York 192, Boston 204, Montreal 205, Toronto 208. That's the line of defense it takes to win. We can do it, and if we do, we're in the playoffs."

Crozier's enthusiasm was rubbing off on his players, because they were feeling the same way.

"I kind of sensed something because at the time, the Sabres were a young team, they had been in the league only two years, so they had nowhere to go but up," said Robert. "For me to come in and play with Perreault and Martin, who I had played against as a junior, I knew there was a lot of potential."

"You could see the confidence in the guys," Carriere remembered. "Perreault was starting to get comfortable, The French Connection was starting to come, and you can't forget Luce and Ramsay who were a big part of the team. And I think it was great the way they injected enthusiastic guys into the lineup. Plus, not only was the team good here, you had a Calder Cup caliber team in Cincinnati with people chomping at the bit to get up here. When you have that competitive edge in an organization, it pushes people to higher levels."

Luce had certainly been pushed to a higher level as he scored seven goals in eight preseason games. "I was confident in training camp, and I was scoring," Luce recalled. "There are times when you can shoot it in the dark and you know you're going to hit the net, and there are other times, you can be five feet away and not hit the net. I think in that training camp, I felt everything was flowing for me, it was going in the net, and I was hoping it would continue for the whole season."

That confidence, Luce said, stemmed from Crozier's tyrannical training camp because the players could see their progress on a daily basis, and they enjoyed first-hand the rewards of their hard labor.

"Joe's training camp that year was extremely hard," Luce said. "He worked us hard to get us in shape so when we came out of the gate, we'd have an edge. You get confidence that way, and if you're in better shape than your opponent for the first little while, mentally you become confident and you start believing in yourself a little earlier.

"I think Joe knew we had a young team, and part of a successful season, especially for a young team, is to get off to a good start."

But no one – not Crozier, Imlach, or any of the players – could have envisioned the success the Sabres encountered at the start of the season. They went unbeaten for the first month, 6-0-4 through the end of October. Instead of being out of the playoff race by November 1 as Mulvoy had forecast, the Sabres were just two points out of first place, trailing only the 7-0-4 Montreal Canadiens.

"That was a surprise, it always is when you go that long without losing," Robert said. "But we knew this team had talent. There were guys there from the beginning who had talent and they had matured over the first two years. The team just jelled very quickly, and it was because of the character of the players, the coach behind the bench, and what can you say about Punch Imlach drafting all these kids. You have to compliment Punch for putting that team together so quickly."

It began on Sunday night, October 8, 1972, when, in front of the largest crowd to ever witness a hockey game in Buffalo to that point – 15,508, thanks to further renovations in the building – the Sabres skated past expansion Atlanta, 5-3, raising Buffalo's all-time record in season openers to 3-0. The Flames had made their NHL debut the night before on Long Island, defeating the other expansion team, the Islanders, 3-2. Against Buffalo, they played pretty well again, but ultimately fell victim to a balanced

Sabres offense that saw every line contribute to the scoring.

Robert snapped a 3-3 tie just 29 seconds into the third period with an assist from Perreault, and then Perreault notched an insurance goal at 6:58 with the help of Robert. The checking line was represented by Ramsay, who beat Atlanta goalie Dan Bouchard in the second period to provide a 3-2 lead. And the other line was led by Lorentz who scored twice within five minutes in the first period after Bob Leiter had opened the scoring for Atlanta.

In addition to the spread-out scoring, the defense played well in front of Roger Crozier, and the penalty-killing units managed to survive a five-minute man-down situation in the third period that preserved the two-goal lead.

On the opening night of the 1972-73 season, Jim Lorentz scored two goals against the expansion Atlanta Flames to lift the Sabres to a 5-3 victory.

While it looked good to the sellout crowd, and to the players themselves, Crozier was able to find some faults. "We played well enough, but we were a little tight," he said. "We missed too many chances and we weren't tough enough killing penalties. There's no way the score should have been 3-3 after two periods."

He reasoned that weak competition from the Flames brought the Sabres' level of play down. "If we'd played the Boston Bruins in our opener, I think we'd have played better," said Crozier. "That's the trouble with playing a new team, you have a tendency to think it's going to be easy."

This, of course, brought a terse reply from Atlanta coach and legendary hothead Boom Boom Geoffrion. "That guy (Crozier) over there thinks he's going to make the playoffs. Who's he going to beat out? I can get out of last place easier than he can make fourth. After this game, I think I've got as good a team as Crozier has."

Naturally, Crozier had to get in the last word. "I don't have to build up a controversy with him. Our building is sold out for the season. At the end of the year, just look at the standings."

Lorentz, who hadn't scored in the preseason, stood out in this game not only because he scored twice, but because he played all three positions on his line, plus took a regular shift as one of the point men on the power play.

"I don't care where I play, wherever they put me, I'll play there," he said. "Sure I enjoyed scoring those two goals after going through some exhibition games where I didn't even get a shot on net, but the important thing this season is to cut down on our goals against. That's what we're all trying to do."

PROFILE - Jim Lorentz

Night after night for nearly a decade and a half, Lorentz has been perched high above the ice in the press box – first at the Aud, and for the past year in the sparkling new Marine Midland Arena – analyzing Sabres games either for television viewers or radio listeners.

His vantage point is vastly different from the one he occupied down on the Sabres bench during his six and a half years with the team, but even though Lorentz now has to squint to see the action, his eye for the game remains perspicacious. He was one of the most intelligent players to ever wear a Sabres sweater, and his knowledge of the game was vitally helpful to his teammates. And now it is his audience that benefits from his innate ability to break down a game on the fly and explain what happened in a simple, direct style.

"I try to teach as I go along, but without preaching," Lorentz said one night midway through the 1997 season, an hour before a telecast. "My philosophy is that people tune in not to hear me or Rick Jeanneret, they tune in for the hockey game, and I don't want to interfere with that. I try to choose my words carefully, say what I have to say, and shut up and let the people enjoy the game."

Lorentz's broadcast doctrine mirrors the concept he lived by as a player. People didn't flock to the Aud in the 1970s to watch Lorentz play, they came to see The French Connection turn opponents inside out, or Danny Gare whistle slap shots, or Schoenfeld and Jerry Korab deliver crushing body checks. Face it, Lorentz's most memorable performance in a Sabres uniform occurred at the Aud during Game Three of the Stanley Cup Finals against Philadelphia in 1975, and it had nothing to do with hockey. A bat

found its way into the fog-filled arena, and after pestering the players and fans for much of the night, the bat made the fatal mistake of flying too close to Lorentz. Lorentz swatted at the airborn rodent with his stick and connected like Babe Ruth, killing the creature and drawing a huge ovation.

Lorentz was a guy who mucked it up in the corners, checked his wing more efficiently than an IRS auditor, and stood in front of the net setting screens and getting his body beaten until it was black and blue. While his contributions may not have been headline-grabbing, they were invaluable to the Sabres. He was a role player whose role was enormous.

Things haven't changed much today as he sits next to the voluble play-by-play man Jeanneret, a Buffalo icon whose voice reverberates all over Buffalo. When he's on the air, just as he did when he was on the ice, Lorentz picks his spots providently and takes full

advantage of his opportunities by expertly dissecting plays.

It was the Sabres' good fortune on January 13, 1972, that New York Rangers general manager Emile Francis was a man of his word.

"Emile Francis promised to trade me if he wasn't going to use me," Lorentz said, recalling the night he was sent to Buffalo in exchange for a second-round draft choice. "That Rangers team was a great team, there really wasn't any room for me, and Emile kept his promise and traded me and it couldn't have worked out any better. I was thrilled to come here, this is where I wanted to go."

Lorentz had won the Central League scoring title and MVP award in 1967-68 by scoring 101 points as a member of the Oklahoma City Blazers. He broke into the NHL with the Boston Bruins in 1968-69, and during their run to the Stanley Cup championship in 1969-70, he contributed seven goals and 16

assists in 68 games and played in 11 of Boston's 12 playoff games. However, he was buried as the fourth center behind Phil Esposito, Derek Sanderson and Fred Stanfield, and wanted out. So two weeks after Bobby Orr went flying across the goal crease while scoring the Cup-winning goal against the St. Louis Blues, the Bruins dealt Lorentz to the Blues in exchange for St. Louis' first-round draft choice in the 1970 amateur draft.

Given a chance to play a regular shift by St. Louis coaches Scotty Bowman and Al Arbour, Lorentz had 19 goals and 21 assists in 76 games, helping the Blues to a second-place finish in the Western Division before Minnesota pulled a quarterfinal playoff upset, knocking the Blues out in six games.

The Blues were a team in turmoil in 1971-72.

Bowman left to take over the Montreal Canadiens, and the team's front office made the mistake of bypassing Rick Martin in the draft in favor of Gene Carr. Three different men – Sid Abel, Bill McCreary and Arbour – wound up behind the bench coaching that season, but Lorentz missed most of the upheaval because in mid-November, after producing just one assist in 12 games, he was part of a six-player trade with the Rangers that also involved Carr.

The Rangers, though, had little use for Lorentz, and he dressed only seven times. Lorentz spoke to Francis and asked that he trade him to a team he could play for, and Francis obliged. With New York playing the Sabres at the Aud and Lorentz in street clothes again, Francis informed him of the deal to Buffalo, which was officially announced the next day.

"I was traded right in the Auditorium between periods of a game, and I couldn't have been happier," he said. "I played my junior hockey in the area at Niagara Falls, I was familiar with the area and I had some friends here, and I knew I was going to play."

During an interview with Randy Schultz for the book Sabres - 26 Seasons in Buffalo's Memorial Auditorium, Lorentz recalled a humorous anecdote from that night.

"I wasn't dressed for the game that night and was waiting in the dressing room for the team to come in after the first period," he said. "Francis took me aside just as the players were heading out for the second period and gave me the good news. I wanted to get to a pay phone and call my family and friends, but I decided to go to the washroom first. When I came out, the room was empty. Everyone was gone for the second period, including the trainer, who didn't realize I was still there and had locked the main dressing room with me in it. I tried banging on the door, but there's about 50 feet of twisting hallway plus a couple of other doorways leading to the ice to eat up the noise, so I just sat there by myself staring at the walls, busting with this great news, and cooled my heels until the Rangers trooped back in

about 45 minutes later."

He played 35 games for Buffalo after the trade and rang up 10 goals and 14 assists. In the six full seasons that followed with the Sabres, he scored 124 goals and 183 assists for 307 points, never playing fewer than 70 games in any year.

Lorentz had played center for most of his career, but it was his willingness to learn how to play both wings that solidified his spot on the Buffalo roster.

"It was out of necessity, really," he said. "I was a natural centerman, had been throughout my career, but suddenly there were situations when they needed someone to start playing wing, and that someone became me. I had no problem with that, except at first because it was a little difficult.

"I came out of the Bruins organization, won a Stanley Cup in 1969-70, then had a pretty good season with St. Louis the following year when Scotty was the coach there. But I really wasn't satisfied with the way I was playing. Then I was traded to the Rangers and, then to Buffalo. The point is, I wanted to play and it didn't matter where I was playing, I wasn't going to complain if I didn't play center, and I wound up becoming adept at playing the wings. I was always pretty good defensively, I could handle the puck pretty well, and I knew what to do in the offensive zone, so that opened up the power-play possibilities."

Twice Lorentz was chosen as the Sabres' Unsung Hero award-winner, first in 1972-73 and later in 1976-77.

Unlike many pro athletes who struggle adapting to retirement, Lorentz had little trouble when he called it quits after the 1978 season. "When I retired, that was it, and I knew it," he said, adding that he doesn't even bother playing in alumni games. "As much as I loved the game, I had no desire to play it anymore. I still go out with the kids, I enjoy that, but as far as competing in the old-timers games, it really didn't do anything for me and still doesn't. Some guys love to keep playing, but when I retired, my career was over, I was willing to accept that and move on with my life and that's what I've done."

His first venture was coaching, and he was a huge success, leading the Buffalo Junior Sabres to a national championship. There was a point where he considered making coaching his new career, but he was happy living in the Buffalo area and didn't want to uproot his family.

"I loved to coach, still do, but I made the decision that I didn't want to start moving around again, and an opportunity to broadcast came along, so I took that," he said. "I tried to coach at the same time, but found I couldn't and had to give up the coaching. After about two or three years of broadcasting, I made the decision that this is what I was going to do. I worked very hard at it, and I still work hard at it, this is my occupation."

Lorentz relies heavily on his playing and coaching experiences in the broadcast booth.

"It makes a huge difference having been a player and a coach, but it's like anything else, you have to prepare," he said. "You get your information, talk to the players and coaches and know what they're feeling, then you try to add your own thoughts to it. Obviously I think when I coached, that helped a lot because I really learned some of the finer points of the game. As a coach, you look at it from a totally different point of view."

When Lorentz is not describing Sabres action, he spends much of his free time writing. He has had numerous articles and stories published in outdoors and literary magazines, and has won a few writing awards for his fictional works.

"I always loved to read and I loved English, but I didn't start writing until about a dozen years ago," he said. "I don't produce very much, but I try to write regularly. I write a lot of fiction, drawing from past experiences. I find it very difficult to do, but it's very rewarding."

Lorentz also is the director of the Lafayette Ice Rink in Buffalo, where he runs skating programs and hockey schools for children. And he helps coach his son Jim's high school hockey team at the Nichols School in North Buffalo.

"He loves hockey, unfortunately a little too much," Lorentz said of his 16-year-old son. *"I'm not saying I don't want him to play hockey, I just want to expose him to other things, and he does enjoy acting and singing, he has a great voice.*

"I find today – and I look back on my experience with the minor kids – that hockey consumes people. That's wrong that it takes over their lives. I always felt if a kid is good enough, he's going to make it, it doesn't matter if he's on the ice 10 times a week or twice a week, he'll be there if he has the talent and the drive. I think so much of the pressure on these kids, the travel hockey, is so unnecessary."

Since retiring from the Sabres, Jim Lorentz has remained with the organization, now serving as the team's analyst on television broadcasts. He is shown here interviewing current Sabre winger Donald Audette.

Lorentz played a major part in the Sabres' second game of the season as well. Robert had suffered a bruised collarbone against the Flames, and when he couldn't practice the day before the Los Angeles Kings were scheduled to visit the Aud, Joe Crozier was going to play Lorentz in Robert's right wing spot on the big line with Perreault and Martin.

When Robert came to the arena, tested out the shoulder and proclaimed himself ready to play, Lorentz was shifted back to left wing on the third line with Meehan and Atkinson. That arrangement lasted barely five minutes into the game. Meehan, who was playing with a pulled muscle in his left shoulder, aggravated the injury, knocking him out for the rest of the night. So Lorentz moved to center between Atkinson and Wyrozub, and contributed two assists to help Buffalo to an easy 7-3 victory.

Perreault had a goal and three assists, Robert had a goal and two assists, and Martin scored his first two goals, giving the threesome a nine-point night and 14 points in the first two games. Yet Lorentz's performance was the one Crozier was most impressed with.

"We lost Gerry Meehan in the first period and bang, Jim Lorentz goes in there and does a standout job between Atkinson and Wyrozub," Crozier said.

For the first time in their brief history, the Sabres were 2-0 in a season. But if any of the players thought Crozier's militaristic style would soften, they were sadly mistaken. Today, physical conditioning is second nature to professional athletes. In the early 1970s, that wasn't the case, unless you were a member of the Sabres.

Every morning, except on game days, the players trooped into the gymnasium at Nichols by 9:30 a.m. for physical training under the guidance of former professional wrestler Fred Atkins, who had been hired as the Sabres' fitness trainer. Atkins put them through a strenuous workout consisting of a two-mile run, stretching exercises, and a 15-station program on a Universal weight machine that included situps, pushups, pullups and arm dips.

Showing off his versatility in the second game of the 1972-73 season against Los Angeles, Jim Lorentz played left wing and center and he recorded two assists in a 7-3 triumph. Here, he is denied a goal by Kings' goalie Rogie Vachon.

"We didn't get to go to practice at 10 or 11 in the morning, we were in early with Fred Atkins, and that was tough to do with a hangover," Robitaille said with a laugh. "That's when physical training was just starting to come in, and Fred would put us through a routine for close to two hours before we even put our hockey equipment on. Then we'd go out and practice, and after that, we'd listen to Joe talk for about 20 minutes. It made for a pretty long day. I used to like it when your biggest worry was where you were going to have lunch, but that changed with Joe. Even when we practiced at the Aud, he'd make us put our sweatsuits on and run those halls before we went on the ice.

"When I look back to those days, I don't think anyone was in shape when you compare it to now. Physical training today is so big and such a huge part of your arsenal. Back then, we had 30 days of training camp to get in shape. Now, they drop the puck the first day and you better be ready to go or you're going to get cut. That's the biggest difference with these players today is the condition they're in."

Had the Sabres not trained so vigorously, Crozier said Robert might not have been able to play against the Kings. "Robert took a good check against Atlanta Sunday," Crozier said. "His shoulder was hurt, but if he wasn't in tip-top shape from the PT, he would have been knocked out for a while."

Given his quick recovery, Robert became a believer in the workouts, too. "We had a good hockey training camp, we are in great shape and it shows," he said. "We can get some quick points against teams that aren't in shape, points we can use later in the season when they come hard."

Although it was something new, and certainly not a lot of fun – especially after a night of celebrating, as Robitaille alluded to – the physical training didn't bother the players as much as Crozier's punitive personality following losses. The man never took his foot off the accelerator, and if the Sabres turned in a particularly lousy effort, he would push that pedal through the metal the next day. In addition to the physical training, he often subjected his team to a no-pucks, two-hour ordeal, er, practice.

"That was the only thing I objected to with Joe is when he used to penalize us after we lost a game," Martin said. "We'd go up the middle for two hours with no pucks. He'd sit there in his chair at center ice drinking his coffee and he'd say, 'Up the middle, gentlemen.' He was always reminding us that we had to keep working harder all the time."

The team didn't work quite hard enough in its first road game of the season. The Sabres traveled to Atlanta and christened that city's new arena, the Omni. In the first event ever held there, the Sabres battled the Flames to a 1-1 tie as Perreault set up Lorentz for a power-play goal in the first period, shortly after Ernie Hicke had scored 2:03 into the game, also on a power play.

But despite a long flight home after the game and another match the next night at home against Toronto, there was plenty of jump in the Sabres' step during a 3-2 victory over the Maple Leafs, Buffalo's first win against Toronto in its own rink after six consecutive losses.

Rene Robert cruised behind the net and got a good view of the puck slipping past Toronto goalie Jacques Plante in the Sabres' fourth game of the 1972-73 season, a 3-2 victory.

Lorentz kept up his scorching scoring pace, assisting on Atkinson's second-period goal that put Buffalo ahead 2-0. Lorentz won a faceoff in the Toronto end and steered the puck to Atkinson who ripped a 20-footer past Leaf goalie Jacques Plante. For Atkinson, it was his second goal of the young season and a sign that perhaps the goal-scoring touch he showed in 1970-71 when he scored 20 times for the Sabres was back after a lapse the previous year when he had slipped to 14.

"I feel a lot stronger, and I'm getting my confidence back," he said. "I just hope I can come back and play like I did two years ago. No, I won't say hope, I'm going to play like that."

That's all Crozier wanted to hear from Atkinson. After Crozier had taken over as coach of the Sabres midway through 1971-72, he had not been impressed by Atkinson, and benched him for the final three games of the year. "I was a little dubious about him," Crozier admitted. "He didn't play that well for me, but he's impressed me so far this year."

Joe Crozier admitted he wasn't overly confident about Steve Atkinson at the start of 1972-73, but when Atkinson scored a couple of early-season goals, Crozier changed his tune.

Wyrozub stole the puck from Brian Glennie and scored on a breakaway to make it 3-0, and after Darryl Sittler beat Roger Crozier twice within 1:06 midway through the second, the Sabres buckled down on defense and Crozier slammed the door the rest of the way. "We showed in the third period that we can check when we have to," Joe Crozier said.

Only the rookies were supposed to show up for practice the day after the Toronto game as Crozier decided to give the veterans their first day off since they had reported to training camp on September 13. Still, half the squad was on the ice at Dann Memorial Rink at Nichols, prompting Schoenfeld to say, "It just goes to show you what kind of spirit we have on this team."

The next day, Crozier was back to his hard-driving self. He gathered the team at center ice prior to practice and told them, "You can play with any team in the National Hockey League if you keep on working as you have been." To make sure they understood his point, Crozier put the team through a grueling two-hour workout that concluded with exhausting sprints. "Take a day off, and no matter how good of shape you're in, you're behind when you return to work," Crozier said.

The Sabres began a tough three-games-in-four-nights stretch at the Aud with a 6-0 dismantling of Vancouver. Perreault was brilliant, scoring two goals and two assists for his second four-point performance in five games.

"I don't think I've ever before seen Gil Perreault play so well so consistently," said Roger Crozier. "He's great every shift he's on the ice. Even from where I stand, it's a treat to watch him play. When Gil has the puck, that's it. The five guys on the other team can just chase him. When he plays like that, it's hard for any defenseman to do anything about it. He's unbelievable."

Crozier wasn't bad himself on this night, turning aside 32 shots, including 17 in the third period, for the shutout. It was just Crozier's fourth shutout as a Sabre. With the win, the Sabres took over sole possession of first place in the Eastern Division with nine points, one more than Detroit and Montreal.

Two nights later, the Sabres managed a 1-1 tie in St. Louis as Perreault assisted on Martin's fifth goal of the year, offsetting a goal by Frank St. Marseille. Crozier made a key strategical move, playing the Perreault-Martin-Robert line for 90-second shifts in the third period, forcing the Blues to backpedal rather than attack, which Imlach really liked. "What Joe did was force St. Louis into playing defensive hockey," the general manager said. "For the last 20 minutes they concentrated on defensing Perreault."

With a flight home to Buffalo after the game, and another game the next night in the Aud against Atlanta, you would have thought all the extra work against the Blues would have slowed Perreault, Martin and Robert against the Flames. Quite the contrary. That line produced all seven goals in a 7-2 blowout of the Flames.

Martin set a team single-game record by scoring four goals and also added an assist; Perreault established a record with six points (two goals and four assists); and Robert chipped in a goal and four assists. In all, the line combined for 16 points, giving them 46 in seven games. In the process, the Sabres' unbeaten streak reached seven, another new team record.

"I'm feeling a little better now," Martin said. "I think I was lucky on a couple of the goals tonight, but I'm not going to refuse them. Gil and Rene are playing superb hockey. If it hadn't been for those two guys, I wouldn't have scored. The whole line is going great."

Thanks to this explosion, Perreault and Robert became the two top scorers in the league, Perreault with 19 points and Robert 15, while Martin's nine goals were a league high. Since they had been thrown together late in the 1971-72 season, the Perreault-Martin-Robert trio had produced 32 goals and 73 points, prompting a furious attempt among members of the local media to come up with a moniker for the group. One night, Lee Coppola, then a reporter for the *Buffalo News* who also worked at the Aud writing catchy little phrases for display on the electronic message boards, struck gold when he came up with The French Connection. The Gene Hackman film of the same name had just come out, and that further enhanced the nickname's appeal.

PROFILE - The French Connection

When the Sabres began their second training camp in September of 1971, it was Imlach's intention to not unite Perreault and Martin on the first line right away. They would play the power play together, but Imlach felt the team would be better balanced offensively if Perreault played on one line and Martin on another. However, when Perreault came waddling into camp after an abundantly caloric offseason, Imlach was forced to alter his plan.

"Gilbert came to camp about 20 pounds overweight, and Punch put me with him and told me to 'Make him skate,'" Martin said with a laugh, recalling Imlach's frustration. "That's how we first got together."

Jenny Craig should be as beneficial. Not only did Perreault get back into shape trying to keep up with Martin, but it became fairly obvious that their coach with the Junior Canadiens had made a mistake not playing them together when they were teammates a couple of years earlier. Their styles were tailor-made for each other as Perreault's strength was weaving through the defense, drawing attention, then deftly passing the puck off to one of his wingers. And who better to be dishing to than Martin, whose shot could burn a hole through the net.

Martin flanked Perreault's left side the entire year and went on to shatter Perreault's NHL rookie record for goals

by scoring 44. But there was still a void on the right side because no one Imlach – and later Crozier – used on that wing was a viable complement. Until Robert joined the club.

"Robert was the guy I wanted for that wing," said Crozier, who played a key role in the acquisition. "It was all discussed ahead of time that it was very important we had a guy in that spot. I knew Rene a long time from the American League, and he was a piece of the puzzle. He had a lot of talent, a lot of experience as far as reading plays. I knew what he could do, what type of person he was, so we went and got him."

After Robert's arrival, Crozier plugged

For obvious reasons, The French Connection loved to play against the Montreal Canadiens. Here, Rene Robert wipes out Guy Lapointe which enables Gilbert Perreault to corral the puck. Rick Martin and Montreal's Jimmy Roberts are in the background. (Photo courtesy of Ron Moscati)

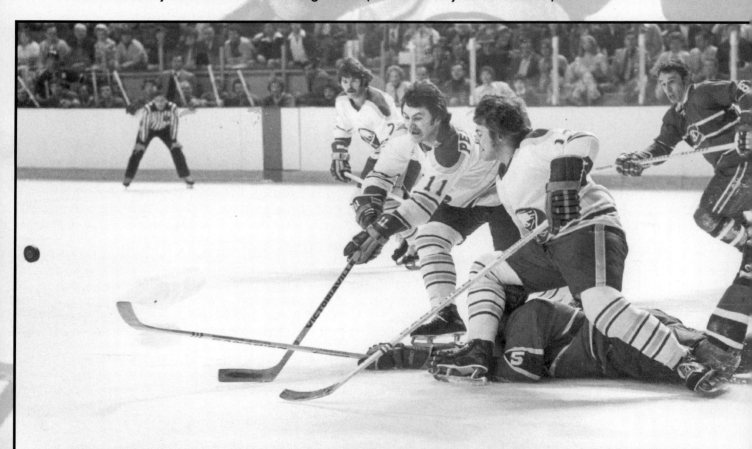

him into the right wing slot with Perreault and Martin for the final 12 games of the 1971-72 season, and he scored six goals.

"I had always played center, but they were looking for a right winger to play with Perreault and Martin," Robert said. "Joe Crozier told me, 'All we want you to do is the backchecking for Perreault and Martin and somehow be the garbage collector.'"

It was plainly apparent that Robert was going to be more than just a "garbage collector." He was the missing link on a line the Sabres could build their team around.

"Punch had always said, 'Concentrate on filling the net, I'm going to find you guys a right winger, just be patient,'" Martin said. "Most of the time he had guys who were there to check. He'd tell them, 'Make sure you're the guy back, these guys (Perreault and Martin) will go on offense.' When Rene came with the team, they kind of told him the same thing, but the problem was that Rene was a great offensive player. It just meshed instantly, it was like we had played together forever."

While Perreault was a magnificent playmaker, and Martin was a dazzling shooter, Robert could pass and shoot equally well, and that brought a neat symmetry to the line. Teams couldn't afford to slide their defense to a particular side because Robert's shot was nearly as deadly as Martin's. And when a team tried to gang up on Perreault, Robert had the ability to move to the center of the ice and become the quarterback. If it was basketball, you would say The French Connection created serious "matchup problems" for the opposing defense.

"Whenever I got on the ice in Buffalo, the home team had the last change, so they would put The French Connection line out, and my coach would be trying his darndest to get me off the ice," former Boston Bruin bad boy Terry O'Reilly said. "I think it had something to do with my skating style. And if I couldn't get off the ice in time, I ended up having to try to cover Martin. My skating was very questionable, and

Crozier knew that, and that was the matchup he wanted, his flying Frenchmen skating against the stumpy Irishman."

O'Reilly was not alone. Very few players could keep up with The French Connection.

"It was kind of fun because we all came from the same Quebec background, but that was about the only fun you had playing against those guys," said Hall of Fame defenseman Denis Potvin, who spent the early part of his career with the New York Islanders dreading the nights his team had to play Buffalo.

"It was unbelievable because they complemented each other so well. Having Gilbert down the middle created a lot of scoring opportunities for them, and he attracted so much attention. And no line in hockey, I don't think, ever had as many finishers, guys who can finish the play. That's the key to the game. There's a lot of good hockey players who can go up and down and shoot the puck, but there's a natural talent to finishing that you just can't teach. And you had all three of them who could finish a play on you, and that's what was so scary."

Another Hall of Famer, Bobby Clarke, enjoyed a measure of success against The French Connection because his Philadelphia Flyer teams of that period were so big and physical, and the Sabres always had trouble against their intimidating style of play. For example, in 1974-75, the year the Flyers beat the Sabres in the Stanley Cup Finals, The French Connection produced only nine points in four regular-season games against Philadelphia, and in the Finals, managed only 11 in six games, including just one point in the three games at the Spectrum when Philadelphia coach Fred Shero had the last line change.

Still, Clarke, now the Flyers' general manager, said The French Connection was not a line anyone liked to face. "Everybody remembers the way Perreault played with his speed, Martin could shoot the puck so well, and Robert was the complete package," Clarke said. "You can't really kill a big line like that.

Speed scares everybody, so we were no different than everybody else, but we were taught to play the game a certain way, that's how we played, and we happened to do pretty well against them."

It got to the point in the mid-70s when Perreault, Martin and Robert could have played with blindfolds on, so adept were they at skating with each other.

"Some people you can play with your whole career and never get used to them," Robert said. "I can't pinpoint why it clicked, but maybe it was because we thought the same way on the ice, we reacted the same way. We just understood each other and knew exactly where each of us were going to be on the ice. We would pass the puck without even looking, knowing the other guy was going to be there."

Martin seconded that opinion.

"Rene could read where I was going, and I could read where he was going. I actually got the puck from him as much as I did from Gilbert, so for me it was great to get him on the line because now I had two people to get the puck to me. I played off those guys so well: I would watch where they were headed, and when I saw an opening, I went for it and they would get me the puck."

Said Perreault, "Rene was an underrated player. He had a lot of talent, good speed and a great shot, and so did Rico. What more can you ask of as a center? It was easy to make plays for those guys. I was more of a tap dancer, Rico had that great shot and great release, and Rene was a smart player who had a great view of the game."

The defending Stanley Cup champion Boston Bruins made their initial visit to the Aud on October 25 and could only manage a 2-2 tie, extending Buffalo's unbeaten streak to eight games. The Bruins, who had the services of injured superstar Bobby Orr only on special teams, took a 2-0 first-period lead against Roger Crozier on goals by Garnet Bailey and Johnny Bucyk. Crozier suffered a pulled muscle in his back, so Dave Dryden played the final two periods and blanked Boston, making 14 saves. Meanwhile, Robert and Meehan scored 31 seconds apart in the second period to produce the tie.

It was Dryden's first playing time of the season, and was the first indication that he was going to have to be in top form because Crozier's durability was a looming question.

"The one who deserves a lot of credit is Dave Dryden," Meehan said. "Dave didn't know whether he would be playing until we went onto the ice to start the second period, about one minute before they dropped the puck."

"I wasn't too prepared mentally," Dryden said. "I didn't know if Crozier could go back in or not. And it's been a long time since I played a game. But the guys were really good. They knew I was in a tough spot."

The Sabres allowed their first shorthanded goal of the season when Don Marcotte stole the puck from Hillman, then fed Bailey just outside the crease. The power-play unit redeemed itself when Perreault set up Robert for a man-advantage goal, but Joe Crozier surmised that, "This was not our best effort. We were a little nervous at first, not moving the puck as we can, holding it for a split second too long before making a play. Maybe it was because we were playing the Boston Bruins, or maybe it was a letdown after seven games without a loss. But we came back against the Bruins after being behind."

As hard as it may have been to believe, when the Sabres traveled to Montreal on Saturday night, October 28, the game featured a battle of two unbeaten teams. And when it was over, no blood had been spilled as the game ended in a 3-3 tie.

"I've said it before and I'll say it again, our club can play with anyone, and that includes the Canadiens," Joe Crozier said after watching his team match the powerful Canadiens shot for shot. Even more inspiring was the play of Dave Dryden, who matched his younger and more celebrated brother, Ken, save for save, each stopping 28 shots.

Martin scored twice on the power play, including the tying goal early in the third period off a feed from Perreault, and Lorentz converted on a 2-on-1 breakaway with Robert. Yvan Cournoyer netted two for Montreal.

Crozier said he feared a letdown when the team came back home the next night for a match with Minnesota, and the Sabres were not as sharp, yet they completed the month undefeated with a hard-fought 2-1 victory over the North Stars as Martin capped a marvelous weekend with another two goals.

And then the Sabres rested. Finally, Crozier gave the entire team a day off after the Minnesota win, and it gave him a chance to reflect on the remarkable start.

"Everything's tough in the NHL, and when you win only 16 games out of 78 as we did last year, you know there are no soft spots," he said. "We've got young players, but they're mature enough to know they can't let down. There are no boys on this team, they're all men."

Left: Dave Dryden goes behind the net to clear the puck around the boards.

Below: Minnesota goalie Gilles Gilbert watched in vain as the puck slid past him, another goal for The French Connection.

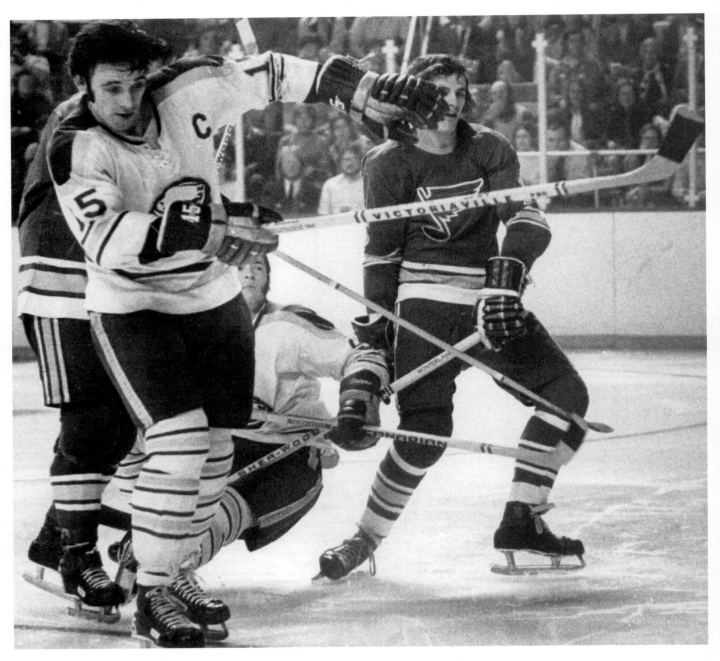

Gerry Meehan fought his way through a maze of sticks and St. Louis Blues. (Photo courtesy of Ron Moscati)

November: You Knew It Couldn't Be This Easy

For the first time in franchise history, the Sabres were in the NHL's spotlight. National magazines, newspapers and TV networks were paying homage to a team that had won just 40 of 156 games in its first two years of existence, but was suddenly knocking heads with the likes of Boston and Montreal and holding its own.

It could be argued that teams just weren't taking the Sabres very seriously early in the season, but Joe Crozier didn't think that was the case.

"I don't think anyone takes anyone lightly in this league," Crozier said. "I think it was the shape that we were in, and we were playing as a unit. They knew more about my system because I was still there, there hadn't been a coaching change. A lot of times you come along with a certain coach, you get to know him, what type of guy he is, what you have to do, how to react, and those guys knew what I expected from them and they did it. I think that had a lot to do with it."

But what also had a lot to do with the fast start was the fact that Buffalo had played three games against expansion Atlanta, two against non-playoff teams Los Angeles and Vancouver, and seven of the first 10 games had been at the Aud. The Sabres had yet to win on the road, playing to three ties, and this point was stuck firmly in Toronto coach John McLellan's craw before his Leafs were to play host to Buffalo on the first night of November.

"Buffalo is playing well, no one can deny that, but I think the bubble will burst for them, and I can't imagine a better time than our game here," McLellan said.

And after the Leafs put a 7-1 whipping on the Sabres to snap the 10-game unbeaten streak, McLellan reiterated his belief that the Sabres were prime for a plucking when he said, "I felt all day we would win. Buffalo couldn't go on forever without losing."

Outside of a poor defensive performance in front of Roger Crozier, the key to the game was the suffocating checking of Toronto's line of Dave Keon, Paul Henderson and Ron Ellis on The French Connection. Perreault's unassisted goal in the first period was the big line's only point of the night as they never got into an offensive flow.

"We knew we had to tie up the Perreault line," McLellan said, "so we put the Keon line on them and they played a hell of a game, kept their big line in check all night."

It was inevitable that teams were going to try to handcuff The French Connection at all costs, and Perreault, Martin and Robert were going to have to find a way to persevere.

"It got tougher every game," Robert recalled. "The more you produce, the more attention you create. The other teams would put their best checkers on us and their job was to make sure that Perreault, Martin and Robert don't touch the puck or go to the net. And what was so hard is that those guys weren't out there to score goals, their coach didn't expect them to, and if they did, it was just a bonus. They were out there just to stop us."

Said Martin, "It was frustrating at times. There were certain games when a team would just throw out a line against us, and all their job was to check us, drape themselves all over us, do anything to stop us. I knew in every game who I was going to get. In Chicago it was Cliff Koroll, in Pittsburgh it was Jean Pronovost, in Philadelphia it was Gary Dornhoeffer, in Montreal it was Jimmy Roberts."

A 5-3 loss in Philadelphia was especially damaging because Perreault suffered an injury to his right hand which made it difficult for him to grip

Mike Robitaille was a sturdy, hard-hitting defenseman whose specialty was laying out fast-moving forwards with his patented hip check.

his stick. Despite the pain, he assisted on all three Buffalo goals, but it wasn't nearly enough as the Flyers' line of Bill Barber, Rick MacLeish and Pierre Plante combined for 14 points.

The Sabres returned home the next night and for the second time this season, played St. Louis to a 1-1 tie with Perreault able to play only a couple of minutes. Without Perreault, The French Connection was held without a point for the first time as Robitaille scored the team's only goal with assists from Luce and Mickey. The tie dropped the Sabres record to 6-2-5 and left them five points behind first-place Montreal after the Canadiens saw their season-opening 13-game unbeaten streak snapped by Detroit.

Blues coach Al Arbour left the Aud very impressed by the Sabres. "Buffalo is catching up to the old clubs," he said. "It's a real fine hockey club, built the way you have to build a club these days, with good draft picks. Gil Perreault, Rick Martin and the others, you have to get guys like that from junior to improve your club."

In their next game, the good news was that the Sabres played terrific on defense. The bad news was that the offensive slump continued.

Buffalo and California wound up in a 0-0 tie, the first such game in the Sabres' 170-game history. "The score should have been 10-0," Joe Crozier said, frustrated by the Seals' 37-year-old journeyman goaltender Marv Edwards, who made 28 saves. Roger Crozier pitched his second shutout of the season for Buffalo.

The Sabres returned to Philadelphia for a date with the Flyers, and one week after getting hammered at the Spectrum, the Sabres were again turned away, this time, 3-1. After an undefeated October, the Sabres were winless in November (0-3-2).

Although their scoring woes continued the next night at home against Pittsburgh, Atkinson managed to slip a shot past Penguins' goalie Jim Rutherford, who otherwise was brilliant with 40 saves, and that was all they needed as the Sabres ended their skein with a 1-0 victory. Roger Crozier posted his third shutout and second in three games, stopping 17 shots including a second-period penalty shot by Lowell MacDonald.

A three-game West Coast trip was next for the Sabres, and it began well enough in Los Angeles as they rallied from a 2-0 deficit to tie the Kings, 3-3, with Lorentz setting up Atkinson for the tying goal with 6:56 left to play.

But the rest of the trip was an unmitigated disaster. First, there was a 5-1 loss to lowly California, which snapped the Seals' eight-game winless streak. Perreault was held without a goal for the seventh straight game, and without a point for the sixth game in a row. If not for Meehan's goal with 2:47 left to play, the Seals would have had two consecutive shutouts against the Sabres. Once again, it was goalie Marv Edwards who made the difference. The former Buffalo Bison stopped 33 shots, including 13 by The French Connection in the first period alone.

And then the team flew to Vancouver and got run out of the Pacific Coliseum as Bobby Schmautz scored four goals to lead a 9-5 Canucks rout in the highest-scoring game in Sabres history to this point. While the Sabres were unbeaten at home (7-0-2), they remained winless on the road (0-5-4). The poor road trip dropped them into fourth place in the East behind Montreal, the Rangers and Boston.

Perreault finally snapped his drought with a goal just 1:50 into the game, but the Canucks scored three in a row over the next 4:45 to take control. "I'm shell-shocked," Joe Crozier said. "I thought we were ready to play hockey. Vancouver is such a small team physically, and there they were, knocking our guys around. We have to start from scratch, get organized all over again."

Crozier wasn't kidding. After the team returned from Vancouver, he put them through a practice that featured the members of The French Connection working on different lines. Perreault was centering for Atkinson and Harris, who had recently been recalled from Cincinnati, while Robert was moved to center, with Martin on his left wing and Lorentz on the right. Crozier's thinking was to spread the offense around, because the flying Frenchmen were the only serious scoring threats the Sabres had, and teams were beginning to clamp down on that one line. In the first 10 games, The French Connection produced 58 points, but in the last nine, they had managed only 12.

"It's OK with me," Martin said. "He had to do something, right?"

NHL STANDINGS THROUGH SUNDAY, NOVEMBER 5

EAST	W	L	T	PTS
Montreal	9	1	4	22
NY Rangers	8	4	1	17
Buffalo	6	2	5	17
Detroit	7	4	1	15
Boston	6	6	2	14
Toronto	5	6	2	12
Vancouver	4	8	1	9
NY Islanders	2	8	1	5

WEST	W	L	T	PTS
Los Angeles	8	6	0	16
Philadelphia	6	5	2	14
Chicago	6	6	2	14
Pittsburgh	6	7	1	13
Minnesota	5	5	2	12
Atlanta	5	7	2	12
St. Louis	2	5	5	9
California	2	7	3	7

EAST	W	L	T	PTS
Montreal	14	2	4	32
NY Rangers	13	5	1	27
Boston	10	7	2	22
Buffalo	7	5	7	21
Detroit	8	7	2	18
Vancouver	7	10	2	16
Toronto	6	9	3	15
NY Islanders	2	13	1	5

WEST	W	L	T	PTS
Los Angeles	10	10	2	22
Pittsburgh	10	9	1	21
Minnesota	9	7	3	21
Atlanta	9	9	3	21
Chicago	9	8	2	20
Philadelphia	9	9	2	20
St. Louis	3	8	5	11
California	3	11	4	10

As it turned out, the plan went awry when Robert came down with the flu and didn't dress for the team's game at Detroit. Ramsay and Meehan scored the only goals in a 6-2 loss that dropped Buffalo's record to 1-6-4 in its last 11 games, and extended its road winless streak to 10.

All was well, though, once the team got back to the Aud the next night for a Thanksgiving Day battle with the Rangers. Robert was feeling better, The French Connection was reunited, and the Sabres looked like the team that tore through October without a loss as they whipped New York, 5-3. It was Buffalo's first victory over the Rangers in their history, breaking an 0-10-2 futility.

Trailing 3-2 in the third, Robert put an end to his five-game goal-less streak when he sizzled a 35-foot slap shot past Eddie Giacomin at the 6:27 mark, and Meehan nailed the game winner with five minutes to go as he took a pass from Lorentz, maneuvered around New York defenseman Jim Neilson, and beat Giacomin from 15 feet out.

After his preseason scoring frenzy, Luce had gone the first 20 games of the regular season without a goal, but he broke through on this night with a pair, one coming in the second period that tied the game at 2-2, the other providing some breathing room in the final minute when he hit an empty net.

Before the game, Luce's 4-year-old son Scotty, recognizing that his dad was struggling offensively, told Don that he could use his stick in the game and maybe that would help him score a goal. "I brought it along in the trunk of the car, and I think I'll bring it along to every game from now on," Luce said. "I knew it was just a matter of time until I scored. I was getting good chances, everybody on our line was, but they weren't going in."

PROFILE - Don Luce

In the spring of 1988, Luce, the Sabres' director of player personnel, attended the world junior hockey championships in Moscow and was mesmerized by a 19-year-old Russian rocket named Alexander Mogilny.

Mogilny had become the youngest Soviet Union player to win an Olympic gold medal when he helped the Central Red Army to victory at the Calgary Games a few months earlier, and now Mogilny was back with the Soviet junior team, dominating play and earning the tournament's designation as best forward.

"He may have been the best player in the world at that time, that was my feeling when I saw him," Luce recalled one day as he sat in his office at Marine Midland Arena.

When Luce returned to America to continue planning for the Sabres' 1988 amateur draft, he discussed with Meehan, then the Sabres' general manager, the

possibility of using their extra fifth-round draft choice on Mogilny.

"At that time no Russian player had come out so it was a gamble, no question, but we had an extra fifth-round pick," Luce said. Meehan agreed it was worth it, even though the chances were remote that the Soviet Union would allow Mogilny to come and play in the NHL.

In January of 1989, Luce and Buffalo's director of scouting, Rudy Migay, traveled to Anchorage, Alaska, to again watch the world junior championships, and they made it a point to meet with Mogilny, give him Luce's business card and make sure he knew the Sabres had drafted him.

At the time, Mogilny had grown frustrated by his treatment in the Soviet Union. He was playing for the third consecutive year in the junior championships, and he felt he had already proven himself at that level. The Central

Red Army team had been touring in North America playing exhibitions against NHL teams, and Mogilny was miffed by his exclusion from that tour. He filed Luce's card away, but not for long.

In the spring, Mogilny stepped up to the national team to compete in the world championships in Stockholm, Sweden, but he wasn't there for hockey only. His dissatisfaction had reached the boiling point, so he came to Sweden with the intention of defecting to the U.S. and playing for the Sabres.

Luce was sitting in his office on May 2, 1989, when he received a phone call from a man in Stockholm claiming to be Mogilny's friend and saying that Mogilny wanted to defect. After being assured that this wasn't some hoax, Luce ran down to Meehan's office and told his boss what was going on. Meehan received permission from the Knox brothers to pursue the matter.

"That afternoon, we got on a plane to Stockholm," Luce said. What transpired over the next 72 hours was straight out of a James Bond movie.

"We spent three days hiding out and changing hotels and negotiating a contract to get him over here," Luce said. "We had to visit the U.S. embassy, which Gerry did, because we didn't want to take Alex in until we had everything in place. And we were checking in and out of hotels to make sure we weren't being trailed.

"It was really exciting. We were told to be very careful, and I guess looking back, it was more dangerous than we thought it was at the time. This had never been attempted before, so what Alex did took an unbelievable amount of courage. It was a scary time for him as well as Gerry and myself."

Though excited about the prospect of luring Mogilny to America, Meehan proceeded cautiously.

"I had never met Alex, so I wasn't convinced that we had the real thing until I got Don in the same room as Alex and Don confirmed that he was the guy," Meehan said. "We went to the hotel where Alex's friend was registered, and sitting on the sofa were two individuals with Alex between them. I asked Don if that was Alex Mogilny, he said, 'That's him' and I said, 'Let's get to work.'"

The first order of business was to make sure Mogilny was serious.

"I wanted to determine Alex's genuine interest in defecting" Meehan said. "Once he was convinced that he was going to come over, that's when everything began to happen in a, shall we say, cloak and dagger fashion."

Meehan's expertise in immigration law effectively facilitated the process, and when the legalities were finalized, Luce and Meehan plotted their final strategy: getting to the airport, and getting the hell out of Stockholm with the player who they felt could turn the Sabres' franchise around.

"We didn't know what was going to happen, we just knew we had to be secretive," Luce said. "We ended up leaving the rental car in the hotel basement when we left to go to the airport and took a cab. We didn't know if we were being followed. Our flight wasn't

until the afternoon, but we left before dawn so we'd get to the airport by six or seven in the morning because once you're in the airport, you're kind of shut off from the public."

Said Meehan, "Once we passed passport control, there was a sense of relief. You can't get on a plane to leave any country without an immigration document. There had been a suggestion that Alex had been kidnapped, and we were concerned we would be identified by anybody who was looking for Mogilny as a kidnap victim, or anybody at passport control who might have been advised to be on the lookout for Alex."

Once inside the terminal, Luce and Meehan learned how narrow an escape they had pulled off.

"Alex had his friend with him who could speak English, and he bought a paper and it had a trail of some of the hotels we had been at," Luce said. "The Russian team had left Sweden and Alex wasn't with them, so there were two or three days where they didn't know where he was. I guess the media found this out so they must have figured Buffalo owned his rights, and they probably checked the hotel registers to see if Gerry was in town, and he was. It was quite a trip, one I'll never forget."

It hasn't always been that exciting for Luce since he traded in his hockey sweater for a suit and tie, but if you think Luce has had to struggle off the

ice to match the gratification he enjoyed on the ice, you would be wrong.

"One thing you realize once you get into management is the amount of work that goes into the off-ice things," he said. "You sort of appreciate what was going on when you were playing, but you don't really see it because you're so involved in the game, you just want to do your best as a player. You don't realize what goes into getting a player, trading for a player, drafting a player, or anything like that. I really enjoy what I'm doing."

As a junior player for the Kitchener Rangers, Luce was a defensive center who could also be a force on offense, as evidenced by his 70 assists that led the Ontario Hockey Association his last year in Kitchener. That rare offensive-defensive combination drew interest from the New York Rangers, who chose him in the third round of the 1966 amateur draft.

Luce spent two years in the Central league toiling for Omaha before earning his first recall to the NHL late in the 1969-70 season. He played 12 games for the Rangers, and in all five of New York's playoff games during their first-round loss to the eventual champion Boston Bruins.

In November of 1970, the Rangers dealt Luce to Detroit, and in May of '71, he and Robitaille came to Buffalo for goalie Joe Daley.

Luce instantly endeared himself to Imlach and Crozier with his stickier-than-a-theater-floor defensive style, and his penalty-killing skills were among the best in the league.

"At any important time in a game when I needed to win a draw in my own end or I needed someone checked, Luce would be on the ice, that's all there was to it," said Crozier. "His skating wasn't as good as some of the other guys, but he had good hands, he could score goals, and he could check anybody."

After surviving the 16-win season of 1971-72, Luce said it was plain to see that the Sabres were going to be a much-improved outfit in 1972-73.

"It was exciting coming here and seeing that there was some talent here and it just had to jell together," Luce said. "I don't think we were looking to win the Stanley Cup at that time, but you realized that there was more talent here than an expansion team would normally have at that time."

Everyone knew Perreault, Martin, and Robert figured to be a key addition, but Luce and Ramsay had become a formidable duo as linemates after Ramsay was recalled from Cincinnati in November of 1971, and entering 1972-73, opposing teams knew the Sabres were more than a one-line team.

"I had a year of experience, Craig had a little more, and Larry Mickey was a proven pro, a guy that added a lot of experience to our line," Luce said. "He showed us a few things in those early years that really helped, he was a gung-ho player and he kind of fit our style, too."

"They were lunch-pail guys," said Ed Westfall. "They wouldn't accept anything less than the best game they could put out, and collectively their work ethic won a lot of hockey games for that team, particularly when they were making that transition from being another expansion team into viability."

How good were Luce and Ramsay? Damn good, said Martin, who had to face them on a daily basis in Crozier's ever-present scrimmages.

"Those guys didn't get half the credit they deserved," said Martin. "We always got a lot of attention as The French Connection. When we'd go on the road, it was always 'The French Connection is coming to town.' But those guys were great checkers, and guess what, we had to play against them in practice every day. They wanted to stop us in practice, they didn't want us to score. We were playing against some of the best checkers in the game, and it made us better, as I'm sure we made them better."

Ramsay agreed, and he said he and Luce thrived on all the accolades that were constantly being bestowed upon The French Connection.

"One of the greatest things was the internal rivalry we had," Ramsay said. "Because of all the press attention The French Connection got, the rest of us didn't want to be hanging on their coat tails and following them around. We didn't believe that's the way it was, we were out to prove that. Don and I went into every game wanting to be the best line out there, and what a great thing that is for a team, to have such a wonderful rivalry, and not a jealousy

thing. It was a rivalry where we wanted to have a great shift, we wanted them to talk about our line after the game."

In 1974-75, Luce set two Sabres' records that still stand. He netted eight shorthanded goals, and he finished with a plus-minus rating of plus 61. He also won the NHL's Bill Masterton Trophy, presented to the player who best exemplifies the qualities of perseverance, sportsmanship and dedication to hockey.

Luce spent almost 10 years in a Sabre uniform and he scored 225 goals and 554 points, earning him a spot in the team's Hall of Fame. He was traded by Scotty Bowman to the Los Angeles Kings along

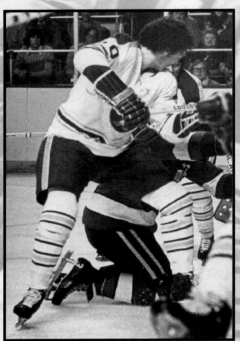

with Martin in March of 1981, went to Toronto a few months later and played half a season with the Leafs, then decided to retire the end of the 1981-82 campaign.

"When you're playing, the end of your career happens so quickly, and you don't want it to end," Luce said. So Luce didn't let his life in hockey end.

"I always wanted to be in the game after I was done playing, so I took a job as coach and general manager of an expansion team in the East Coast League called the Spruce Pine (N.C.) Bucks. It was a town of about 2,500 people, so it was quite a challenge."

As it turned out, a challenge far more difficult than trying to contain Guy LaFleur, Phil Esposito or Bobby Orr. The league started with six teams, and two days into the season, two of the

franchises folded. By Christmas of 1982, Luce returned to Buffalo, out of hockey for the first time since before kindergarten.

He opened his own printing business in Buffalo and tried to keep himself abreast of hockey matters by attending the amateur draft and talking to various coaches, general managers and players. A couple of job possibilities didn't pan out, but Luce persisted, and in August of 1984, Bowman called to offer him a position in the Sabres' scouting department.

In 1985-86, Luce left the offices and moved down to ice level to serve as assistant coach to Schoenfeld, and later for Bowman, who took over behind the bench in January of '86 after he fired Schoenfeld. But coaching didn't really interest Luce, so in 1987, he was bumped back upstairs to the position he still holds – director of player personnel.

In that role, Luce is the man largely responsible for deciding what players Buffalo picks in the annual amateur draft. It is an occupation that stimulates his senses even more than scoring a goal, winning a key faceoff, or delivering a solid body check. Imagine what Luce was feeling last season when the 1996-97 Sabres shocked the hockey establishment by winning the Northeast Division, and they did so in the era of free agency with 11 original Sabres' draft choices – all players Luce made a decision on – contributing heavily to the team.

"There's a lot of enjoyment in going out there and watching the players, working the draft, and making trades," Luce said. "Looking at it from both sides, having played and now doing what I do now, it's a job that is very important to the organization. I think it's just as valuable a job as being a player.

"You're not only working for today, but you're working for next year, the year after, and three, four and five years down the road. I don't think people realize that it takes a tremendous amount of planning to keep an organization running along smoothly, and that doesn't always mean winning the Stanley Cup, but just to keep it at a level where you're in the playoffs, and you're contending. The fan sometimes doesn't realize that there's going to be a little bit of up and down, you may have to take a slide down in the standings in order to rebuild and get back up there."

Luce was back in the scoring column a few nights later, but then again, almost everyone was as the Sabres played the expansion Islanders for the first time and set team records for goals scored and shots (50) in a 9-2 demolition. Robert, Martin and Lorentz each scored twice while Luce, Perreault and Meehan had one each, and The French Connection combined for 10 points as Buffalo extended its home-ice unbeaten streak to 12 games (9-0-3). The only bad news was that Horton suffered a shoulder injury which would keep him out of the next five games.

After the game, Joe Crozier pointed out that his team played fine, but "We have to start winning on the road if we're going to make the playoffs." And on Tuesday, November 28, they did just that. They traveled to Long Island for a rematch with the Islanders and snapped their 10-game road winless skein with a 7-2 blowout. Luce scored again, and The French Connection tallied another four goals and six points, Perreault leading the way with two goals and an assist. That performance led Crozier to say, "I wouldn't trade Perreault for the entire Montreal team."

While Horton's absence didn't matter too much against the Islanders, it was a big factor in the next game as Buffalo lost in Boston, 5-4. The Sabres were unable to hold a 4-3 lead as Johnny Bucyk scored with 4:29 left to play to tie the score, and then 2:19 later, Don Marcotte tipped Bobby Orr's slapshot from the point past Roger Crozier for the winner.

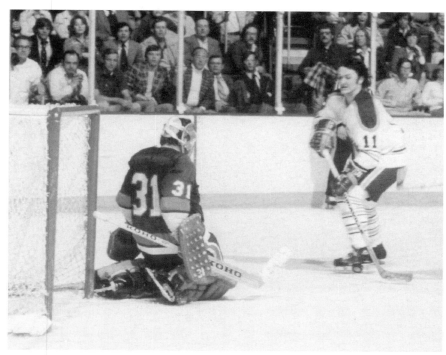

New York Islanders goalie Billy Smith made a save on a shot by Gilbert Perreault during a 9-2 Buffalo victory in which the Sabres set a team single-game scoring record.

The game was a typically hard-hitting Buffalo-Boston affair, yet referee Bryan Lewis called only two minor penalties all night. Carriere suffered a concussion in the first period when he was checked by Wayne Cashman and did not return, further depleting the defensive corps that was also minus Pratt, out with an ankle injury. And Perreault had his nose broken in the third period when he was smashed into the boards by Don Awrey. Both Carriere and Perreault were cut and bled, yet Lewis did not assess penalties on either play, which had Crozier fuming afterward.

Three times the Sabres rallied from one-goal deficits to tie it, the last when Hillman beat Eddie Johnston at the 11:38 mark of the third period. Less than two minutes later, Martin steered the puck to Perreault who stick-handled neatly through the Boston defense before slipping a pass across the goal crease to Robert. When Orr and Johnston got tangled up in the crease, Robert found an opening and put Buffalo ahead for the first time. Bucyk then batted in a rebound of Bobby Walton's shot, and Marcotte scored to break the Sabres' hearts.

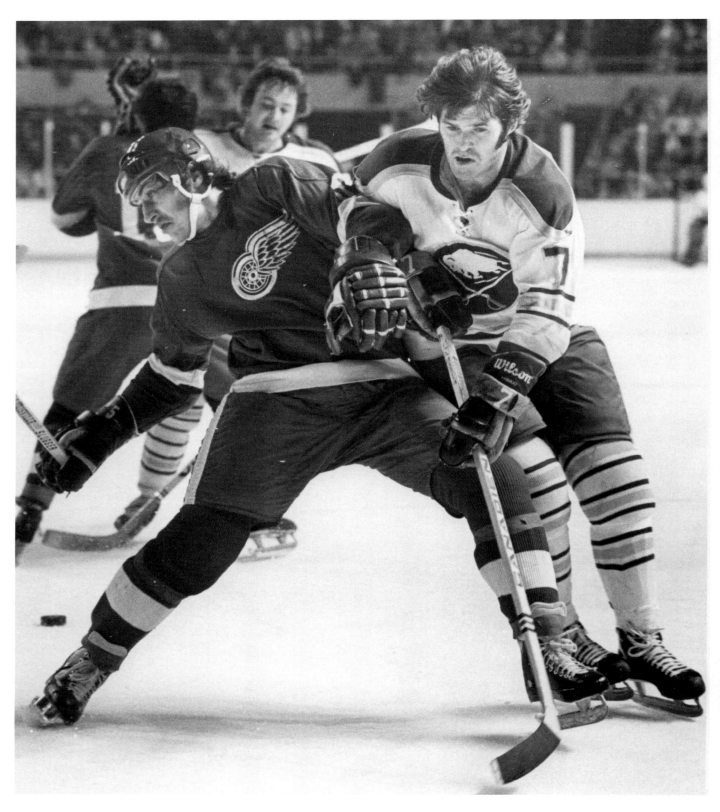

The more The French Connection scored, the more attention they received from opposing checkers, as Rick Martin found out against the Detroit Red Wings. (Photo courtesy of Ron Moscati)

December: Eight Straight Wins, and the Fight

The Sabres opened the month of December with a brutal 8-6 loss in Minnesota, and closed it with a 4-2 defeat in Chicago on New Year's Eve. In between, there was a team-record eight-game winning streak, highlighted by a 7-3 victory over the Bruins that remains today one of the most unforgettable games in Sabres history.

The loss in Minnesota further illuminated how important Horton was to the defense as the North Stars seemed to score at will. Thanks to hat tricks by both Robert and Meehan, Buffalo owned a 6-5 lead heading into the third period, and once again it couldn't hang on as Jude Drouin tied it 45 seconds into the period, Dean Prentice netted the winner with 7:35 left, and Bob Nevin chipped in with an insurance marker with 4:25 to go.

"Horton settles us down," Meehan said. "When he has the puck he won't give it up until he can make a good play. He makes the defensive end of our game go."

The teams both flew to Buffalo after the game for a return date at the Aud, and this time the Sabres came out on top, 7-4. The result snapped Minnesota's winning streak at six games, and started the Sabres on their eight-game winning streak. Luce scored twice, giving him six goals in six games, and Meehan also scored twice, giving him five goals in two games, 11 in 10 games, and an 11-game point scoring streak.

"I remember early in that season I hadn't been playing very much, and I was coming off what I considered to be not a very good year the season before," Meehan said, recalling his hot streak. "This was an important year for me career-wise. I had just gotten to the point where I had established myself in the league the first year (1970-71) and then I slipped a bit (in 1971-72), so I sensed this was a pivotal year.

"I had some issues about ice time that I took up with Joe Crozier early in the season and I suggested that even though The French Connection was a powerful and explosive line, someone else had to contribute some offense and I just kind of consulted with him on the possibility of playing a little more."

Crozier respected his captain and he gave Meehan more responsibility. So much so that he made this statement after the Minnesota victory: "It's up to Gerry whether we make the playoffs. We're counting on him to take some of the pressure off Gil Perreault's line."

PROFILE - Gerry Meehan

A couple of weeks before the 1970 expansion draft, Meehan came to the conclusion that his hockey career was on the brink of extinction. And he was prepared for that inevitability.

"I was 23 years old, I wasn't going to bang around the minors anymore," Meehan recalled. "I was going to stay at home in Streetsville (Ont.). I had been offered a position with a local drug company as a management trainee, and I would go to school in the evenings."

After a stellar junior career with the Toronto Marlboros, Imlach selected Meehan in the fourth round of the 1963 amateur draft for the Maple Leafs, but it took Meehan five years before he got a chance to play in the NHL as two of the Stanley Cups Toronto won in the 1960s came after he had joined the organization.

Unable to crack that superb roster, Meehan labored in places like Rochester, Tulsa, Phoenix and Seattle before finally being promoted to Toronto in 1968. Even then, he played sparingly in 25 games, collecting a mere two assists and two penalty minutes before Imlach traded him in March of 1969 to Philadelphia.

Meehan played 12 games for the Flyers accumulating three assists, and he went scoreless in four playoff games. Because he played in the postseason, he thought he might have a chance the following year in Philadelphia, but he was back in the minors for the entire 1969-70 season, and then was left off Philadelphia's protected list prior to the 1970 expansion draft. Seeing that the Flyers thought so little of him, Meehan was ready to move on with his life and join the real world.

"I believed it was my last chance to play in the NHL," Meehan said of the expansion draft. "If I wasn't picked up by another team, I was not going to go to training camp. I had decided that summer that if I didn't play in the NHL

that year, I wasn't going to continue playing. And then I got drafted, and being drafted by the Sabres and playing here basically gave me my career."

After years of trying to make a Toronto team that was loaded with all-stars, Meehan sized up Buffalo's personnel that first year and knew he wouldn't be taking that job with the drug company.

"Having gone through camp those first few weeks, and then going through the process of conditioning, you could

see that after the top 24 or 25 guys, there wasn't a lot of competition for jobs," Meehan said. "So if you didn't get cocky, played hard and worked hard, it was a real opportunity."

And in Buffalo's inaugural season, Meehan made the most of his opportunity. He scored 24 goals and his 55 points were fewer than only Perreault (72) and Goyette (65).

His numbers dropped in 1971-72, but he joined forces with Lorentz and Harris in 1972-73 and enjoyed the greatest

goal-scoring year of his career with 31.

"That was a year when I was able to capitalize playing basically in a second line position behind Perreault," Meehan said. "We didn't get as much quality ice time as Gilbert's line, and deservedly so; they were the Connection, but we were able to chip in some pretty decent numbers as a second unit.

"Jim was a terrific player, but people tend not to remember Hughie. He was the same type of player as Lorentz, but while Jim was more wily in the corners, Hughie was bigger and stronger and he could crash the corners a little better. We played together for about two-thirds of that season, and we really worked well as a unit."

Harris jumped to New England of the WHA in 1973-74 and was replaced on the line by a variety of players including Rick Dudley, Norm Gratton and Steve Atkinson, and as the chemistry changed, so too did Meehan's scoring touch as he managed only 20 goals and 46 points.

The following year, Joe Crozier left to coach Vancouver in the WHA, and Floyd Smith took over as head coach of the Sabres. Three games into the season, Imlach traded Meehan and Robitaille to Vancouver for defenseman Jocelyn Guevermont and minor leaguer Bryan McSheffrey, who wound up playing only three games for Buffalo.

Meehan had been an original Sabre, one of only three – Perreault and Roger Crozier were the others – left on the roster, and the trade to Vancouver prevented him from participating in the Sabres' greatest season ever. They won a team-record 49 games, captured their first Adams Division crown, and advanced all the way to the Stanley Cup Finals before losing to the Flyers in six games.

"Well, I never had a sense that that was going to happen to the team," Meehan said. "At the time I was more disappointed about leaving and having to go as far away as we did. It was something that had probably been in the works because my last season didn't match up to my previous one, and I think they were looking at ways to add components to the team which included a big shot from the point, which Guevermont could provide."

Meehan's travels were far from complete. Later that year, the Canucks sent him back to the East Coast in a deal with Atlanta, and then midway through 1975-76, the Flames traded him to Washington. With the Capitals, Meehan enjoyed two more productive years, scoring a career-high 64 points in 1976-77.

"There were some good things happening in Washington my second year there, similar to the way things started building in Buffalo," he said. "We had a pretty good young team with some pretty solid veterans, and we took a run at the playoffs for about three months. Then as the season wore on, we started to fade because of our lack of depth. That's what usually happens with teams that challenge early, they don't have the depth to carry it through to the end in an 80-game schedule.

"I had some very gratifying moments there, I had my best offensive year in Washington points-wise, and I was sort of a community guy, did a lot of work there, was an alternate captain. But then age and time ran out."

He began the 1978 season with the Capitals, but the young team was moving in a new direction, and the 32-year-old Meehan was not part of the future. Washington general manager Max McNab told Meehan he could trade him to Cincinnati of the WHA, and Meehan approved the deal, mainly because it was almost a certainty that the WHA was going to merge in some way with the NHL the following year. However, after just two games in Cincinnati, he suffered a shoulder injury, then spent the next few weeks stewing about his future. Just before Christmas, he decided to retire.

"When I got to Buffalo, I spent a couple years enjoying the life of being in the NHL and not having to worry about

where the money was coming from, so I played golf in the summers and worked at a few hockey schools," he said. "But after I got traded from Buffalo, I realized this was going to be it, I wasn't going to be able to waste my summers anymore, so I enrolled at Canisius for summer school, and continued the undergraduate degree that I had started in Toronto, and I concluded it just about the time my career ended.

"When I quit hockey, I didn't have anything to do, but I also had no immediate financial concerns because I had planned for the day when my career ended and made sure that I wouldn't have to jump into the first situation that came along just to pay the bills. So one day I was just out driving around doing a few errands and I thought maybe I should go over to UB Law School and see what I have to do. It turned out that was the very last day to apply for admission and write the law school aptitude test. If I had gone the other direction on that drive, I probably wouldn't have done it. I managed to get in my application by the end of the day.

"I'd always had plans when I was playing junior and going to the University of Toronto that I'd end up in law. I thought about not playing pro hockey and going into law school right after junior hockey. When the decision came to go to a pro camp and I was offered a contract, I thought I could always come back to law school, but if I don't give hockey a shot, I'll never find out if I could have made it."

Meehan graduated from law school at the University of Buffalo in 1982, and his appetite for working in the sports law area was satisfied when he took a position with the firm of Cohen, Swados, Wright, Hanifin, Bradford and Brett.

Robert Swados had been a key player in the Sabres organization since its inception. Swados had made a name for himself on the Buffalo sports scene by serving as vice-president of the Buffalo Bisons baseball club, and also as one of the driving forces in Buffalo's bid to get a Major League Baseball franchise in the 1950s. He was later retained as counsel by the Knox brothers when they

made their first attempt to enter the NHL in the expansion of 1967, and when the Sabres were finally accepted in 1969, Swados was named vice-president of the team.

So with Swados' firm doing the bulk of the team's legal business, Meehan was able to work on player contracts, assisting then-Sabres general manager Scotty Bowman. In the summer of 1984, the Knoxes asked Meehan to come work for the team directly as Bowman's assistant general manager and Meehan accepted, thus becoming the first ex-Sabres player to work in the team's front office.

On December 2, 1986, Meehan ascended to the general manager's position when Bowman was fired, beginning a six-and-a-half-year term that was filled with many accomplishments, but was also tainted by the Sabres' inability to make a dent in the NHL playoffs.

The year Meehan took over as GM was without question the poorest in Sabres history. On November 6, 1986, Bowman relinquished his coaching duties and put his assistant, Ramsay, in charge. Three weeks later, Perreault abruptly announced his retirement, ending his Hall of Fame career. And a week after that, the Knoxes announced that Bowman was being relieved of all his duties. Sadly, the front office turmoil wasn't the worst of it, because on the ice, the team was floundering horribly. With a pitiful 7-22-4 record, Meehan made his first major move on December 22, 1986, when he demoted Ramsay back to assistant coach and brought in Ted Sator to run the team.

The Sabres went on to a last-place finish in the NHL, but in Meehan's first full year on the job, the team zipped up the ladder to No. 7 overall in the league, and Meehan finished second in balloting for The Sporting News NHL Executive of the Year Award.

"The coaching change was important, and Ted Sator came in and did an excellent job," Meehan said. "Craig was the interim coach when I came in, and Craig really wasn't, at that time I didn't think, comfortable being the coach of an NHL team. He had taken the job under some degree of pressure, and the team just didn't respond, there was some uncertainty, the players were wondering what's going to happen next. My thought was to stabilize the uncertainty, bring in a coach who can be perceived as a career coach.

"Ted had done good things in New York, he was a strong disciplinarian, and conditioning was an important part of his program. He had the kind of approach that team needed at that time."

In 1988-89, Buffalo leaped to third in the NHL standings. However, just as they had been eliminated in the first round of the playoffs by Boston the previous season, the Sabres were sent packing again by the Bruins, and this was a trend that only became more disturbing as the years went on.

"My job as a general manager was to make sure we had a competitive team that represented Buffalo in the playoffs every year, and we made the playoffs every year I was there as general manager," Meehan said.

That was because Meehan knew how to put a team together. Among the players he acquired via trades: Mark Napier, Doug Bodger, Rick Vaive, Clint Malarchuk, Grant Ledyard, Dale Hawerchuk, Pat LaFontaine, Randy Wood, Petr Svoboda, Dave Hannan, Dominik Hasek and Grant Fuhr. And he presided over the drafting of players such as Pierre Turgeon, Alexander Mogilny, Rob Ray, Kevin Haller, Derek Plante, Donald Audette, Brad May, Richard Smehlik, Jason Dawe, Steve Shields, Brian Holzinger and Matthew Barnaby, and of course, was instrumental in bringing Mogilny to America.

But the only playoff series the Sabres won during his tenure came in 1993 – Meehan's last year as GM – when May's overtime goal completed a four-game sweep of the Bruins. And then in the second round, Montreal swept the Sabres.

"We beat Boston and got to the second round, and that was the year we had a healthy, strong, well-motivated group of players," Meehan said. "That was a team that I believe was a Stanley Cup contender. But then we lost the first two games in Montreal, and in Game Three, we lost Mogilny and LaFontaine to injuries. Grant Fuhr had been injured and Dominik Hasek was playing net for the first time, and I still believe that team,

had we stayed healthy, could have won the Stanley Cup. Was I disappointed? Sure I was, what might have happened didn't, but that's a fact of life."

In June of 1993, Meehan was ready to take on a more prominent role, not only with the Sabres, but with the entire sports empire being operated at the Aud.

"I approached the ownership and told them there were things about this job I loved, and things I didn't like, but here's the job I'd really like to have," Meehan said of his proposal to the Knoxes to become executive vice-president of sports operations.

John Muckler, who had been hired as director of hockey operations in 1991 and then took over as head coach in December that year, was perfectly capable of assuming the general manager's position, so the Knoxes agreed to promote Meehan. Thus, Meehan had a hand in running the Sabres and their farm club in Rochester, as well as the Buffalo Blizzard of the National Professional Soccer League, and the Buffalo Bandits of the Major Indoor Lacrosse League.

"I was responsible for all aspects of their sports activities, and that's what I wanted to do, to be more involved in the business and legal affairs of the corporation rather than just the hockey department," Meehan said.

Meehan thrived on those duties, but he was also hoping that one day he would be promoted to president of the operation. Those dreams were shattered in December of 1994 when Doug Moss

was hired for that newly created position. Within six months, Meehan resigned his position and left the organization.

When he left the Sabres, he and his wife Mirella and their three children, Danny, Adam and Katie, moved back to Toronto. Meehan is licensed to practice law in New York State, so he deals primarily with international law and also does consulting work. But his passion for hockey remains, so when a former junior teammate requested his help in a bold new venture, Meehan could not resist.

Meehan spent the vast majority of the last year helping to build an expansion junior team in the Ontario Hockey Association, the premier development league for the NHL. The St. Michaels College Majors were a storied team in the 1940s and 50s, but went out of business in 1961. With Meehan's help, the club is being reformed 36 years later.

"It has been quite a challenge, but it's doable," Meehan said prior to the team's debut this fall. "I was looking for something to do, and this was an area that I'm familiar with. An old friend of mine called me and said, 'We need your help,' so I agreed to do it."

Meehan does not sound bitter as he talks about his departure from the Sabres, but when asked if he thinks he should still be a member of the organization, he says, "The guy (Moss) who didn't want me there is no longer there, so I would say that if he hadn't been brought in, yes, I probably would still be there."

As Joe Crozier looked at the four games scheduled between December 6-13, he knew this was going to be as crucial a stretch as his young club had ever faced. First there was a trip to Madison Square Garden, where the Sabres had never won in six previous tries. Then it was back home to face Detroit, the team the Sabres were probably going to have to beat out for a playoff spot in the East, followed by dates with the two best teams in the NHL, Montreal and Boston.

To this point, 17 of the Sabres' 26 games had come against teams with sub-.500 records – five against the two expansion teams – so there was reason to believe the Sabres had fattened up on a weak early schedule. This stretch would give Crozier an accurate barometer of how far his club had come, and perhaps how far it still had to go.

In New York, Dryden made his third consecutive start, and after a pair of clunkers against the North Stars, he turned aside 31 shots and kept the Sabres in the game long enough for Meehan to win it, 3-2, with a bad-angle goal that caromed in off New York goalie Gilles Villemure's stick with 2:43 left to play.

There was no time to relish the victory, though, because the next night, the Sabres hosted the Red Wings. With Horton back in the lineup, and Dryden again tending net after his strong effort in New York, the Sabres cruised to a 6-1 victory. Meehan and Robert, the two hottest

NHL STANDINGS THROUGH SUNDAY, DECEMBER 3				
EAST	**W**	**L**	**T**	**PTS**
Montreal	15	4	7	37
NY Rangers	16	7	3	35
Boston	15	7	3	33
Buffalo	11	8	7	29
Detroit	11	10	2	24
Toronto	8	13	4	20
Vancouver	8	15	2	18
NY Islanders	3	18	2	8
WEST	**W**	**L**	**T**	**PTS**
Minnesota	14	8	3	31
Chicago	14	9	2	30
Pittsburgh	13	11	2	28
Los Angeles	11	11	4	26
Philadelphia	11	11	4	26
Atlanta	10	13	5	25
St. Louis	7	11	5	19
California	4	15	5	13

Hugh Harris was one of the unsung players on the 1972-73 team. He was a grinder in the corners who helped Jim Lorentz and Gerry Meehan get numerous scoring chances.

offensive performers, scored twice while Harris and Ramsay had the other goals.

Dryden's hot streak couldn't have come at a better time, what with his brother Ken and the Canadiens coming to town next. In four games against Ken, Dave had never come away a winner, but in front of an electrified sellout throng at the Aud, Dave made 26 saves to backbone a 4-2 victory, Buffalo's fourth in a row, a new club record.

"I had myself convinced before we went on the ice that we were just playing a bunch of guys in red shirts," Dave said. "I had a nice nap in the afternoon and felt as ready as I ever have before a game. But every once in a while I would look up and see Ken making a good save down at the other end of the ice and then I'd feel I had to make a good one, too."

Luce and Robert scored in the first 6:18 of the game, but Montreal battled back to get even before the period ended on goals by Jacques Lemaire and Rejean Houle. After a scoreless second period, the Sabres took control in the third, firing 16 shots at Ken Dryden and getting two behind him. At 1:19, with Buffalo on a power play, Dryden stopped shots by Robert and Martin, but he couldn't stop Lorentz on a rebound. And then with 5:31 remaining, Martin let the air out of the building when he rifled a 15-footer over Dryden's glove.

Montreal coach Scotty Bowman was upset by the officiating. When Lorentz scored, the Canadiens were, in effect, two men short. Guy Lafleur and Pete Mahovolich were both in the penalty box and Buffalo enjoyed a two-man advantage for 51 seconds. Lorentz's goal came just two seconds after Lafleur had returned to the ice, and before he could get himself back into the play.

"That double penalty was the game," Bowman complained. "And the crowd influenced those penalties, definitely. I have yet to get what I consider a good game by an official in Buffalo."

Three games into this crucial stretch, and the Sabres had won every game. If anyone in the NHL was questioning the Sabres now, Joe Crozier said they were crazy.

"If we play like we did tonight, we're going to be knocking at the (playoff) door," he said. "We're a third-year expansion team working hard to win and we've beaten the Montreal Canadiens and the New York Rangers within five days."

And three days hence, Crozier was able to add the Boston Bruins to that impressive list. In a game that is still talked about to this day, the Sabres beat the stuffing out of the Bruins – literally – 7-3.

Forgotten was the fact that Buffalo extended its home-ice unbeaten streak to 16 games, or that the loss ended Boston's unbeaten streak at 12 games, or that Perreault scored twice, or that Robert had three assists, or that league scoring leader Phil Esposito was held without a point, or that Atkinson spent the whole day at a hospital with his pregnant wife Lola, left her at 5:45 p.m. to come to the Aud, and scored a goal just minutes after it was flashed across the message board that Lola had given birth to a baby girl.

No, what people remember about that night were the three fights

SCORING THROUGH DECEMBER 10

PLAYER	G	A	PTS
Perreault	12	27	39
Robert	18	21	39
Martin	21	17	38
Lorentz	9	16	25
Meehan	15	7	22
Hillman	3	11	14
Luce	7	6	13
Harris	4	9	13
Atkinson	5	7	12
Ramsay	6	3	9
Robitaille	1	7	8
Horton	0	7	7
Mickey	1	5	6
Schoenfeld	1	5	6
Terbenche	0	5	5
Wyrozub	2	2	4
Pratt	0	4	4
Carriere	0	3	3
Deadmarsh	1	0	1

GOALIE	GM	GA	GAA
Crozier	22	57	2.85
Dryden	11	29	3.22

Schoenfeld got into, most notably his battle with Wayne Cashman when both players went crashing through the doors to the Zamboni entrance, and continued their melee on the concrete as the Aud rocked with glee.

"That was a strange thing that happened when Cashman and Schoenfeld went through the boards," recalled Fred Stanfield, who played for the Bruins in that game, but later joined the Sabres and was a key member of the 1974-75 team. "It was just one of those crazy games. It was a great rivalry between Buffalo and Boston, and you could feel that coming into the building, the friction in the stands, the crowd, you just knew you were in for a good hockey game.

"That's what it's all about, having that competition out there between Boston and Buffalo. It got you more up for the game, playing against a team

Steve Atkinson got off to a great start, but he slumped near the end of the season and his goal production fell off.

like that one in Buffalo. That game gave the Buffalo fans quite a spark. It showed them their team wasn't afraid to fight the Boston Bruins, who were No. 1 at that time. It got the fans even more interested in hockey, and the interest has stayed forever. That was one of the outstanding games that was ever played in the Aud."

Schoenfeld also duked it out with Carol Vadnais and the incomparable Bobby Orr, who rarely lost his cool, but did so on this occasion. In fact, when Schoenfeld and Vadnais had their set-to, Orr left the Bruins bench with a bunch of his pals in tow, and skated to the Buffalo bench looking for action. Orr found Hillman to be a willing partner, and when Crozier tried to pry them apart, he wound up on the floor underneath the two combatants.

Interestingly, Terry O'Reilly, the most pugnacious Bruin, never got involved with Schoenfeld. However, there was a reason.

"Jim and I had squared off in junior hockey," O'Reilly said. "He played for Niagara Falls when I was playing for Oshawa. We had a real heavy bout to the point where I don't think we were ever going to do it again, and we didn't. In our professional careers, we never scrapped with each other, just out of mutual respect. In fact, eventually he ended up in Boston as my teammate, and it was a great experience for me. So when he and Cashman went through the boards, I think I just went right down there to the edge of the ice to watch. Besides, I didn't want to get my skates all scuffled up on the concrete."

The Bruins had jumped to a 2-0 lead, scoring twice within 11 seconds in the first period, the second goal coming on a power play after the Schoenfeld-Cashman brawl, the result of an extra minor assessed to Schoenfeld. But the Sabres rallied to tie it on goals by Hillman and Ramsay, and when Meehan and Perreault scored before six minutes had been played in the second period, Buffalo was on top, 4-2.

Orr blasted one past Dryden to cut the Bruins deficit to 4-3, but three minutes later Atkinson celebrated his daughter's birth in high style, and then Perreault and Luce scored in the third period to put an exclamation point on a crazy evening.

"All I want to do is play the game," Schoenfeld said that night. "Truthfully, I would like to have people come into the dressing room and say, 'You played a good game,' instead of talking about what a great fight I was in. I admit I sometimes turn into an animal during a game, but when the game is over, it's all forgotten with me. I like to see and talk to any guy I fight with and see that he's a human being just as I am."

PROFILE - Jim Schoenfeld

Twenty-five years have passed since Schoenfeld and Cashman waged their epic battle, but the memory remains fresh, mainly because people still ask them about it to this day.

"It gets magnified because the Zamboni doors flew open," Schoenfeld said. "If the doors don't fly open, then it's just another night, a hockey game with a couple of scraps. The fact that the doors flew open adds a definite signature to the night, but to me it was nothing more than two hungry teams battling hard.

"Too much was made of that fight. It certainly didn't change my career nor did it change Wayne Cashman's career. Wayne was a player I had a great deal of respect for as a kid watching him with the Bruins and then playing against him, and that respect probably grew after the fight. It wouldn't have mattered to Wayne if he would have spanked me in that fight and it wouldn't have mattered to me if I would have spanked him. It was just part of the game.

"That's just hockey and people who aren't in the game, they may not understand. You can get brothers on opposing teams who will scrap because this is a very emotional game. But it's one of those things where, when it's over, you might see a fella in a bar or restaurant afterward and it's immediately done. It's finished on the ice, you don't carry it off the ice."

Contrary to popular belief, Schoenfeld said he wasn't looking to make a statement that night by going toe-to-toe

with the big, bad Bruins.

"I wasn't really looking for things. Boston was a tough team, they had great team courage, and their strength was playing a physical game, so you didn't have to go looking for physical confrontations against a club like the Bruins.

"We were a young team trying to be like that, trying to compete in every game, trying to play through the physical aspects of the game. This was just one of those nights where we happened to be playing the Bruins and our team really pulled together and we won the hockey game."

Schoenfeld was born and raised in Galt, Ont., about 65 miles west of Toronto. As a child, he took a liking to hockey, and he remembers following Horton's exploits when Horton was helping the Leafs win four Stanley Cups in the 1960s, "so Timmy being my mentor in Buffalo was a nice turn of events," Schoenfeld said.

Hockey wasn't Schoenfeld's only passion. He liked all sports and he and his friends changed with the seasons. "In autumn there was football, in the spring you fished and in the summer you played baseball," he said. "We didn't play hockey year-round the way kids play nowadays."

However, by the time he was 10 years old and playing organized hockey, he knew he wanted to play in the NHL.

Schoenfeld's junior career was unique in that he played for three different organizations. He started with London, but late in his first year, the Knights were pushing for a playoff spot and decided to trade some of their youth for a few more established junior players, so Schoenfeld and future Pittsburgh Penguin Rick Kehoe were sent to Hamilton. In Hamilton, Schoenfeld had a run-in with the owner of the team, and he was dealt again, this time to Niagara Falls. It was with the Flyers where Schoenfeld began to make a name for himself as a sturdy defensive defenseman who could provide muscle. In his final season, he led the OHA with 225 penalty minutes.

"I don't think I ever really had a reputation of being a tough guy in junior," Schoenfeld said. "I don't think I was a player who went out of the way to look for a fight. Once in a while you have to fight and if you do well, people might think that's something you might be suited for."

Although he had played in nearby

Niagara Falls, Schoenfeld didn't particularly have a desire to play for the Sabres, although once he arrived in St. Catharines for his first training camp, he knew he was in the right place.

"I was just happy to be drafted, period," he said. "The thing that was fortunate for me is that this was an expansion team that I was drafted by, and it was a team that I was able to play on right away. A lot of players that were better than I was who may have been drafted before or after me, perhaps they went to a stronger team, but they didn't get an opportunity to play right away. I was able to go to Buffalo and be a member of the team right off the bat and be paired with a real good teacher like Tim.

"And it wasn't only Tim. Larry Hillman was another guy who was a strong influence on me. I was fortunate, I sat in the corner of the dressing room with Tim to my immediate left and Larry to my immediate right. I was surrounded by experience, by players who had won Stanley Cups, by players who played hard every game and knew what it took to be winners. As a young kid coming in, these were men I had watched and looked up to, so it was a terrific growing and learning environment for a young player."

Schoenfeld was an instant hit with the fans in Buffalo. His rugged, hard-hitting style sent shock waves throughout the Aud, and also gave his teammates an added air of confidence knowing that if they got into a tussle, Schoenfeld was there to lend a hand.

"Obviously that year we had a great addition with Schony," said Martin. "He let people know he was on the ice. But he wasn't just a fighter, he was a solid defenseman."

After getting off to an impressive start, which had people around the league touting him as a possible Rookie of the Year candidate – potentially the Sabres' third such winner in a row – Schoenfeld took a step back at midseason. A Christmas Eve automobile accident cost him about two weeks of playing time, and when he returned, he struggled and his plus minus rating actually dipped into negative numbers for the first time.

"When you're a rookie, everything is so new, every game has its own life," he said. "I never looked at statistics, I was just trying to play my best each game and just trying to get by. What happened – as what happens with a lot of young kids – is that you come into the league, you're gung ho, but as the season wears on, you're not used to playing an 80-game grind, or whatever it was back then, against well-conditioned men.

"I think I went through a period of adjustment where the game catches up and surpasses you a little bit, and sometimes it takes until the next year or the following year to regain your footing. A lot of kids come in and have a great rookie year or great first half of their rookie year and then don't follow it up with a good second year or even a good third year. That's just the growing process. Having been in the game, I see that happen a lot. It's difficult for a kid to start well and then continue to improve the entire season. You're bound to have some ups and downs."

The downs didn't last long. Schoenfeld fought back, with the help of Horton, Hillman and Joe Crozier, and down the stretch he was back playing the way he did early in the season.

"He was a tough kid," Crozier said. "He and Horton were great buddies and I played them together and Schony really looked up to Horton. I could play Schony under any circumstances, even when he was a rookie, because they all respected him and were afraid of him. He fought them all."

Schoenfeld finished his first year with a plus 12 rating which tied him with Horton for third-best on the team. But the 1973-74 season was, to say the least, a tragic one for Schoenfeld. Not only did he battle injuries all year that limited him to 28 games, but he lost his friend, his mentor, Horton.

"We got a call early in the morning from the office," Schoenfeld says, recalling that unforgettable day that remains, in his mind, the low point of his career. "We were living over in Fort Erie in a beach house and there was a patio out back, and I remember spending most of the day shoveling snow off the patio and

then shoveling it back on, just trying to occupy my time with something physical. Then I took my dog for a long walk on the beach just trying to reconcile things.

"I thought I had a pretty good handle on it, I thought I was OK and I'd go to the rink and play, but I remember being on the ice as part of the starting lineup during the national anthem, and they had the moment of silence for Tim. It was strange, it was almost like you could feel the compound grief of everyone in the building and it was kind of overwhelming.

"I remember trying to play the first shift with tears coming out of my eyes. I remember finishing the shift, going to the bench and Joe Crozier came down and comforted me. He recognized the situation and told me it was going to be OK. From that point on I was OK. You never know when your emotions are going to catch up to you. I thought I had a handle on everything and could keep my emotion inside, but that wasn't the case.

"The loss of Tim was not only felt then, but it's been felt ever since. Tim was not only a great mentor and hockey player and someone I looked up to in that way, he was also a hell of a guy. He was a great example. If you want to look for a person who did everything to the max, whether it was playing the game, working in his business, Tim did everything all out. He lived a very full life and for a young, impressionable kid, that was good to see. In the short time we were together, he had a real strong impact on my life."

Schoenfeld put the misery of 1973-74 behind him and returned with a vengeance in 1974-75. He was awarded the captain's C after Meehan was traded, and he and Jerry Korab became one of the most feared defensive pairings in the league. When opposing skaters brought the puck into the Buffalo zone against those two, they never did so with their heads down because Schoenfeld and Korab would knock them into the next millennium.

Over the next four years, Schoenfeld was a cumulative plus 127 and he played in one All-Star game, and after an injury-shortened 1978-79 campaign, he turned in one of the greatest seasons in Sabres history in 1979-80, Scotty Bowman's first year with the club. Schoenfeld posted a plus 60 rating, second all-time to Luce's plus 61 in 1974-75. He earned second-team NHL All-Star honors and played in his second All-Star game. In addition, he produced career-highs with nine goals and 36 points as Buffalo won the Adams Division and advanced to the Wales Conference finals where it lost to the New York Islanders.

Schoenfeld slipped a bit in 1980-81, and after the Sabres made a disappointing second-round playoff exit, it was obvious Bowman was looking to make changes in 1981-82. Sure enough, even though the team lost only five of its first 24 games, Bowman made what was at that point the biggest trade in team history.

He sent Schoenfeld, Danny Gare, Derek Smith and Bob Sauve to Detroit in exchange for Mike Foligno, Dale McCourt and Brent Peterson. Schoenfeld and Gare were considered the heart and soul of the team, and Sabres fans were livid. In the 24 hours after the deal was consummated, the team's tapeline received almost 800 calls. In a memorable scene at the Buffalo airport, Schoenfeld broke down and cried while being interviewed by Channel 7 sports anchor Rick Azar, and the normally stoic Azar was visibly shaken as well.

"I'd been traded in junior, but I wasn't married and didn't have any children and at the time of this trade, we had two kids and my wife Theresa was expecting our third in about a month," Schoenfeld said. "They couldn't come with me because the kids were in school and she had to stay back with her doctors, so I was going off alone. It wasn't only leaving the team, but I was leaving my family. It's funny at the time how traumatic things seem, but then when you look back, it's nothing more than a slight inconvenience because we went on to Detroit and made

some new friends there, then went to Boston and you find the beat goes on. But sure, it was a big hurt when I had to leave Buffalo."

As Schoenfeld looks back on his nine and a half years in Buffalo, none of the highs were higher than his rookie season when he helped the Sabres make the playoffs for the first time.

"It was something the franchise had never done before," Schoenfeld said. "It was the culmination of an exciting first

year and a first look at the NHL and to be there and experience it with Tim and Larry Hillman and Larry Carriere and all the guys, that was really something. I was going to war with Horton and Hillman and you feel like you're a part of that accomplishment. That to me was the greatest highlight of my time there."

Schoenfeld played in Detroit through 1983, spent one year with his former foils, the Bruins, and then retired from the game. Or so he thought.

After accepting the head coaching position for Buffalo's farm team in

Rochester and guiding the Amerks to a superb record of 17-6-2 in early 1984-85, Bowman talked Schoenfeld into returning to Buffalo as a player to help out the struggling Sabres defensive corps.

"It was a situation where the Sabres weren't playing as well as people expected and I think Scotty thought a veteran player on the blue line could help out a little bit," Schoenfeld said. "I was termed a senior defenseman which meant I'd be a guy who would play defense for the Sabres, be in and out of the lineup, and work with the young kids."

The brief stint as coach in Rochester proved to be one of the turning points in Schoenfeld's life.

"I was offered the job in Rochester, but I didn't think I would be interested. I had a friend who said, 'Why don't you try it and if you hate it, at least you'll know that's what you don't want to do for the rest of your life and you can move on to something else.' So I said, 'What the hell, I might as well try it.' I had no other plans. And as it turned out, I really liked it in Rochester. We had a real hard-working team and we got off to a sensational start that year. It was a great first experience, and I thought this coaching thing was pretty nice."

At the end of the 1984-85 season, Schoenfeld retired from playing, this time for good, and a couple of months later, Bowman decided he no longer wanted to stand behind the bench, so he turned the Sabres coaching reins over to Schoenfeld, even though the big redhead's only coaching experience at any level were those 25 games in the AHL the year before.

Unlike his team in Rochester, the Sabres didn't produce the same type of results. They started well, but then began to slip into a funk that Bowman decided Schoenfeld wasn't capable of pulling them out of. In a very surprising move, Bowman fired Schoenfeld with the team's record at 19-19-5, and he coached the remainder of the season. Bowman's record over the final 37 games was 18-18-1, and the team finished last in the Adams, missing the playoffs for the first time in 11 years.

"That's the way it is in sports," Schoenfeld said. "When the expectations are greater than the realization, something has to give. The expectations that year were for a much more successful season. Whether the expectations are realistic or not really doesn't matter, that's not the point, and it happens all over the place, not only in hockey but in all sports.

"So either you trade players, or change coaches and/or general managers. And that's OK, that's the business. If you want to be a coach, you have to understand going in that that's part and parcel of what being a coach is. If push comes to shove, there's a good chance the coach is the guy who will be moved rather than a group of players, even if they're underachievers or malcontents or players who have been overrated that aren't ever going to be good."

After spending almost two years away from the game, working primarily as a spokesman for the City Mattress bedding company, Schoenfeld accepted the New Jersey Devils' head coaching position after Doug Carpenter was fired 50 games into the 1987-88 season.

"I really thought that (Devils' general manager) Lou Lamoriello showed a great deal of courage in hiring me. Here I was, a guy who had coached 43 games in the NHL and had been fired, and now it's a couple of years later and I wasn't involved in the game for two years, and he took a chance on me."

Schoenfeld guided the Devils to a 17-12-1 record and when John MacLean scored an overtime goal to win the final game of the year in Chicago, the Devils reached the playoffs for the first time.

"That was the greatest highlight of all my time in hockey," Schoenfeld said. "That meant so much to so many people who had been with the organization for a number of years and always fell short of making the playoffs. That was the most emotional night I've ever had in the game. The only thing that could

surpass that would be winning a Stanley Cup as a coach, it was that meaningful."

After MacLean's goal, the Devils got on a roll in the postseason and advanced to the Wales Conference finals against the Boston Bruins, then coached by Schoenfeld's old rival, Terry O'Reilly.

"All I know about Schoenfeld is that he doesn't pay his bets," O'Reilly said recently with a laugh. "I had a bet for dinner with him on the outcome of that series when he was coaching New Jersey and I was coaching Boston. We won and he hasn't paid up yet."

Countered Schoenfeld, "I took him out to dinner in Boston last year (1996), that bum. I picked up the tab, and as usual, he over-ate."

It was during that series that Schoenfeld made one of the most famous wisecracks in NHL lore. Unhappy with the performance of referee Don Koharski in the Devils' Game Three defeat, Schoenfeld called Koharski a "fat pig" and told him to "eat another donut."

"I look back now and I don't think it was warranted," Schoenfeld said of his remarks. "The thing I regret most is that I made a personal comment in a professional argument and I shouldn't have done that."

The Devils slipped to fifth place in the Patrick Division the following year and missed the playoffs, and when the team started 6-6-2 in 1989-90, Schoenfeld was fired and replaced by John Cunniff.

Schoenfeld joined ESPN as a studio analyst for the cable network's hockey telecasts, and his good looks combined with his honest and insightful commentary made him a popular figure for the two years he was on the air. But just when he thought his days at the rink were through, the Washington Capitals came knocking at his door midway through the 1993-94 season.

"I really felt I had put coaching behind me, that it was out of my system," Schoenfeld said. "I was enjoying what I was doing, and I didn't pursue coaching at all. I wasn't sending out resumes or making calls or asking anyone to put in a word for me, I just wasn't interested, and then I got a call from David (Poile, the Capitals' general manager) out of the blue, and he was contemplating

making a change.

"The minute I was asked if I would like to be the coach, a spark went off and said, 'This is probably what you should be doing.' Even though I was enjoying what I was doing, coaching was still kind of in my blood. So I came back, and I'm still at it."

Schoenfeld completed his third full season behind the Capitals' bench last year and for the first time since he came aboard, Washington failed to make the playoffs, narrowly losing a tight race with Montreal and Ottawa.

In the aftermath, Schoenfeld and Poile were both fired, and Schoenfeld landed on his feet in Phoenix as coach of the Coyotes.

He hasn't been part of the Sabres organization for more than a decade, but you'll never hear Sabres' fans boo Schoenfeld no matter what club he's with. He was a fan favorite as a player and coach, and Buffalonians haven't forgotten what he meant to the team, and to them.

"I was extremely proud to be a Buffalo Sabre. I have a high regard for the people who owned the team, the late Seymour Knox, and Norty, and I still do. I was fortunate to break in with players who I immediately had a great deal of respect for, and found out that my respect for them was warranted. Sometimes in life you find it goes the other way, you look at people that you have a high regard for and then as you get to know them, maybe it wasn't really warranted, but in this case, my respect grew for these people.

"The whole introducton to the Sabres organization was one of class for me, a real positive entry into the NHL. I thought, 'If every franchise is like this, it might be a great league.' And then you find out every franchise isn't the same. The one regret, and it will always be with me, is that we didn't give the Buffalo fans a championship season. Selfishly I would have loved to have won the Stanley Cup, but unselfishly, I think it's something that the Buffalo fans deserve. They gave us such great support, and have continued to give the team great support, so you'd like to see that rewarded."

Had the Sabres' winning streak come to an end at five, they would have had a few good excuses. After all the emotion expelled during the Boston win, a letdown would have been natural. Plus, they were scheduled to play next in St. Louis, where they had never won in seven previous attempts. Add to that a harrowing trip caused by a snowstorm that delayed their arrival into the arch city until 1:30 p.m. the day of the game, and all the ingredients were there for a defeat.

Instead, Meehan scored with 7:36 left to play, and Roger Crozier, back in the nets after a two-week layoff, stopped 35 shots to key a 4-3 triumph. Perreault had his second straight two-goal game, even though Martin was sidelined for the final two periods due to a hand injury. It was Buffalo's 16th win of the season, matching its total from 1971-72.

The next night, the Maple Leafs came to the Aud, and the Sabres disposed of them, 4-0, behind Dryden's 21-save shutout. Their seventh win in a row also extended their home-ice unbeaten streak to 17 games (14-0-3), and it was the first time they had beaten Toronto twice in a season.

Dryden talked about his increased workload, the most he had ever had in the NHL.

"I never before had the feeling I have here," he said. "I never actually talked about it with Joe Crozier, but he gave me the feeling that I'm going to play, so get out, have some fun, enjoy yourself."

The team's winning streak and exciting style of play brought to the forefront an unfortunate, but understandable, oversight on the part of the NBC television network which at the time was broadcasting NHL games. NBC was contracted to televise 15 regular-season games (12 Sundays, one Saturday and two Fridays), and nowhere on that schedule were the Sabres. Five Detroit games were going to be shown.

"Well, let's be honest about it," Imlach remarked. "Nobody in radio or television was aware that we were gonna be as good a drawing card as we've turned out to be. You can't blame the network for it because these TV schedules are made up as early as June sometimes. Naturally we as a team are upset about it, but right now, the TV people are well aware of us and we won't be overlooked in the future. Anyway, we'll be on NBC in the playoffs this year, you can count on it."

The push for that playoff spot continued with a 6-3 win over Vancouver, Buffalo's eighth in a row, as Hillman assisted on the first three goals, Martin recorded his seventh two-goal game of the year, and Harris also chipped in with two goals. The victory was a solid one for the Sabres because after wading through a difficult schedule the past couple of weeks, the team was ripe for a letdown against the lowly Canucks.

"After playing teams like New York, Boston and Montreal, you seem to have a letdown no matter how hard you try not to," Hillman said. "You don't want to have a letdown, yet you do, and you don't know why. A club like Vancouver shouldn't beat you and you know it. So there's a different sort of pressure. You have to beat these clubs to make the playoffs."

This was a point Joe Crozier wholeheartedly agreed with. "Everybody is expecting a Boston-type game every night, which means everyone is expecting too much. Everybody is happy when we beat Boston. Me, I'm

NHL STANDINGS THROUGH SUNDAY, DECEMBER 17				
EAST	W	L	T	PTS
Montreal	19	5	8	46
Boston	20	8	3	43
NY Rangers	20	10	3	43
Buffalo	17	8	7	41
Detroit	13	14	3	29
Toronto	9	17	5	23
Vancouver	9	19	4	22
NY Islanders	3	24	3	9
WEST	W	L	T	PTS
Chicago	19	10	2	40
Minnesota	17	12	3	37
Philadelphia	15	14	4	34
Pittsburgh	15	13	3	33
Los Angeles	14	14	4	32
Atlanta	13	16	5	31
St. Louis	10	14	6	26
California	4	19	7	15

happy when we beat Vancouver."

Lorentz, who tipped in a long shot by Hillman in the second period to give Buffalo a 3-0 lead and also assisted on two goals, said the Sabres had been fortunate because, "we haven't played too well the last three games, but we won them. I don't think we'll go into any prolonged slump or anything like that. We have confidence now, we have proven we can play with anybody."

Except, of course, the woebegone California Golden Seals. Incredibly, the Sabres had a 0-0 tie in Buffalo, and a pitiful 5-1 loss in Oakland against a team that had won just four of its first 31 games. It was with that baggage that they flew to the left coast for the second time in a month with games scheduled against the Seals and Los Angeles Kings.

The Sabres had won eight games in a row, California had not won in its last nine starts, and virtually no one in the Bay Area even knew the Seals existed. Yet in front of a sparse gathering of 3,080 at the Oakland Arena, the Seals had the Sabres shaking their heads in disbelief again following a 4-2 loss.

"I don't know why they are in last place," said Joe Crozier, who saw the Seals hold The French Connection without a point for the third time this season. "They just check, check, check us all night. They play well against us."

Larry Hillman provided veteran leadership to the young defensive corps, and he was a tough player who kept the front of the crease clear.

After a quick flight down to Los Angeles, the team spent the afternoon of December 23 at their hotel watching the National Football League playoffs, and rather than be inspired by Pittsburgh Steeler running back Franco Harris' Imaculate Reception that beat the Oakland Raiders, the Sabres turned in another flat effort that night against the Kings, losing 2-0. Rogie Vachon had to make only 20 saves as the Buffalo offense was stagnant.

"Nothing worked," Crozier said. "I didn't think any lack of hustle was apparent, they just didn't make the right moves. I'd like to nip this thing in the bud before it becomes an actual slump."

On the flight home, the team received some unsettling news as Roger Crozier – who had played pretty well against the Kings despite the loss – experienced serious stomach pains, and when the plane landed in Toronto, he was rushed to Toronto General Hospital. Crozier had undergone surgery on his pancreas and for removal of his gall bladder in the summer of 1971, and ever since he had been forced to follow a strict diet. He would remain hospitalized through the Christmas holiday.

A day later, Schoenfeld wound up in Deaconess Hospital after suffering a concussion in a Christmas Eve auto accident, so Terbenche made the trip to New York for the team's next game against the Rangers.

Without Crozier, the Sabres recalled Rocky Farr from Cincinnati to be Dryden's backup, but Farr wasn't needed at Madison Square Garden as the Sabres ventured into the hallowed arena for the second time in three weeks and beat the Rangers, 4-1. Dryden made 32 saves and so frustrated New York that coach Emile Francis said, "We could have played until tomorrow without doing any better."

The Western Division-leading Chicago Blackhawks had the same feeling the next night as the Sabres put together a dazzling performance, breaking free from a 3-2 game with five third-period goals for an 8-2 rout. The Sabres

SCORING THROUGH DECEMBER 31			
PLAYER	G	A	PTS
Perreault	17	34	51
Robert	23	27	50
Martin	23	21	44
Lorentz	14	25	39
Meehan	22	9	31
Hillman	4	17	21
Luce	10	10	20
Harris	6	12	18
Atkinson	8	8	16
Ramsay	7	8	15
Robitaille	2	8	10
Mickey	2	6	8
Schoenfeld	1	6	7
Horton	0	7	7
Pratt	1	5	6
Terbenche	0	5	5
Wyrozub	2	2	4
Carriere	0	3	3
Deadmarsh	1	0	1

Jim Lorentz and the rest of his teammates blitzed Chicago goalie Gary Smith during an 8-2 blowout at the Aud.

Blackhawks goalie Tony Esposito, shown here making a save in a game at Buffalo, stymied the Sabres in a New Years' Eve game at Chicago Stadium.

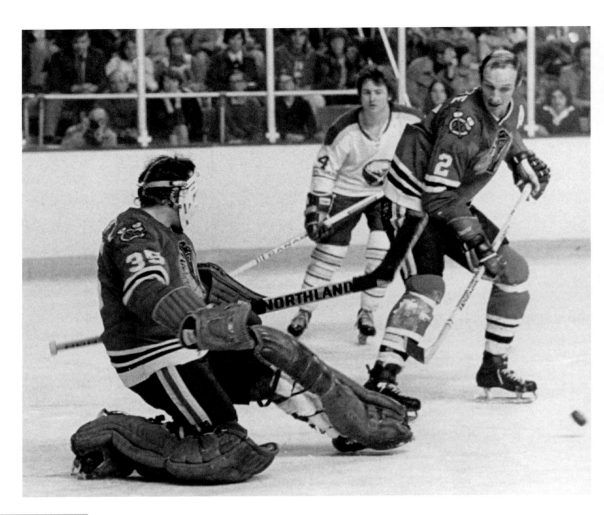

NHL STANDINGS THROUGH SUNDAY, DECEMBER 31				
EAST	**W**	**L**	**T**	**PTS**
Boston	25	8	3	53
Montreal	22	6	9	53
NY Rangers	23	12	3	49
Buffalo	20	11	7	47
Detroit	15	16	6	36
Toronto	12	19	6	30
Vancouver	11	21	6	28
NY Islanders	4	28	4	12
WEST	**W**	**L**	**T**	**PTS**
Chicago	22	13	2	46
Minnesota	19	14	4	42
Los Angeles	18	16	4	40
Philadelphia	16	17	6	38
Atlanta	15	18	6	36
Pittsburgh	15	16	6	36
St. Louis	12	18	6	30
California	6	22	8	20

extended their home-ice unbeaten streak to 19, and they now owned seven straight victories in December against the original six teams – New York, Boston, Montreal, Toronto, Detroit and Chicago – including at least one against every team.

Meehan scored a hat trick within 5:30 of the third period to set a new team record for fastest three goals by one player, and Robert scored twice.

Despite the fact that Schoenfeld was still hospitalized and Horton was out again with his recurring knee injury, Imlach decided to send Carriere back to Cincinnati. Carriere had not played since getting his head slammed into the glass against Boston back on November 30, and though he was ready to go again, Imlach decided he should get back into game shape with the Swords, where he would receive larger chunks of ice time.

The calendar year came to an end with a 4-2 New Year's Eve loss at Chicago Stadium as Blackhawks coach Billy Reay decided against using Gary Smith in net as he had done a few nights before in Buffalo. For this game, he went with Tony Esposito, and Espo blocked 30 shots to record the victory. The game was tied at 2-2 until Pat Stapleton ripped a 40-foot slap shot past Dryden with 4:40 left.

January: The Aud Unbeaten Streak Finally Ends

Since the start of the 1967 season, 10 expansion teams had joined the NHL. But until January 3, 1973, none of those clubs had ever won 11 straight games at home. That is, until the Sabres soared past the New York Islanders, 4-1.

The new NHL mark for longest home winning streak by an expansion team also extended Buffalo's unbeaten skein in the Aud to 20 games. For the Islanders, it was their 30th loss in 38 starts and one sportswriter summed up their gloomy situation best when he said, "They can't even ice the puck with authority."

The next night in Detroit, Joe Crozier decided to give Farr his first NHL start. Dryden had been carrying the burden with Roger Crozier still recuperating from his latest stomach ailment, and because the team was scheduled to play four games in five nights, the coach decided to give Dryden a rest against the Red Wings.

When Farr stopped all 15 first-period shots he faced, the coach looked like a genius. But then the Red Wings scored three goals on their first five shots in the middle period, and Crozier quickly brought an end to the experiment. He inserted Dryden 8:47 into the period after Alex Delvecchio scored, and Dryden blanked Detroit until Marcel Dionne's goal with just 1:05 left in Buffalo's 4-2 loss. Farr was sent back to Cincinnati at the end of the week when Roger Crozier returned, and never played another minute for the Sabres that season.

Joe Crozier was not blaming Farr for the defeat, though. "He had a hell of a first period, but it was his first NHL game and since I didn't feel we were giving him good support, I didn't want to see them run up the score on the kid. I didn't want him to lose his confidence because I think the kid has a fine future in this league."

The lone bright spot for the Sabres was the two-goal performance of Robert, who now had scored a goal in five straight games and had a team-high 26 for the season, already the most by any right winger in the team's brief history.

PROFILE - Rene Robert

It is Robert's fervent feeling that if Scotty Bowman had swallowed his massive ego and left the Sabres' roster intact when he took control of the team in the summer of 1979, Robert and his teammates would have been skating around the Aud holding the Stanley Cup aloft in the spring of 1980.

"If he had left that team alone for one year, just said, 'I'll leave my feelings aside and let the players play for one year and then I'll evaluate things at the end of the year,' we would have won the Stanley Cup," said Robert, an irascible tone to his voice that is easily detectable. "Instead, he went the other way. He wanted to prove a point that he was the boss, so he got rid of me. He wanted to build his own team and prove to the organization that he could do it on his own, and he ruined the franchise."

On October 5, 1979, Bowman struck a deal with the Colorado Rockies that brought defenseman John Van Boxmeer to Buffalo in exchange for Robert. The trade simultaneously disconnected The French Connection forever, and ripped open a gaping wound in Robert's heart that nearly two decades later hasn't fully healed.

"Yes, I'm still bitter," Robert said. "I loved it here and I never wanted to leave Buffalo, but that was beyond me, I couldn't control my destiny. The only reason he traded me is because he never saw eye-to-eye with me, yet we didn't even know each other aside from All-Star Games or when I played in the Canada Cup. We built a franchise from scratch here, and some pretty good hockey players came through this organization, and to let one guy ruin everything that was built in the first 10 years, it was hard to swallow. That's the grudge that I carry."

For more than seven years, Robert was one of the cornerstones on which the Sabres were built. Teaming with Perreault and Martin to form the dynamic French Connection line, Robert's slick skating, pinpoint passing, sharp shooting and gritty determination had Aud crowds bowing in "We're not worthy" deference long before Dana Carvey and Mike Myers popularized that form of flattery in the movie Wayne's World.

Robert had been a scoring prodigy in his native Three Rivers, Que., accumulating 69 goals and 150 points in his final junior season. Oddly, he had not been picked in the NHL amateur draft, so he spent four years bouncing around the minor leagues, making stops in the Central (Tulsa), Western (Vancouver) and American (Rochester) Leagues before earning his first trip to the NHL at the start of the 1970-71 season with Toronto. He played just five games before being demoted to Tulsa, and later that year he was traded to Phoenix of the Western League.

At the start of 1971-72, Robert was back in the NHL having won a spot on the Pittsburgh Penguins roster, but in 49 games he scored only seven goals and 18 points. He was unhappy in coach Red Kelly's system, and Kelly wasn't exactly enamored with Robert's play.

Imlach had heard that Kelly and Robert were not getting along, so Imlach – sidelined by his heart attack – told Fred Hunt to call Kelly and offer him Eddie Shack and cash in exchange for Robert. Kelly – who had played 20 years with Detroit and Toronto, won eight Stanley Cups, and who had been inducted into the Hockey Hall of Fame in 1969 – accepted Imlach's proposal. Soon thereafter, Robert's career, and the fortunes of the Sabres, took off faster than one of Robert's rising slapshots.

"I guess it was a lot of luck," Robert said of his fateful fusing with Perreault and Martin. "It's the luck of the draw, it could have been anyone else, really. Perreault could make anyone look good."

But Robert made his linemates look good, too. Because he had been a center for most of his career, Robert could carry the puck with ease and his thought process very often was pass first, shoot second.

"What would happen is when people would start concentrating on Perreault, we would switch places on the ice," Robert said. "Gilbert would take my wing and I would cut over to center, and a lot of times I wound up making the plays."

Robert was particularly effective on the power play as the point man.

"Rene was the best point man on the power play to ever play in a Sabres sweater," said Lorentz. "He had the ability to skate the puck into the zone, he made great decisions with the puck, and he was accurate putting his shot on the net. I scored on a lot of deflections because of him."

Robert's first full season with the Sabres was 1972-73, and he scored a team-high 40 goals and finished second to Perreault in points with 83. The entire team slumped in 1973-74 and Robert's production dropped to 21 goals and 65 points, but the following season, he became the first Sabre to amass 100 points (40 goals, 60 assists). He also scored two of the most memorable goals in club history, both in overtime playoff games. The first one beat Montreal in Game Five of the Wales Conference finals to give the Sabres a 3-2 series lead. The other came in Game Three of the Stanley Cup Finals against Philadelphia that got the Sabres back into the series after they had dropped the first two games.

Numerically, Robert never approached his milestone 1974-75 season, but in the last four years he played in Buffalo, he was still second, second, third and fourth on the team in scoring.

Robert was about to turn 31 in 1979, and, he said, "I was still at the peak of my career, I still had five or six years to give." Bowman didn't see it that way. Bowman saw a player whose point total in 1978-79 had dipped to 62, his lowest figure as a Sabre.

Plus, the Sabres had never finished lower than eighth in the NHL in power-play percentage until that year when they ranked 13th, and Robert had provided only one man-advantage goal after having scored 52 in his previous six-plus years. Bowman deemed it necessary to bring in someone with a booming shot from the point to shore up the power play, Van Boxmeer fit the bill, and Robert was the price Bowman was willing to pay.

Hockey was never the same after that for Robert. He cried the day he was traded. It saddens him today.

"I considered Buffalo my home," he said. "The best years of my life I spent in Buffalo, I became a man and a professional in Buffalo. It's very difficult to walk away from something that's been so good to you. I said it when I left Buffalo, and I still say it today, the Buffalo fans are the greatest fans in the world. They'll support you win or lose, so long as you put the effort in."

Putting the effort in was difficult in Colorado. Even though four weak, stripped-down teams from the folded WHA were absorbed into the NHL in 1979-80, none were worse than the Rockies. Colorado finished tied for last in the league with 51 points and Robert's 28 goals and 63 points were almost all meaningless.

Robert started 1980-81 with Colorado, was traded midway through the year to the equally non-competitive Maple Leafs, and managed only 14 goals combined. Finally, after playing for the Leafs in 1981-82, Robert decided to retire.

"I still had a two-year contract, but I couldn't take it anymore," he said. "Once you lose your heart, you lose your desire to play, you don't enjoy your job and it's time to move on because you're cheating the people. I wanted to retire after I was traded from Buffalo, and if I would have been financially secure, I would have."

Robert's first post-hockey job was with Molson Breweries in Toronto, working in sales and marketing. After a couple of years he accepted a position as president of Canadian operations for Carreira Eyewear, and spent nine years with that company before moving on to his current job as director of event marketing and promotions for Liberty Canada Holdings Ltd., a division of Liberty Mutual of Canada.

"Life has been very good to me," Robert said. "I've been very fortunate after I quit hockey."

Until December 2, 1986, the day Bowman was relieved of all his duties with the Sabres, Robert made himself an outcast from the organization. "When Bowman was here, I wouldn't come near the building. As much as I wanted to, I just stayed away because of what had happened in the past. Now that the organization has changed, we're welcomed here whenever we want. It's nice that the organization wants to do things for the alumni and work hand in hand with us. Yes, I enjoy coming here, but if you had asked me 10 years ago, I'd have had a different answer."

His relationship with the Sabres healed, Robert was given the tribute he so richly deserved on the night of November 15, 1995, when his No. 14 was raised to the rafters of the Aud along with Martin's No. 7. Like long-lost friends, they were reunited with Perreault, whose No. 11 had been retired in a 1990 ceremony. Together again, The French Connection, and when the Aud closed its doors in the spring of 1996, the three symbols of Sabres' supremacy from the 1970s were simply toted down the block to the new Marine Midland Arena.

"It's the pinnacle of my career," Robert said, recalling that tear-filled night. "How many athletes have had their jersey retired in any sport, and to have us all together, it was a great thrill."

"It's very gratifying, my accomplishments in Buffalo. I was very fortunate to be born with a given talent to be a pro athlete. God gave me a talent, and I had to make the best of it and appreciate it, and I did."

Robert extended his goal-scoring streak to six games when he flipped in an empty-netter to cap a four-goal third period in the Sabres' 4-1 victory over the Rangers at Madison Square Garden. The Sabres thus remained unbeaten in 24 games played within the state of New York. They hadn't lost in 20 games at the Aud, were 1-0 at Nassau Coliseum against the Islanders, and improved to 3-0 at Madison Square Garden, outscoring the Rangers 11-4 in those games.

The New York State streak reached 25 the next night when Buffalo completed a terrific weekend, shutting out the Flyers, 2-0. Robert was finally blanked, but all the Sabres needed were goals by Lorentz in the second period and Martin in the third. Dryden turned aside 35 Philadelphia shots, and during the now-completed four-games-in-five-nights haul, he played a total of 211 of a possible 240 minutes, and stopped 95 of the 98 shots he faced.

The Sabres couldn't have been happier for Dryden. He had struggled to make an impact in the NHL, but had never really done so until now. And then just when his time had come, his little brother Ken burst onto the scene and became recognized not only as the best goaltender in the family, but in the league, and perhaps the planet.

"Dave Dryden, without question, is one of the nicest human beings in the world," Ramsay said of his teammate. "He was so good for all of us. Anybody who was in a slump or struggling went over to talk to Dave. If you spent time with Dave, you walked away feeling great about yourself, about the team, about everybody because he was such a positive guy. He was a better player than he ever got credit for."

Joe Crozier will never forget Dryden's kindness.

"I'll tell you what kind of guy Dave Dryden is," Crozier began. "After I got fired by the Maple Leafs (in 1980), who called me on the phone but Dave Dryden. He said, 'Joe, how'd you like to go to the OHA and coach Kitchener?' He had some connection up there and he said I should go there. He was the guy who got me that job, and we won the Memorial Cup (in 1982) with Scott Stevens and Brian Bellows. Dave was a super guy."

It had been an exhausting week for the Sabres, and Joe Crozier acknowledged that in the locker room after the Flyers game when he said, "After that super effort in New York, and with this being our fourth game in five nights, we were a little fatigued."

So with three days off before their next game, did Crozier ease up and give his troops a break? Of course not. He brought the team back to their training camp site at Garden City Arena in St. Catharines for a two-day midseason refresher camp consisting of a one-and-a-half-hour physical training session the next two mornings, followed by three-and-a-half hours of on-ice practice each day.

"This is not a punitive measure," Crozier explained. "It's a period of review and instruction on basic fundamentals to prepare for the final half of the season. With our busy schedule, you don't really have a chance to work on mistakes and straighten things out. This is to help ourselves. I did it in Vancouver, and I did it in Rochester."

Schoenfeld remembered that midseason camp this way: "Looking back, we had probably lost focus a little bit and it was a way of zeroing back in. You get away from your normal environment, those with families are away from their wife and children and the rest of us that were living in apartments are back in a hotel, and so it becomes just the team again. I'm sure Joe was just trying to get our focus back on hockey. We were a young franchise and certainly a collection of players who were just being molded into a team and I think Joe felt that was necessary. As it turned out, I think it was a good thing for us."

Roger Crozier was back in uniform for the first time in slightly more than two weeks but said it was going to "take a couple of days to get my timing back." So Joe Crozier selected Dryden to start in goal when the team returned to action on Thursday night, January 11, against the Rangers.

It was almost a year ago to the day when Joe Crozier had made his NHL coaching debut at the Aud after being named the interim replacement for the ailing Imlach. That Buffalo team was in last place with just eight victories in its first 42 games, and in Crozier's first game, the first-place Rangers inflicted a one-sided 5-2 defeat on the Sabres. Interestingly, the Rangers were back in town to help Crozier celebrate his anniversary. While times had certainly changed as the Sabres entered this game with only 12 losses in their first 42 games and were battling the Rangers for sole possession of third place, the result was eerily similar to the one a year before. New York cruised to a 4-2 victory, thus bringing to an end Buffalo's home-ice streaks of 12 victories and 21 games without a loss, still team records.

Pete Stemkowski scored a pair of second-period goals to give the Rangers a 3-1 lead, and after Robert scored early in the third, New York goalie Ed Giacomin held off a furious Buffalo rally until Stemkowski iced the game by completing a hat trick with an empty net goal one second before the final horn.

In a prelude of what was to come at the end of the season, the sellout crowd rose as one and sent the Sabres skating off the ice with a thunderous standing ovation ringing in their ears, the chant of "Thank You Sabres" tugging at their hearts.

"We've got some first-class people in this building," Meehan said that night. "It was like they were saying, 'Thanks boys for winning so many, now let's start again.' We figured we'd just keep winning and winning, there wasn't really any pressure. What hurts most was that we missed a chance to move up in the standings, not that the streak is broken."

Joe Crozier was appreciative of the fans' gesture, but as he said in his post-game press conference, "It was great, but it didn't give us the two points. I think if we had played Boston or Montreal tonight, we would have won, but the Rangers played very well. I only wish it could have gone another 20 minutes because we were coming in waves in the third period. We had enough chances in the first period to win three hockey games, but then so did they in the second period."

PROFILE - Memorial Auditorium

One February 1997 day, Joe Crozier sat in a luxury suite high above the ice surface at Marine Midland Arena watching then-Sabres coach Ted Nolan put the team through a game-day morning skate. The place was glimmering in its newness, and the vacant mid-air expanse where the Jumbotron scoreboard used to hang before it tumbled to the floor in a $4 million pile of wreckage was hardly noticeable.

The arena is a marvelous monument to downtown Buffalo and there is no doubt the Sabres are happy in their plush new home. But Crozier sat back in the comfortably cushioned seat he was sitting in, and smiled in rememberance of his old friend, the Aud.

"The Aud had charisma," Crozier said. "It was a smaller rink, the people were closer to the ice, so you had a lot going for you in that place. There was so much enthusiasm in that building that year, we couldn't lose. We just went on and on with that streak. I remember I'd come in and there would be people lined up in the lobby waiting to buy tickets. The fans were great, they really helped us. There was a hell of a difference for us playing at home with those people behind us."

Later that same day, as Lorentz was preparing to broadcast the game on television from the spacious and state-of-the-art press box, he too dipped into his memory bank to talk about what the Aud meant to the players.

"That 1972-73 season was one of the most exciting, enjoyable years I ever had in hockey because in those days, the fans were really a part of it," Lorentz said. "They were like an extra teammate out there, and that's what made it so much better, all the support we got."

"The crowds were awesome," remembered Danny Gare, who joined the Sabres in 1974-75 and is now the team's radio analyst. "You look at Boston, Philly, Chicago, all tough places to play, but I would put the Aud right

up in the top three or four in advantage. When we skated out on the ice, you were so pumped, they were playing that Sabre dance. And the people and their proximity to the ice, they were loud and vocal and you could feel the energy. When we needed them, they would lift you."

Outside of Perreault, no player in the history of the franchise spent more time on the Aud ice than Ramsay. Starting with the 1972-73 season, the building was sold out for the rest of the decade, a period of 359 games, and Ramsay played in every one as his team-record consecutive-games-played streak of 776 began that year. Ramsay seconded Gare's opinion about how huge the home-ice advantage was for Buffalo.

"Teams hated playing at the Aud," Ramsay said. "There were a lot of games that were over in the first 10 minutes. We'd have teams down 3-0 in the first 10 minutes and that was it, and it was a matter for them of just keeping from getting hurt. And when we had those quick starts, the crowd would just be jumping, they loved it.

"Teams would come in there, and there was nowhere to go, nowhere to hide, there was no open space. The fans loved the banging from our big people, they loved our speed with our counter attack. We were an exciting team to watch, the people loved it, and we felt such a great relationship with them during those years. It was fun for all of us to be in the building."

Beyond the crowd noise, what Ramsay really enjoyed was the smaller-than-regulation configuration of the ice. At 193 feet long by 84 feet wide, it was seven feet shorter and one foot less wide than the standard 200-by-85 NHL rink. With his penchant for defense, Ramsay was more effective against the high-flying opposing lines he routinely had to play against.

"My style was to attack, not to follow people around, so playing in a

smaller building where everything is so intense and things happen in a hurry was perfect for me," he said. "I liked to play in big buildings too so I didn't get hit as much, I wasn't that big a guy and that could take its toll. But as far as cutting off angles, angles were absolutely vital in a place like Buffalo. And when you could attack people when they didn't expect it, when you could use your feet and your stick to get in the way and steal pucks, you now had a good offensive chance in a real hurry. I could get after people in that building and put pressure on them easier than in the other big buildings.

"It was all speed and quickness, and if you were able to play that aggressive style, which our whole team was, it was a big advantage for us. We were in their face so fast and we had such speed, this rink was ideal for us. People said we'd have been even better in a big rink with our speed and stickhandling, but what people forget is that it's not just size that wins. A lot of big teams came in here and we beat them because we were quicker. If you look back, the Sabres tried to go with a bigger team a few years after that and it wasn't nearly as successful."

During the unbeaten streak in 1972-73, Robitaille remembered the electric feeling in the building every night as the streak extended further into the season.

"I think we as players got caught up in the excitement of it," Robitaille said. "All of a sudden, everyone was talking about the Sabres. The fans, the media, people around the NHL. It really started getting bigger and bigger and bigger and holy cripes, before you knew it, you realized this was really a big deal. You're on the street and everyone was talking about it. It became a monster of a subject and you got caught up in it."

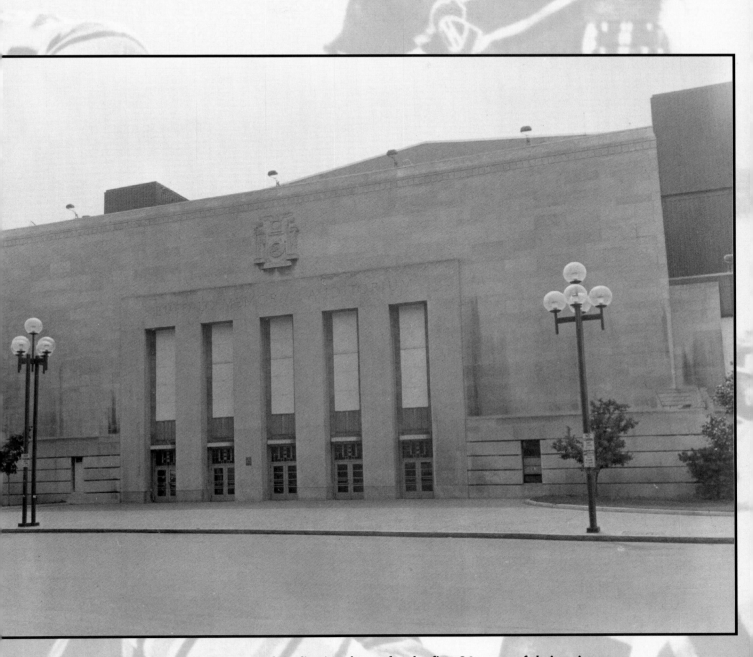

The Sabres called Memorial Auditorium home for the first 26 years of their existence.

Playing before sellouts on a nightly basis, the Sabres posted a 30-6-3 record at the Aud during the 1972-73 regular season. Along the way they were unbeaten in their first 21 games on home ice.

In their first two years in the NHL, the Sabres were about as enticing a draw to Boston Garden as the rats that called the old arena hard by North Station home. And you couldn't blame the Beantown faithful for not getting too pumped up to watch a Bruins-Sabres game. After all, the Bruins had been waging war against the Canadiens, Rangers, Red Wings, Maple Leafs and Blackhawks for decades and those old fellow original six teams were their real rivals. Who were the Sabres? A punk expansion team that should feel honored to be skating on the revered Garden floor, that's who.

Odds are that if you asked even the most ardent Bruins supporter to name 10 players who played for Buffalo in the team's first two years, he'd be hard-pressed to do it. But Bostonians knew more than they wanted to know about the 1972-73 Sabres, especially after Buffalo had brawled its way to a victory over their beloved defending Stanley Cup champions a month earlier.

So when the Sabres flew into Boston for a January 14 date with the Bruins, they took it as a compliment to be greeted by a "Cream the Sabres" campaign orchestrated by a couple of Boston radio stations. As the players themselves always said, you know you've earned respect if the other team's fans go to extraordinary lengths to boo you.

Unfortunately, the Sabres did not deserve to be respected on this night, and they were indeed "creamed" by the Bruins to the tune of 6-0. Phil Esposito scored four goals – two of them while his team was shorthanded – and assisted on the game's first goal by Johnny Bucyk. He also took 11 of Boston's 40 shots on Dryden as nothing Joe Crozier tried defensively worked.

"We played terrible, and Boston played one hell of a hockey game," Crozier said. "Boston was ready for us and went out and skated and had the puck all night. Esposito had 11 shots on goal. I never had anyone who had 11 shots on goal in one game."

Roger Crozier made his first start since December 23 when the Sabres hosted the Blackhawks, who had done Buffalo a favor the night before by defeating Detroit, 6-4. The Red Wings had won six games in a row to get within five points of fourth-place Buffalo. The Blackhawks then did the Sabres another favor, playing horribly during a 5-1 loss as Crozier was called on to make only 18 saves.

After the Boston loss, Joe Crozier had again split The French Connection up during the ensuing practices, but he didn't follow through on the plan and had the unit back together for the Chicago game and Martin scored the final goal on a power play. But the Frenchmen were overshadowed by Meehan's line, which produced four goals – two by Meehan, one each by Lorentz and Harris. In all, they combined for 10 points, which led Chicago coach Billy Reay to say, "That Meehan, if he had to play against us every night he'd score 70 goals."

Meehan, his line, and the rest of the Sabres weren't nearly as sharp two nights later in Detroit as the Red Wings had little trouble posting a 4-2 victory to pull back within five points of Buffalo. And the next night, the Sabres lost at home for only the second time all year as Philadelphia's Bill Flett scored the first three goals of the game and the Flyers held on for a 4-3 victory, Buffalo's fourth loss in its last five games.

The Sabres finished with a flurry, pouring 20 shots on Flyers goalie Bob Taylor in the third period with The French Connection producing three goals, but Rick MacLeish's goal midway through the period was the fly in the ointment and was just enough to hold the Sabres off.

"We got in a big hole tonight, had some defensive lapses, and Philadelphia capitalized on them to run up that early lead," Joe Crozier said. "The Perreault line (20 shots combined) was the only one I had going for me tonight."

The Sabres were fortunate in that Minnesota defeated Detroit, preventing the Red Wings from cutting their deficit to one point. "Naturally we're feeling pressure from Detroit," Crozier said. "I told them we have to make our own breaks, we can't expect anyone else to do it for us."

There was more bad news after the game as Perreault found out he had been left off the Eastern Division all-star team after having played in the All-Star Game his first two years in the league. Martin and Robert had been chosen by the media, but East coach Tom Johnson of Boston selected Jean Ratelle of the Rangers and Dave Keon of the Leafs as his backup centers behind Phil Esposito and Jacques Lemaire, even though Perreault had finished third in the media balloting, and was tied for sixth in the NHL in scoring.

"I talked to Tom and he said he considered Gil," Crozier said. "He also said he considered Ratelle and Keon. I guess he considered them more."

Rene Robert, shown here taking a tumble against Atlanta, was chosen to play in the 1973 NHL All-Star Game along with Rick Martin. Gilbert Perreault was snubbed.

PROFILE - Gilbert Perreault

Jerry Korab tells a story about the first time he played against Perreault in an NHL game. It was at Chicago Stadium during the 1970-71 season, both players' rookie year, and though the Blackhawks had little trouble defeating the newborn Sabres, Perreault left an indelible impression on everyone who was there, especially Korab's spouse, Mary Ann.

"My wife said after the game, 'Who's number 11?'" Korab recalls with a smile. "She recognized him right away. He was just starting out, but she wanted to know who he was. She even went on further to say, 'You better be aware of that guy in future years.'"

Mary Ann Korab would eventually get to see plenty of Perreault as Jerry was traded to Buffalo and spent nine seasons as Perreault's teammate during two separate stints (1973-80, 1983-85). But long before the Perreault and Korab families became best of friends, Mary Ann Korab obviously had a pretty keen eye for talent. From her seat that night in Chicago she knew she was looking at a superstar, and over the next 16 years, Perreault proved her right.

For anyone who saw him play in person, it was a privilege, because the moment Perreault jumped over the boards, you got the feeling that something remarkable might happen at any moment. Say what you want about any Little 3 scoring fest between Bob Lanier and Calvin Murphy, any Braves-Celtics NBA showdown, or any Bruce Springsteen concert, but there was nothing more exciting at the Aud than the sight of Perreault cruising behind his own net to pick up the puck for the start of one of his patented end-to-end rushes.

"Gilbert Perreault, when he went behind the net and took that puck, we stood up on the bench half the time, this guy was so thrilling," said Ramsay.

It would begin with him wheeling through the Sabres' zone, gathering speed with every mighty stride as his

skates cut into the ice like miniature chain saws. It was usually in the neutral zone where he'd meet his first resistance, and at that point, the level of excitement jumped a few notches and your rear end crept closer to the edge of your seat as Perreault would manuever his way through the opposition like a skier negotiating a slalom course.

With the first wave of defenders drowning in his wake, he would cross the enemy blue line with the puck

seemingly glued to his stick, his hair blowing in the gusty breeze he was creating, and your muscles began to get tense with anticipation. One defenseman would try to make a play and Perreault would zoom past him the way Jeff Gordon dusts his NASCAR pursuers.

Now there was only one man to beat, so Perreault would beat him, and you rose to your feet thinking the same thing the panicked goaltender was thinking, that he had no chance.

A deke to the left, another to the right, maybe a third just for the hell of it, and when the carnage was over, the puck was in the net, Perreault was being hugged by his teammates, your eyes were bulging from their sockets, and you couldn't wait to get home and watch the replay on the 11 o'clock news.

"To this day, there isn't anybody that I talk about, even Orr with the great speed he had, there's nobody who gave me more trouble than Gilbert," said former Islander Denis Potvin. "He was an outstanding athlete and with that wide stride and the way he handled the puck, he was the toughest one-on-one player I ever had to deal with.

"The key was to try to contain him, because guys like that you can't stop. There were other guys you could hit early and stop them from doing anything, get them off their game, but with Gilbert, you couldn't figure that was going to happen. If I did get a piece of him, he was so strong, he could always still get by. You had to get all of him because if you didn't, he was going to make the play, either taking a shot or making a pass."

Said Korab, "First let me say it was a lot more fun being on the same team with him than it was playing against him. But when you're playing against

Bert, when you're on the ice with a player like that, you sort of peak yourself, because you know you have to play your best. He probably did that to a lot of players. He was just an amazing player, a great skater. If you couldn't see him coming, you could hear him. His skates would fly, he was one of the most powerful skaters I ever saw."

Like Korab, Jocelyn Guevremont knew first-hand the difference between playing with and playing against Perreault. Guevremont was a teammate of Perreault's at the midget and junior levels, became an opponent when he began his NHL career with Vancouver, then teamed up with Perreault again when he joined the Sabres via a trade at the beginning of the 1974-75 season.

After he had played a few games in Buffalo, Guevremont said of Perreault, "When he was in midget hockey, he had fun with everybody, controlling the puck and fooling everybody. When he moved up to junior, they told him he wouldn't be able to do that in a tougher brand of hockey, but he did it, he still played the same way. Then they told him no way he'd be able to do it in the pros, but he's still making the same super moves."

When Northrup Knox was interviewed by writer Ross Brewitt for the book *Sabres – 26 Seasons in Buffalo's Memorial Auditorium* he shared some wonderful recollections about his nights at the Aud watching Perreault dazzle the masses.

"One of the things that was a constant source of enjoyment for people sitting behind and near the Sabres bench was watching the reaction to things Gilbert Perreault did on the ice," Knox said. "He'd come barrelling up the ice with those powerful strides and make some of his best moves in the neutral zone, right in front of both benches. Teammates and opponents would look at each other, sometimes roll their eyes or shake their heads in amazement. I especially got a kick out of the players coming off the ice after a whistle. They'd smile, wink and make faces that said, 'Wow' to one another."

Martin knows exactly what Knox was

talking about, because on many occasions he was guilty of such acts.

"He'd come down and make a move, and you'd say, 'How the hell did he do that?'" Martin said. "The toughest part about playing with Gilbert is that you had to guard against just standing there watching him. He could take the puck from one end to the other and sometimes he'd deke the same guy three times. But you had to keep in motion and make sure you were in position because eventually he'd decide that he was tired enough and now he was going to make a play."

Perreault was born in Victoriaville, Que., the town where Victoriaville hockey sticks are produced, and he had one of those sticks in his hands at a very early age. He became a child prodigy, and by the time he joined the Montreal Junior Canadiens, he was a can't-miss NHL prospect. His last season as a junior in 1969-70, Perreault was named MVP of the OHA as he had 51 goals and 70 assists for 121 points in 54 games. Combined with his output of 37-60-97 in 54 games the year before, Perreault had 88-130-218 in 108 games.

Imlach remembered a scouting trip to St. Catharines just after he had become general manager and coach of the Sabres. The Junior Canadiens were in town, and when Imlach saw Perreault play, he wrote in *Heaven and Hell in the NHL*: "I wanted Gilbert Perreault as I had never wanted a hockey player before. The hair just stood up on my neck at what he could do. He was a superstar in the making, the man the Buffalo franchise could be built around."

When Imlach was fortunate enough to win the spin of the wheel, Perreault was given the same No. 11 he had worn as a junior, and no one else ever has or ever will wear that number for the Sabres.

In his first season, he won the NHL's Rookie of the Year award when he scored a then-NHL rookie record 38 goals. In his second season, the team took a step back, but while Perreault was considered the franchise, he does not remember feeling any pressure to perform.

"The first two years I didn't think too much about anything," he said. "I just went on the ice and tried to do the best I could do."

When the Sabres reached the playoffs in 1972-73, Perreault was their leading scorer – as he had been the first two years – and he won the NHL's Lady Byng Trophy, presented to the player who exemplifies sportsmanship and gentlemanly conduct. After a disappointing fourth season in which he missed almost two months with a broken leg and the Sabres failed to make it back to the playoffs, he led the team to the Stanley Cup Finals in 1974-75.

"In 1973 we made the playoffs for the first time and we all had confidence," he said. "We were all 22, 23, 24 years old, we knew we were an expansion team making the playoffs in its third year, and that was great. And we gave the Montreal Canadiens a good run that year. It was a lot of fun to play that year.

"We had some good trades, some good draft choices with Martin and Ramsay and Schoenfeld and Gare and within five years, we were a great team that went to the Finals. And I think we had great teams every year into 1980."

But despite their talent, the Sabres were unable to take that final step and win the Cup, and during the 1980s, the Sabres' yearly playoff flameout became an annual rite of passage. Starting with that run to the Cup Finals in 1975, the Sabres qualified for the playoffs 11 years in a row, but the furthest they ever advanced was the Wales Conference finals in 1980 when they lost to the New York Islanders, a team that would go on to win the first of its four consecutive Stanley Cups.

"Through the '70s we were building up to it so we thought we would be back even when we didn't win," Perreault said. "After we lost in 1975, I really thought we would be there for the next four or five years, but it didn't happen. I don't know why."

Martin has an idea. In his opinion, management didn't do what was necessary to put the team over the hump.

"It happened so quickly that we

became a contender, we just never realized how good we were or how good we were capable of being," Martin said. "If someone had just gotten ahold of us after we lost the Stanley Cup Finals and done a little tweaking. We needed a rushing defenseman, and we needed a cementhead. Not that we didn't have any tough guys, but all our tough guys were good players. Schoenfeld was more valuable to us on the ice than he was in the penalty box.

"The intimidation factor was there against the Flyers. We needed a good, tough forward that could have been intimidating. They (coaches and management) knew what we needed. Had they gone out and spent a little money, gone out and gotten what we needed, who knows. But they didn't, and we never won the Cup."

The lack of a championship is the only thing missing from Perreault's Hall of Fame career. "I just wish we could have had more years in the Finals," he said. "We only had one shot at it, and sometimes if you get there three, four, five times, you might win one."

The Sabres sank to last place in the Adams Division in 1985-86, Perreault's final full season with the team, and after playing 20 games at the start of the 1986-87 season, he knew he wouldn't have any more chances to win that elusive Cup. On November 24, 1986, he decided to retire, and unlike Buffalo

It wasn't hard to figure out who the most popular Sabre was in 1972-73. Hundreds of fans lined up at a department store to get Gilbert Perreault's autograph.

Bills quarterback Jim Kelly's lavish farewell announcement in January of 1997, Perreault said goodbye in the typically quiet, low-key manner he had conducted himself throughout his career. There wasn't even a press conference.

"It was enough for me," Perreault said that day. "I was not happy with the way I was playing and I lost, very quickly, the desire to play. I knew it was over for me. I felt like I just didn't have it anymore."

Because he was a silent superstar, Perreault was often misunderstood by fans and media in Buffalo. He was considered aloof by many, uncooperative by others, but the truth was he was uncomfortable speaking English early in his career, and he was basically shy around strangers.

He was not, however, a shy guy with his teammates. In fact, if the Sabres had given out an award for team clown, Perreault would have been an annual recipient.

"Gilbert was a character," said Joe Crozier. "We had a lot of fun with him, he really kept the guys laughing. We'd be in an airport and he'd drop a dollar on the floor, and as soon as someone went to pick it up, he'd pull it away with his foot.

"There was another time it was Gilbert's birthday and we had a road game. So before we left, Mrs. (Seymour) Knox had put four bottles of champagne in his luggage. We're at the airport and we're fooling around and I picked up his bag and it was really heavy. I said, 'What the hell's in this bag?' and I drop it on the ground and there goes all the champagne, all over his clothes. I laughed like hell because he shouldn't have brought it with him in the first place.

"People said he didn't like to talk or that he was quiet, but people didn't know him like we knew him. Everybody loved him."

Perreault has revealed more of his boisterous personality in recent years, especially during his appearances with the Hockey Legends team that tours the country playing exhibition games against various NHL alumni teams. In February of 1997, the Sabres invited the Hockey Legends to Marine Midland Arena to play their alumni in a game to benefit the family of the late Ted Darling, the longtime voice of the Sabres.

Perreault naturally played for the Sabres and was reunited with his French Connection linemates, Martin and Robert. The goal Perreault scored that day on assists from Martin and Robert was certainly an electrifying blast from the past, but it wasn't what the sellout gathering of more than 18,000 will remember years from now. During the second period, Perreault grabbed the microphone from referee Red Storey – who provides comical play-by-play commentary during the Hockey Legends games – and skated over to where the Zamboni comes on to the ice. Accompanied by a rock band, Perreault belted out an impressive rendition of Proud Mary that had the appreciative and somewhat stunned crowd roaring its approval.

When he retired, Perreault, his wife Carmen and their two sons, Marc and Sean, moved back to his native Victoriaville where he has kept busy with a number of activities, although he admitted being away from the NHL was a difficult transition at first.

"The first year after I retired was pretty tough," he said. "It takes a while to adjust to life after you've played for so long. You need that year to find out what you're going to do in hockey."

For awhile, he thought his career path was going to be coaching. There were rumors around Buffalo for more than a few years that Perreault would someday return to the city as coach of the Sabres, and when he became coach, general manager and part owner of the Victoriaville Tigers of the Quebec Major Junior Hockey League, it was viewed as the start of his ascension to the NHL coaching ranks.

But after two years, Perreault grew disenchanted with coaching and got out of the hockey management game, although he still retains part ownership of the team.

"It was a great experience for me," he said. "It's something that I wanted to do after I retired, and I had a chance to do it in my hometown. I had a chance to see what my reactions would be behind the bench and how I would handle situations. I really did enjoy it, I learned some experiences from it, but now I'm out of it. Maybe in the future I'll have another shot at it, who knows."

Perreault moved into real estate and made such sound investments that he has time to play in about 25 games a year with the Hockey Legends.

And in the summer of 1997, Perreault picked up a part-time job as he returned to the Sabres organization for the first time since his retirement in 1986. He will make appearances on behalf of the team in an effort to boost the team's public relations and marketing efforts.

"I enjoy every minute of retirement, I don't miss the game because I still play," he said. "And both my sons play, so I enjoy it through them."

His career numbers are astonishing, and they are likely to remain Sabres records for many years to come. When he quit, he was sixth on the NHL's all-time points list with 1,326, eighth in assists (814) and 11th in goals (512). In 1990, he was inducted into the Hockey Hall of Fame, and he also had his jersey number retired by the Sabres in a moving ceremony at the Aud.

"It's a great honor when you have your number retired," he said. "I had a lot of great moments, and that was one of the greatest."

When asked what it means for him to look into the rafters at Marine Midland Arena and see his number hanging there, Perreault, with that dry sense of humor that he kept hidden from the public for so many years, said, "I guess that means I had a pretty good career, eh?"

EAST	W	L	T	PTS
Montreal	32	7	11	75
NY Rangers	33	13	4	70
Boston	30	15	4	64
Buffalo	25	17	7	57
Detroit	24	19	7	55
Toronto	15	26	7	37
Vancouver	14	30	7	35
NY Islanders	6	39	4	16

West	W	L	T	PTS
Chicago	28	17	5	61
Philadelphia	23	21	7	53
Minnesota	22	19	8	52
Atlanta	21	22	9	51
Los Angeles	21	23	7	49
St. Louis	19	21	9	47
Pittsburgh	20	25	6	46
California	9	28	12	30

It was the Minnesota North Stars' misfortune to be next on Buffalo's schedule following Perreault's all-star snub, because the flashy center played at a level most NHL players were not capable of reaching. He scored two goals to snap a 13-game drought, assisted on a score by Schoenfeld, took 11 shots, and was a unanimous first-star selection as the Sabres, after falling behind 2-0, breezed to a 5-2 victory in the Aud. It was the 25th win of the season, breaking the record of 24 set in the inaugural year.

"I've shown already what I can do," Perreault said, trying not to get into a war of words about the All-Star Game. "They have an All-Star Game every year, I've got lots more years." About his recent slump he added, "Yes, I had been pressing. I guess I really haven't been skating as well as I can the last month."

Perreault set up Schoenfeld for a power-play goal that turned the game around at the 16:26 mark of the second period. Twenty-seven seconds later, Lorentz set up Meehan for the tying goal, and then 1:40 after that, Perreault beat Gilles Gilbert with what proved to be the winner. His second goal came with just 1:04 left to play.

While Perreault was dazzling the crowd, Schoenfeld was fighting his way out of Joe Crozier's doghouse. The big rookie had been struggling the past month and had seen his plus-minus rating drop to minus four, second-worst on the team. Crozier had played him only two shifts in the first period, then decided to stir things up in the second period, playing Schoenfeld in a forward position on the power play.

"I wanted someone in front of the net to cause a little disturbance," Crozier explained. "And he did. He scored a goal and got us going. After that, he started playing like he was two months ago."

Said Schoenfeld of his experience on the forward line, "I went out there afraid. I was just praying to God as I went on the ice, asking Him, 'Just don't let me look bad out there.' That's what it is to believe. When I scored, I almost broke down. I was the closest I've been to crying since I was 12 years old."

The whole team was close to crying when expansion Atlanta hung an 8-5 defeat on the Sabres, the second-highest scoring output ever by a team visiting the Aud. After going the first 51 games of their history without one player recording a hat trick, the Flames got two in this game, by Rey Comeau and Keith McCreary.

Detroit had upset the Canadiens in Montreal earlier in the day to get within two points of Buffalo, and for the first time, it looked like the pressure of being in a playoff race was finally starting to show on the young Sabres.

"We're a third-year expansion team, we have to crawl before we can walk, but we should start thinking about moving up the ladder rather than worrying about the club behind us," Joe Crozier said. "Ever since we knocked off the Rangers the last time in New York (on January 6), we haven't put three good periods together."

Jim Schoenfeld was a pillar in front of the Sabres net and his toughness kept opposing forwards honest as they skated near the Buffalo crease.

Michael Jordan has the trademark tongue while Gilbert Perreault, when he reached maximum speed, would often skate with his mouth wide open. (Photo courtesy of Ron Moscati)

February: Playoff Pressure Begins to Mount

The NHL took its annual three-day break for the All-Star game, and Robert scored the East's first goal in a 5-4 victory at Madison Square Garden. He and Martin combined to take 10 of the East's 34 shots, and matched with their center, Ratelle, were the most prolific trio in the game, even though Greg Polis of the Western Division was voted the MVP because he scored twice.

Just one year earlier, Robert was a teammate of Polis' in Pittsburgh, but while Polis was playing a regular shift, Robert was spending much of his time glued to the bench.

"It's hard to believe, really, that things could change so much in less than a year," Robert said after the game in reference to his career path. "Playing with these guys, the best in the NHL, and doing all right. It was a thrill.

"When you don't get a chance to play, you get down on yourself. You hope and you wonder. The biggest break I ever got was when I came to Buffalo."

The Sabres returned from the All-Star break well-rested, and they needed to be as they were about to start a stretch where they would play seven games in the first 11 days of February, which had Joe Crozier excited. "We can't stay sharp just practicing," he said. "When we're playing all the time, we're playing better."

This hectic period began very impressively as the Sabres defeated Los Angeles at the Aud, 5-3, and after a lackluster 1-1 tie with the Islanders at Nassau Coliseum, they came back to Buffalo the next night for a rematch with the Islanders and dominated them in a 5-1 victory. It gave the Sabres five of a possible six points, yet the Red Wings gained in the standings and now trailed Buffalo by just one point as they won three in a row over the same span.

Lorentz keyed the win over Los Angeles with two goals and two assists, and Mickey scored the only goal in the tie with New York as Islanders goalie Billy Smith made 36 saves.

It was before the second game of the home-and-home weekend series with New York that Joe Crozier sent Perreault out alone for the pre-game warmup.

SCORING THROUGH FEBRUARY 4			
PLAYER	**G**	**A**	**PTS**
Robert	30	34	64
Perreault	21	41	62
Martin	28	27	55
Lorentz	22	31	53
Meehan	27	21	48
Harris	11	22	33
Luce	12	14	26
Hillman	4	18	22
Atkinson	9	9	18
Robitaille	3	14	17
Ramsay	7	9	16
Mickey	6	7	13
Schoenfeld	3	8	11
Horton	0	9	9
Pratt	1	8	9
Terbenche	0	6	6
Wyrozub	2	3	5
Carriere	0	3	3
Deadmarsh	1	1	2
Rombough	1	0	1
Gould	0	1	1

GOALIES	**GM**	**GA**	**GAA**
Dryden	27	62	2.50
Crozier	30	81	2.99

GOALIES	**W**	**L**	**T**
Dryden	13	8	4
Crozier	14	8	4

"You guys stood around watching Gil skate last night," Crozier bellowed before the game as he flicked on the power button on the television monitor inside the team's locker room. "Tonight you can watch him before the game and maybe you'll do a little skating yourself."

This little ploy seemed to work wonders as Buffalo skated circles around the overmatched Islanders, firing 49 shots at Smith. Although Smith was again marvelous, he couldn't stop the Sabres all by himself.

"The Sabres were flying tonight," said new Islanders coach Earl Ingarfield, who had replaced the fired Phil Goyette a week earlier. "They would have beat anybody the way they were going."

The line of Lorentz, Meehan and Harris picked up six points and swept the three-star awards, something not even The French Connection had done.

The only negative note to this cheery song was the continued slump of The French Connection. Although Perreault scored on a breakaway, there was some concern over the big line's inability to finish plays around the net in recent weeks.

"You better believe we're in a slump," Robert said. "Gil is back skating as well as ever, but we're just not going, not playing as we were early in the season. We need a three- or four-goal game, I guess, to get us started again."

Meehan offered this explanation for the Connection's troubles: "The other team doesn't try to score when the Perreault line is on. It just tries to stop them from scoring."

That was certainly the strategy Chicago used a few nights later in a 2-1 victory over Buffalo, although it was a little easier for the Blackhawks because Martin missed the game after being hospitalized with an acute upper respiratory infection. Joe Crozier tried three players in Martin's left wing slot next to Perreault – Bob Richer, Randy Wyrozub and Ramsay – but no combination worked as the Sabres managed only 21 shots and didn't get one past Tony Esposito until 32 seconds remained in the game when Schoenfeld ruined his shutout bid.

The game was scoreless for more than 50 minutes as Dryden matched Esposito save for save, but then Jim Pappin and Dennis Hull scored twice within 32 seconds. The loss, coupled with Detroit's win in Atlanta, dropped the Sabres into fifth place by one point, the first time all year they had been below the playoff qualifier line.

Twenty-four hours later, the Sabres were back in fourth place, though, as Dryden pitched his third shutout of the year in a 4-0 victory over California, their first win against the Seals this season. Martin was again out of the lineup, and for awhile it looked like Perreault might be, too. He did not skate in the pre-game warmup because he was at the Burn Treatment Center after spilling hot coffee on himself. However, he made it back to the Aud in time for the game and assisted on the first of Robert's two third-period goals.

Buffalo then endured a lost weekend, falling to Montreal, 2-1, at the Forum, and dropping a 5-2 decision to the Red Wings at the Aud which leap-frogged Detroit back ahead of the Sabres.

The Sabres did not have Martin's services for the third straight game in Montreal, but his absence was more than offset by the Canadiens being

Dave Dryden's career goals-against average of 3.06 ranks fourth-best on the Sabres all-time list.

without goalie Ken Dryden and center Peter Mahovolich. Michel Plasse tended goal for Montreal, and the only Buffalo score he permitted was Robert's rebound goal off a Schoenfeld shot in the second period. Frank Mahovolich had managed to get around Horton to score in the first period, and Henri Richard netted the winner at 3:25 of the third, ripping a slap shot from the faceoff circle past Dave Dryden.

The pain from that loss was soothed by the news that Detroit had been beaten by Minnesota, but the next night, the Red Wings took care of business with four goals in the third period to overcome a 2-1 deficit.

Martin was back in the lineup and he made his presence felt by scoring twice, giving him 30 goals for the year. And both of his goals were aided by Perreault and Robert, as The French Connection was flying. But Martin's first goal since January 21 and his first two-goal game since December 20 weren't nearly enough against a red-hot Detroit team that had lost only six of its previous 28 games.

The loss was the Sabres' third in four games, but as Meehan pointed out, "We didn't play bad in any of these four games, yet we lost three."

Joe Crozier agreed, commending his team's effort, and then he singled out Martin for particular praise. "There was Martin coming out of the hospital leading the parade. Maybe I should put them all in the hospital for a couple of days."

NHL STANDINGS THROUGH SUNDAY, FEBRUARY 11

EAST	W	L	T	PTS
Montreal	36	7	13	85
NY Rangers	38	13	5	81
Boston	34	16	5	73
Detroit	29	20	7	65
Buffalo	28	20	8	64
Toronto	18	30	7	43
Vancouver	15	35	7	37
NY Islanders	7	45	5	19

WEST	W	L	T	PTS
Chicago	33	17	6	72
Philadelphia	25	23	9	59
Minnesota	25	23	8	58
St. Louis	23	22	10	56
Atlanta	23	26	9	55
Los Angeles	23	27	7	53
Pittsburgh	22	28	6	50
California	9	36	12	30

PROFILE - Rick Martin

Every winter morning of Rick Martin's youth, he would trudge off to school with his books in one hand, his hockey stick in the other, and his skates tied together and slung over his shoulder. That was the way it was in Quebec where the passion for hockey burns hot enough to melt the province's frozen ponds in the dead of February. You studied, you skated, you slept, and you repeated the process day after bitter cold day.

"We didn't play in organized leagues, most of the hockey that I played when I was a little kid was pretty much what you'd call sandlot ball," said Martin, who was born in the Montreal suburb of Verdun, but grew up just outside Ottawa in Hull, a town about 50 miles west of Montreal, located right on the Ottawa River which serves as the border separating Quebec and Ontario.

"We'd bring our sticks to school and go right from there to the outdoor rinks. Then we'd go home, eat, do our home-work, and go back out and play because the rinks were lit at night. There were parish rinks every two or three blocks, so there was always somewhere to play.

"We'd play every day, it was a lot of fun growing up. There'd be 30 guys out there, 15 on each team. Just think of it, when there's 15 guys on your side, you're going to run into your own guys half the time. You developed some good quickness and skills in tight. That's why guys like Perreault and Lafleur were so good with the puck, that's the way they were brought up. Usually, one guy

would get the puck and just go."

While Perreault was skating circles around his pals in Victoriaville, Que., and Lafleur was doing the same thing on the rinks in Thurso, Que., the guy dominating those densely populated pickup games in Hull was Martin. Yet despite his obvious skill, Martin didn't lay in bed at night dreaming of playing

in the NHL. When he was growing up, the NHL was a six-team league, and only the best of the best of the best ever reached the sport's highest level.

"I only played hockey because it was a lot of fun," Martin said. "The first organized league I played in, we won the championship and I scored a lot of goals, so I knew I was better than most of the other players, but as far as playing in the NHL, I didn't start thinking about

it until I started playing junior hockey."

From the moment he strapped his first pair of blades on, Martin was different than the other kids he competed against. Sure, those long days on the outdoor ice surfaces in Hull did wonders for his skating, but what really set him apart was the incredible velocity and accuracy of his shot. Oh, what a shot it was, and it only became more fear-some the older and stronger he got.

"I didn't slap pucks at walls (the way Bobby Orr said he used to when he was growing up), but I shot a lot of pucks during practice," Martin said. "I always had a natural shot, but as I started playing junior, then I really worked on it. I always had a lot of speed on it, so I started working on quickness and accuracy. I'm not going to say I didn't have a natural ability, but I also worked a lot harder on it than most guys. Every day after practice, I'd stay out there a little longer. I'd shoot more pucks in one year than some guys shoot in 10.

"When I got to the NHL, I found out right away that if you want to play at this level, it was all about quickness and reaction. The opening is only there for a second, so you're talking about trying to gain just fractions of seconds, but that was the difference between getting the shot off and getting your ass flattened."

As a 15-year-old, Martin left home to play Junior B hockey in Tetford Mines because there was no junior team in Hull like there is today. But when he was 16, his father, who was in the trucking business, was transferred to

Photo courtesy of Ron Moscati

Montreal, home of the Junior Canadiens. So Martin gathered his belongings and moved back into his parent's house, soon to be joined by one of his Junior Canadien teammates, Perreault, who lived with the Martins for one season.

"He used to play his stereo real loud," Perreault said of Martin. "The neighbors would knock on the walls. They didn't like it too much."

Martin enjoyed two reasonably productive seasons, scoring a combined 45 goals and 107 points, but he still didn't know what to think about his future in hockey. By then the NHL had expanded to 14 teams, more than doubling the number of job positions in the league. But Martin hadn't put together a monster season, like, for instance, the one Perreault choreographed in 1969-70 when he was named the OHA's MVP.

That is until 1970-71. By the end of that year, Martin knew the NHL was not only attainable, but probable. He scored an OHA-record 71 goals and added 51 assists for 122 points to lead the Junior Canadiens to their second straight Memorial Cup championship. That was enough in itself to convince him he could make it, but his confidence was buoyed even further when he glanced at the NHL amateur draft lists from the previous couple of years and saw that former teammates such as Perreault, Rejean Houle, Marc Tardif, Andre Dupont, Art Quoquochi, Norm Gratton, Serge Lajeunesse, Bobby Guindon and J.P. Bordeleau had all been drafted.

"I played three years in Montreal, we won two Memorial Cups, and I saw a lot of guys I played with in my first couple years who wound up getting drafted into the NHL," Martin said. "I saw some of those guys that were playing in the NHL and I looked at them and I said, 'Geez, he's a good player, but I know I'm better than he is.' So that's when I started to focus a little more on that goal of making the NHL."

Buffalo used the fifth pick of the first round to select Martin, and over the next nine years, his lowest goal-scoring output was 28 during an injury-plagued 1977-78 season. Twice he

topped 50 goals, and nearly made it three seasons in a row, but he stayed stuck on 49 for the last three games of 1975-76.

Martin still holds the team record for most goals (44) and points (74) by a rookie, most goals by a left winger in a season (52) and a career (382), while his goal total is second only to Perreault, and his 695 points are third behind Perreault and Dave Andreychuk.

Impressive numbers indeed, yet sadly, they could have been so much better, Martin says, if not for Mike Palmateer and Scotty Bowman.

"When Scotty came here, we were excited, we knew his reputation and we thought maybe he'd take us to the next level and maybe we'd win a Cup with him," Martin said, recalling that first year under Bowman. "We were willing to respect his talents and his leadership, so whatever he threw at us, we took it. We worked for him, but unfortunately on his side, he didn't respect us.

"There were guys he hated because of things that happened against Montreal when we used to beat them, so he already pre-judged some players without giving them a chance. Like Robert and Korab, he had strong personal differences with those guys off the ice, and they were immediately gone when he came in. He wanted to prove to the world that he could build his own team."

Bowman had taken over as coach and general manager in 1979, and one of the first duties he performed was breaking up The French Connection by trading Robert to Colorado. He left the other two components of the line alone, and Martin and Perreault enjoyed terrific seasons, Martin scoring 45 goals, his most since 1975-76, and Perreault ringing up 106 points, his most since 1974-75.

While Martin had played well, Bowman entered the 1980 season intent on making more personnel moves, and Martin was high on his list of players who could be used as trade bait. For whatever reason, Bowman was not a fan of Martin's, and that became abundantly clear in the weeks after Martin's career was dealt a cataclysmic blow.

On November 9, 1980, in a game

against the Washington Capitals at the Aud, Martin was racing in on a breakaway against Palmateer, the former star Toronto goalie who had moved on to Washington. Capitals forward Ryan Walter managed to trip Martin to the ice – although no penalty was called – and the puck skidded away. Just as Martin was regaining his feet, Palmateer, already way out of his crease, knocked Martin back down by kicking his knee, causing cartilage damage that basically ended Martin's career.

"Palmateer kicked me on purpose," Martin said. "I was on a breakaway, I was tripped up at the blue line and the puck was going into the corner, and he came out and hit me at the top of the circle. When you're going in on a breakaway and the puck is going into the corner, you don't expect the goalie to hit you. I didn't have the puck."

Tests failed to reveal any damage, so Bowman assumed Martin was OK. When Martin was unable to play, or couldn't give 100 percent when he did dress, Bowman insisted that Martin was faking the injury.

"I skated for about two weeks after the injury, and it wasn't all right, it was pinching, it hurt, I didn't have full range of motion," Martin recalled. "They kept doing tests, but the tests they were doing couldn't find the kind of tear that I had. I should have had arthroscopic surgery, but everything kept coming up negative. When your knee is injured, you should see a knee specialist. I mean if you hurt your brain, you don't go see a podiatrist, right? I wasn't with the right doctor, that's the thing that really frosted me."

While Martin was in and out of the lineup, Bowman was more intent than ever on trading him, and he nearly had a deal worked out with the Edmonton Oilers that would have sent defenseman Paul Coffey to Buffalo. Alas, Oilers GM and coach Glen Sather backed out at the last minute.

Eventually, Martin sought a new doctor and had surgery performed in Toronto, but once he did that, "It got a little sticky because at the time you didn't seek another opinion on medical matters," he said. "After I had the surgery out of town, I knew the handwriting was on the wall."

On March 10, 1981, Bowman traded Martin and Luce to the Los Angeles Kings for a pair of draft choices, one of which the Sabres used to select goalie Tom Barrasso in 1983.

"It's always tough to get traded, you want to play for the same team you came up with, but I looked at it as a fresh start," Martin said. "I had met (then-Kings' owner) Jerry Buss, had a talk with him and he laid out what he wanted out of me. He said a lot of flattering things about me, so I was looking forward to playing there. And it could have been good because I would have played with Marcel Dionne and (Dave) Taylor, so that would have been a nice line."

However, Martin's knee would not cooperate. "My skating was never the same after the surgery. I had a whole summer of rest, but even with an electrical stimulator, everytime I skated, I would get fluid on the knee, and then I'd have to stop for four or five days and I couldn't do anything. Then I'd try again, skate a few days and boom, it would swell up again and I'd be back to square one."

He wound up playing four games for the Kings before calling it a career, then named the Sabres, several doctors, a Buffalo hospital, and Bowman in a $10 million malpractice lawsuit that was ultimately settled out of court in Martin's favor about 10 years later.

"Did Scotty share in the blame? Well, he was absolved because of New York State compensation laws, but you're damn right he did, he was the one who was calling me a faker, telling me if I didn't skate he was going to trade me or suspend me," Martin said.

In December of 1986, Bowman was interviewed for a story on Martin by Buffalo News writer Jane Kwiatkowski that appeared in Buffalo magazine and had this to say:

"All I can tell you is that we never played any player that was injured. I acted on the advice of the medical department, whether it was Rick Martin or any other player. He's got

sour grapes. It's strictly because of the trade, there's no question about that. You'll have to understand that any player that gets traded is very bitter. Why wouldn't they be? It's a simple case of life in the hockey arena."

"I can't change what happened, and as far as I'm concerned, it's water under the bridge now," Martin says. "Do I wish things would have been different? The only sore spot is that when I stopped playing, it wasn't because I wanted to, but because I had to. I finished with 384 goals and 500 wasn't that far out of range. I was only 29 when I got hurt, and I had a lot of good years left. My last two seasons were a wash, they didn't really count. After everything was said and done, that injury shouldn't have ended my career if it was handled properly. That kind of thing would have never happened today."

Since retiring, Martin has been involved in a variety of ventures. He briefly owned a bar, he worked for a brokerage firm for a few years but found the 9-to-5 lifestyle wasn't to his liking, and then spent time with a friend, Jim Reece, manufacturing copper refrigerator parts. None of this work fulfilled Martin, but his next job certainly did.

"I went on a gold-mining project for six months along the Ivory Coast in West Africa," he explained. "A friend of mine had options on a company over there. There was surface gold, a fairly large expanse with tremendous potential. He wanted to go back and do drill holes to verify that they were correct. It was a French-speaking country, I spoke French, and I was familiar with mining from when I was younger.

"It was very interesting. I missed my wife and kids, but it ended up being a very worthwhile experience. It puts things in perspective because no matter how bad you feel things are, there are always people who have it far worse than you do. I'm very happy for what I have, I feel very fortunate."

The journey to West Africa provided him with a refreshed attitude, so when he returned to Western New York, he was focused on finding an occupation he could enjoy until his working days

were over. He thinks he has done that. He is partnered in a computer consulting company called Kieffer, Martin Ltd. in Buffalo.

"Of course I'd like to change certain things, but overall, things have turned out great," he said. "I have a great wife and kids, and I found something that I really enjoy doing. It took a while, but I finally made the transition. It was pretty tough there for a while. When I had the lawsuit going, and it dragged on and on, I was pretty much outcast. You don't sue the NHL and the Sabres and think they're going to welcome you back with open arms. It was a strain, even with some of the players, because you can't hang around. You're viewed as, 'How dare you.'"

It has been more than 16 years since Martin last wore the Sabres sweater, not counting appearances in alumni games, of course. But because he has remained a part of the Western New York community, he continues to be a recognizeable face.

"Being a pro athlete is a totally different lifestyle than anything you can imagine," Martin said. "When you're in a public life, a lot of people know who you are, there's a lot of notoriety, you have to act a certain way, and you have to be aware that you're well-known and there isn't any privacy. When you stop playing, you don't get it as much, but here in Buffalo, I still do to this day. I have tons of people coming up to me, and I love it.

"For years around here, people were only used to seeing good, exciting hockey, so when the 80s came around and the teams were deteriorating, and they ended up hitting rock bottom, it was hard to watch. Even today when the fans talk about it, the worse things got and the team couldn't turn it around, a lot of fans would tell me 'We didn't realize how good you guys were.' That's nice to hear.

"In all honesty, I have to say that we didn't either. I think we could have had a dynasty. The regret I have is that we didn't win a Stanley Cup. We had the talent, and I think if we could have added to it, we could have won."

Martin was reunited with his old Junior Canadiens linemate, right winger Norm Gratton, the day after the Detroit game when Imlach obtained Gratton from Atlanta in exchange for Butch Deadmarsh. Gratton had been a first-round draft choice by the Rangers in 1970, 11th overall, while Buffalo had taken Deadmarsh four slots later at the top of the second round in that same draft. Imlach said he "always rated Gratton very high because he is a fast skater with a hard shot who just needed ice time."

Gratton spent two years in the Central League playing for Omaha and played only three games near the end of the 1971-72 season with the Rangers. And after being chosen by Atlanta in the expansion draft, he scored just nine points in 29 games for the Flames prior to the trade.

Gratton arrived too late to play in the Sabres' 3-2 victory over Toronto at Maple Leaf Gardens, but he was in the lineup the next night and helped the Sabres defeat the Rangers for the fifth time in six meetings, 4-1, at the Aud. Gratton exacted sweet revenge against the team that had buried him in the minors during his first two professional seasons, scoring the last goal of the game late in the third period.

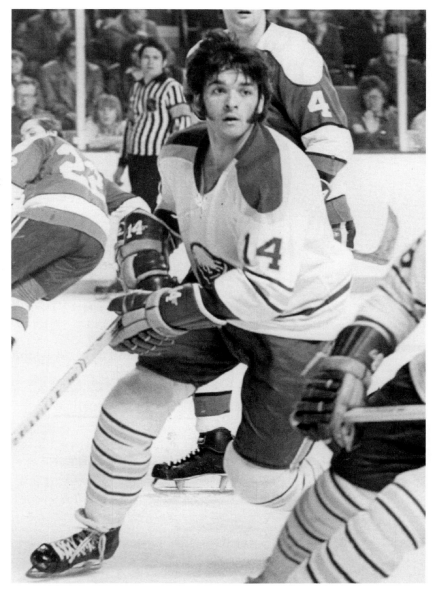

Norm Gratton, a former junior teammate of Gilbert Perreault and Rick Martin, was reunited with his friends after being traded to the Sabres by Atlanta.

"Scoring like that takes a lot of the nervousness away," Gratton said. "It helps my confidence. It's good to be back with Rick and with Bert. Bert Perreault, that's what we all called him in junior."

Outside of his personal gratification, Gratton's goal meant little to the outcome because Roger Crozier had spent the night befuddling the Rangers. After a 28-save performance against the Leafs, Crozier was able to come back 24 hours later and stop 30 New York shots. His back-to-back first-star awards were a hopeful sign that perhaps he was ready for the stretch run.

"I've seen Crozier play a lot of good games over the years, but I don't think I ever saw him play better than he did tonight," said Rangers coach Emile Francis. "Crozier was the difference. We haven't had better chances to score on their club all year than we had tonight, but we couldn't capitalize on them. He stopped everything."

After a day off, the Sabres traveled to Pittsburgh for a home-and-home weekend series with the Penguins, and Roger was only able to play part of the first period at Pittsburgh allowing one goal, before exiting with more stomach troubles. Dryden was touched for two goals in the first period as Pittsburgh jumped to a 3-1 lead, but he blanked the Penguins the rest of the way while Martin scored twice in the second period to forge a 3-3 tie. That enabled the Sabres to remain unbeaten in seven games lifetime in Pittsburgh (3-0-4).

The next night, Joe Crozier monitored the pregame warmup closely, and decided at the last minute to start Roger in goal, and this time, he went the distance, stopping 24 shots in a 4-1 victory that saw Gratton score again.

The team had played four games in five nights and earned seven of a possible eight points. And with Detroit playing three consecutive ties during that same span, Buffalo catapulted back into fourth place.

"There's no way, in my thinking, that we'll miss the playoffs," Joe Crozier said. "We'll be there because we should be there. There's no justice in this world if this club does not make the Stanley Cup playoffs. This team has worked harder than any team in the league and that's why they deserve to be there."

With 18 games left in the regular season, the players were aware that every game was crucial, but Martin remembered that the key to the Sabres' ability to rise above the pressure was to focus on the game at hand each night.

"We were trying to play one game at a time," Martin said. "We were reading the newspapers, we knew where we were, we had stats coming out of the ying-yang, so we all knew where we stood. But the thing we had to do was play the game that was in front of us, we couldn't afford to look three games down the road and say, 'Ooh, we're playing Detroit.'"

Said Ramsay, "I remember we were thinking, 'How great is this to really have a shot at making the playoffs.' Especially in our division. We'd look at the other side and we'd say, 'Holy mackerel, we'd be in second place in the other division.' We had built a level of confidence on our team and we were going hard for every game no matter who, what or where. We believed we were good and that we would win."

Martin added that Joe Crozier's influence on the team had become vital by now, because down the stretch, defense was going to win games, not offense. During the four-game unbeaten week, the Sabres were outshot in just one game (which they won anyway over the Rangers) and yielded only seven goals in 12 periods.

"The first couple of years, the team allowed a lot of shots, so the goalies were really overworked," Martin said. "But in the third year, our defense got better and we started playing more and more as a team. We could play it tight, we could play that style, and we won some 2-1 games. We were well-coached, we had good discipline, we had a lot of talent and guys who really took pride in what they did."

Said Robitaille, "When I see this team (the 1996-97 Sabres) and how they're playing defensively in their own zone, I think of Joe a lot because we seemed to be in the same positions on the ice that they're in today. A lot of loose pucks used to come our way because Joe made sure we were in position."

PROFILE - Mike Robitaille

When Robitaille played, a lot of loose pucks came the Sabres' way courtesy of him wiping out an opposing puck carrier with one of his patented hip checks.

"I learned checking in junior hockey from a little guy who played in the AHL named Terry Ball," Robitaille said. "I watched him and learned and carried it over, and I was doing something very few people could do. I was quite effective, especially in open-ice hitting. I knew if I didn't hit, I wouldn't be playing. After the games, the first thing I would look at is how many hits I got, that's what was important to me.

"The problem was, people started getting used to it and they started going around you, or they end up dumping the puck in because you've flipped them so many times. But there was about four or five years there where I was really nailing guys left and right."

It was a style that Joe Crozier loved.

"He was a hell of a hitter," Crozier said. "Not many people beat him, they were afraid of him because he would catch them on the outside with his hip, and they didn't want to go along the boards because he'd get them. So they'd go to the middle and Carriere or Pratt, whoever I had paired with Robitaille, would be on the other side."

After a fine junior career with Kitchener, Robitaille was signed by the New York Rangers and sent to their farm club in Omaha, Neb. In his second year there, he was named the Central League's Defenseman of the Year, and led the Knights to the playoff championship, recording a postseason-leading 14 assists.

That showing earned him a promotion to the Rangers, where he appeared in his first four NHL games at the end of the 1969-70 season. In 1970-71, while

battling a chronic shoulder injury, he split time with Omaha and the Rangers, but like Lorentz, Gratton and Luce, Robitaille was watching his NHL career melt away either from the bench or in the press box in New York. Therefore, when he was traded to Detroit along with Arnie Brown and Tom Miller in exchange for Bruce MacGregor and Larry Brown on February 2, 1971, he was thrilled.

The excitement didn't last long, though. While he played 23 games for the Red Wings that season, scoring four goals and eight assists, Robitaille didn't think he was going to become a regular on Detroit's back line. He was right. After the 1970-71 season, the Red Wings went looking for a competent goalie to back up Al Smith, and when Imlach offered Joe Daley and asked for

Robitaille and Luce in return, Detroit general manager Ned Harkness agreed.

"You get to a point where you have a lack of confidence, because until you've played, until you've done good things on the ice and you start to feel better about yourself, your confidence isn't going to grow," Robitaille said. "I never had that opportunity with New York or Detroit, but when I came to Buffalo, I felt I could play somewhat of an important role with the team."

His first season in Buffalo was sabotaged by injuries. He underwent an operation on his shoulder, and after recuperating and then spending a few weeks in Cincinnati getting into playing shape, he returned to Buffalo and suffered a knee injury. He was limited to 31 games with the Sabres, but using his accurate and powerful shot from the point, he amassed 12 points, and his defensive play and checking style were certainly assets the team could use.

"I liked the way he played, especially in our small rink in the Aud because they didn't have much room to move and he'd hammer guys," said Joe Crozier.

Robitaille spent the next two seasons hammering opponents for Buffalo, but three games into the 1974-75 campaign, he and Meehan were traded to Vancouver for Jocelyn Guevremont and Bryan McSheffrey. With the Canucks, Robitaille continued to play the same bruising style and he was a key contributor in Vancouver until his career came to a sudden, sad and bitter end midway through the 1976-77 season.

Robitaille suffered a fractured neck during a game, but in what was — looking back — an eerily similar prelude to Martin's problems with Scotty Bowman, Robitaille was forced to play by Vancouver coach Phil Maloney.

Robitaille says that Maloney did not believe his injury was very serious, and because the Canucks were fighting for a playoff spot, it was Maloney's contention that Robitaille should shrug off the pain in order to help the team.

"I shouldn't have been playing and the team knew better because they had advice from the doctors that I shouldn't have been playing," Robitaille said. "But I was coerced into playing. Phil Maloney threatened to send me to the minors. That's kind of the dark side of hockey."

Robitaille followed orders, and actually made it through two games without incident, although he was in great discomfort, not to mention danger. His worst fears were realized in a game against Pittsburgh, when he collided with Dennis Owchar, and his body went limp as he crashed to the ice. For three or four minutes, he had no feeling in his outer extremities, and though his senses did return before he was taken off the ice, he knew his career was over.

"I had to hold my head a certain way in order to skate, I couldn't hit anyone and if I did, I had to push with my hands," he said. "There's no way I should have been on the ice for any of those games, but it was more important for them to make the playoffs. When Owchar hit me, it didn't matter how hard it was, because all I had to do was fall down and it was going to finish me off."

Since that night, Robitaille has lived with a permanent physical disability. Tests revealed that his brain stem had been injured causing motor damage, and he had a fracture in his third vertebrae.

"I can't skate because I'd just fall down as soon as I tried to stride out," he said. "I have to walk because if I run, I'll fall down. It's just something that I've learned to live with and work around."

Robitaille became the first player to sue the NHL, and not only did he win a judgement in the $500,000 range, but a new law was enacted in British Columbia which made businesses adhere to stricter standards when dealing with injured employees. Robitaille's victory also transformed the NHL's thinking on injured players, although when you review the facts of Martin's situation a

few years later, you tend to believe Bowman must not have been paying attention to what had happened in the Robitaille case.

"It really paved the way for players being better taken care of," Robitaille said proudly. "Right after that, all of a sudden you didn't just drag players off the ice, you took them off properly. It snapped the league to attention and woke them up to the fact that they have a duty to care for their players. I'm really ashamed and embarrassed by the way Vancouver handled it. It left such a bad mark on hockey, just because certain individuals thought they were doctors."

In an interview for the story on Martin that appeared in Buffalo magazine, Robitaille said the verdict gave him peace of mind.

"More than anything else, it gave me my dignity back," he said. "You can't call me a liar anymore, you can't call me a con artist. The word that was out around the NHL was Mike Robitaille was a malingerer. All it was was a big hoax on my part, that I didn't want to play. They also, at one point, said I was going through a nervous breakdown, which wasn't the truth. My own teammates, players in the NHL, some of my friends in hockey, wouldn't believe me until I actually could hold the judgement up and say, 'Here, read it.'"

For more than two years after the injury, Robitaille was unable to work, and his exorbitant medical bills drained his savings. He thought his medical insurance through the Canucks organization would pay the bills, but he says, "the hockey club cut me off without even telling me."

He and his wife Isabel and their daughters, Sarah and Anique, moved back to Buffalo, and eventually, Robitaille rejoined the Sabres organization in 1983 as an analyst on radio and television with Ted Darling. While his hard-hitting style was the reason he lasted eight years in the NHL, that same no-holds-barred technique didn't sit well with Sabres management. After more than a decade of telling it like it was, Robitaille was let go during an organizational restructuring before the 1994-95 season.

"They (the Sabres' front office) wanted more of the company line on the broadcasts, and I wasn't about to sell out," he said. "I preferred, and still prefer, not to insult the public's intelligence and try to pass something on to them that's not true. If you lose 7-2 you played pretty bad, and I didn't want to sit there and make up excuses for them.

"If they win 7-2 I'll praise them to heaven. I preferred to keep my integrity intact, and I really feel good about that. I've been about as honest as anyone could possibly be and I took an awful pounding from management for doing it, to the point that I was fired. I just went down my own path, I did what I thought was right and what was right for the people who were listening. I didn't sell them a bill of goods."

Robitaille quickly moved into a new field, becoming general manager of Fort Erie Race Track, a position he still holds. He manages a staff of over 300 people, and oversees a $100 million a year business. But hockey remains Robitaille's first love, and to quench that thirst for the game, he joined the Empire Sports Network and along with broadcaster Brian Blessing, co-hosts Hockey Hotline, a call-in show that airs between periods and after every Sabres game.

"When I moved over to Empire, they looked at it totally different than the Sabres did," Robitaille said. "They wanted me to keep my integrity, be as honest as I could be, and talk about what I see. I spare no prisoners, and that's why I think the ratings have been up for the show. It's one of the highest-rated shows they have.

"I was very sour right after I was let go by the Sabres for a lot of reasons. But it got better after about a year when I realized they weren't sitting around thinking about me and getting sick about what happened. So I decided I'm sure as hell not going to give them the pleasure.

"Right now, I don't have any animosity. I feel wonderful, I like what I'm doing, I like my TV show. I can't wait to get up every morning and go to work in management at the jockey club, especially now that we were just granted a casino for the race track. These are pretty exciting times for me."

When the Sabres defeated Vancouver, 3-1, on February 22, they officially eliminated the Canucks from the playoff race, which gave Joe Crozier a thrill.

Exciting times are exactly what the Sabres continued to enjoy in late February as they stretched their unbeaten streak to five games with a 3-1 victory over Vancouver. As an added bonus for Joe Crozier, the loss officially eliminated the Canucks from playoff contention.

Roger Crozier stopped 30 of 31 shots and said afterwards, "Yes, life is easier for me now because we're a good hockey team. We've come quite far quite fast because of the great job management has done – Punch Imlach and Joe Crozier. At the beginning of the season when we went through 10 games unbeaten, we really didn't know how good we were and we wondered if we were just lucky. Now that we've gone through 60 games, it's different, we know we're not just a flash-in-the-pan team."

Gratton played his third game in the Aud, and his goal in the second period, which turned out to be the game-winner, gave him a goal in each of those three games. He spent much of the night playing right wing paired with Perreault and Martin as Joe Crozier split The French Connection by putting Robert with Meehan and Lorentz.

"It's OK with me wherever I play," said Robert, the team's leading scorer to this point. "It's getting close to the playoffs and we need more scoring balance. If I can help the team playing on another line, fine. I'll play defense if they want me to."

The Gratton experiment was continued when the Sabres traveled to Minnesota, but following a 4-2 loss that ended the unbeaten skein, Crozier reunited the Connection the next night in Buffalo and Robert's pretty behind-the-back pass – "my Yvan Cournoyer pass," he said – set up Perreault for the winning goal as the Sabres edged Pittsburgh again, this time, 2-1.

The Red Wings also split a pair of weekend games, losing a shocker to the pitiful Islanders before defeating St. Louis, thus leaving them four points behind Buffalo.

"Five weeks from today we play Montreal," Joe Crozier said, again exuding unbridled confidence in his club's ability to make the playoffs.

Tracy Pratt was nicknamed "Tree" because of his imposing 6-foot-2, 195-pound frame.

11
March: The Slides of March

There was a reason why Joe Crozier was confident enough to boldly cast aside the advances of the experienced Red Wings and continue to predict that his upstarts would be Montreal's first-round opponent. The Sabres had managed to avoid any prolonged slumps as their longest winless streak had been five games, that coming on the heels of the 10-game unbeaten streak which had opened the season.

The difference was, that was November. This was March, and the pressure was starting to mount on Crozier's young club.

"We tried to keep it as cool as we could so as to not get too uptight about this thing," Crozier remembered. "We knew what was happening all right."

What was happening is that every game had become a struggle. Although the calendar said the playoffs didn't start until April, the Sabres had essentially been playing games with playoff-type ramifications ever since the Red Wings had overtaken them briefly a few weeks earlier.

And it all began to catch up with the team when the month of March roared in. During the first 25 days of the month, a span of 12 games, the Sabres won only once. There was an eight-game winless drought to start, and after a 5-1 victory over Toronto on March 18, another three-game skid ensued. Incredibly, Detroit was also going through some tough times, and the furthest Buffalo ever fell behind the Red Wings was by one point.

The Sabres visited Atlanta on March 1 and after falling behind 3-0 and 4-1, rallied for a 4-4 tie as Martin and Mickey scored 1:45 apart in the third period and the Buffalo defense clamped down after a sloppy start, allowing only three Flames shots in the final 20 minutes. Joe Crozier was grateful for the one point his team earned, yet said it should have been two as Perreault rang a slap shot off the post with 27 seconds left that would have given the Sabres the victory.

The team returned to Buffalo and had two days to prepare for an invasion by the Canadiens, and it looked as if the Sabres spent their time wisely. Although they lost, 4-2, it was one of their best games of the season. Buffalo played dead even with Montreal until 1:44 remained when a clearing pass by Robitaille accidentally ticked off Roger Crozier's stick and caromed directly to Jacques Lemaire who promptly scored the winning goal.

"Luce was wide open up center," Robitaille explained. "Roger was going from one side of the net to the other and his stick was dragging. I tried to send a pass to Luce and it nicked Roger's stick and deflected right to Lemaire. Well, I can't sit and sulk about it. Maybe I'll get it back the next game."

Lemaire couldn't believe his good fortune.

"I didn't know what was happening until I heard the crowd yelling," Lemaire said. "Then I turned and saw the puck rolling toward me. As far as I knew, Buffalo had control of the puck and had two defensemen back there."

Gilbert Perreault maneuvered behind the net as a Los Angeles defender was about to chop him with his stick.

The freak play spoiled a fabulous effort by the Sabres against the league's best team. They fired 35 shots at Ken Dryden, but Dryden was his typically superb self, allowing only goals by Hillman in the first period and by Ramsay while the Sabres were shorthanded in the second.

When the Sabres departed the following day for a three-game West Coast trip with their lead over Detroit down to one point, Robitaille and Schoenfeld were left behind due to injuries. Schoenfeld had missed the last two games with a foot injury and Robitaille had taken a shot off his foot against Montreal. With a sudden depletion of his defensive corps, Joe Crozier recalled Carriere from Cincinnati, and told the rookie to meet the team in Los Angeles.

Carriere did just that, and after Buffalo fell behind 2-0 to the Kings, Carriere assisted on a second-period goal by Lorentz, then scored the tying goal – his first in the NHL – early in the third to give the Sabres a 2-2 tie despite the fact that Crozier dressed only five defensemen.

"I didn't know what to expect when I got here," Carriere said that night. "I didn't realize so many guys were injured. I didn't know I'd play a regular shift. I wasn't playing much for Buffalo before I was sent down, so I wasn't shooting much. With Cincinnati, I was on the ice a lot, regular shift plus the power play, so I gained a lot of confidence.

"I have to admit I was a little disappointed over not having scored that first NHL goal when I was up with the Sabres for the first half of the season. But I'm really happy that when it finally came, it was an important game for the team."

PROFILE - Larry Carriere

Carriere leans back in his chair with his hands clasped behind his head, rhapsodizing about that night nearly a quarter of a century ago. The sun is shining brilliantly through the window in his Marine Midland Arena office, and you have to squint to see the man who is now the Sabres' assistant general manager. But even with your vision impaired, it is easy to recognize the sheer joy that engulfs Carriere when recalling the memory of his first NHL goal.

"I stayed here through December that first year and then they sent me to Cincinnati until about March 5," Carriere recalls. "I got called up because we had some injuries and I was told to meet the team in LA. So I went out there and I scored a tying goal to grab us a point and that was my first NHL goal. I'll never forget that date."

That goal against the Kings in his rookie season was the first truly significant contribution Carriere made to the Sabres. There have been many more since then.

Carriere was born in hockey heaven, Montreal, but he did not take the normal path that most young Canadian boys followed to the NHL. He played just half a season of junior hockey with Verdun before attending Loyola University in Montreal where he played four years of college hockey for the Warriors in addition to graduating with a degree in business administration.

While the junior leagues churned out the vast majority of NHL prospects in those days, Carriere said he felt playing for Loyola gave him an advantage over many junior players in terms of the experience and maturity level of the competition he was facing.

"It was all former major junior players who were a little older, so I was the youngest one of the bunch," said Carriere, whose coach at Loyola was Dave Draper, currently the director of player personnel for the 1996 Stanley Cup champion Colorado Avalanche. "We used to beat some of the junior clubs because our guys were a little older and more experienced. There were

some advantages, mainly because I was playing with more experienced players.

"The only down side was that we only played 35 to 40 games as opposed to 70 that they play in junior, but we had a lot of practice time and a lot of exhibition tours in the U.S. against some of the best Division I teams, and to my recollection we used to beat most of them."

As a collegian, Carriere logged ample ice time and by his senior year, he was the team's best defenseman. He played a tight, hard-hitting style in his own end, but he also showed an ability to skate, carry the puck, and shoot, as evidenced by the 20 goals he scored from the back line. That was enough to bring NHL scouts to Loyola in droves, and once

they were there, Carriere became a hot property, not only because of his talent, but because he hadn't toiled in the junior leagues before going to college so he was one of the few Warriors young enough to be eligible for the 19- and 20-year-old amateur draft.

"In my draft year, there were a lot of scouts watching me, and I tried to crank up my play a lot, and I guess I did," said Carriere, who was inducted into the Loyola Sports Hall of Fame in 1987.

One scout who came away very impressed was Mike Racicot, at the time

the Sabres' Quebec region talent hound. The Sabres were in desperate need of defensive help going into the 1972-73 season, and after Imlach selected Schoenfeld with the fifth pick in the first round, he grabbed Carriere in the second round, No. 25 overall.

Imlach and Joe Crozier did not think Carriere would make the club out of training camp, but he was one of the big surprises at St. Catharines as Horton had taken him under his wing and helped him immeasurably.

"That was old school hockey with Tim," Carriere said. "We (he and Schoenfeld) didn't say much in training camp, we just listened to Tim and worked hard. We came to camp not knowing if we'd make the team, but we did.

"I think Punch designed it that way, and having a guy like Tim out there probably sped up the development of the team. We were young guys and we moved in there and took over a couple spots from veterans like Al Hamilton and Jim Watson who had gone to the WHA."

At the end of November, Carriere was injured in a game against Boston, knocking him out of action for about a month. A couple of days before New Year's when he was ready to return, he was sent down to Cincinnati, until his recall for that game in LA. The Sabres never sent him to the minors again.

Carriere spent two more full years with Buffalo. In 1973-74, he had six goals and 30 points, and was a plus three, and in 1974-75, he dipped to one goal and 11 assists, but played all 80 games and was a plus 12. He had become a solid defenseman, described by Joe Crozier as "a tough guy who worked very, very hard. He didn't have as much finesse as Schoenfeld, but he'd get there. He was a player I could use in tough moments, or on the penalty kill, and he'd come through for me."

But before the 1975-76 season, Rick Dudley left the Sabres to play for Cincinnati in the WHA, and feeling the need to fill that void on left wing,

Imlach obtained Jacques Richard from the Flames in exchange for Carriere and a second-round draft pick. It was not one of Imlach's more prudent deals as Richard, a former first-round draft choice of Atlanta, proved to be a bust.

Defenseman Bill Hajt said in Celebrate the Tradition by Budd Bailey that while Dudley's departure hurt the Sabres, so too did the trade involving Carriere.

"Larry Carriere was also a big part of our team, a muscle guy, a super team player," Hajt said. "All of a sudden we had lost two key players and got nothing in return."

Carriere wasn't exactly thrilled by the deal, either.

"It was right after we had almost won the Cup, and I was higher than a kite, I loved playing here," Carriere said. "But in training camp the following year, they decided they needed to make some changes. I had just gotten married, and it was pretty traumatic because it was the first time I had been traded. I was very disappointed and I let Mr. Imlach know that, and he said, 'One day we'll get you back.'"

Carriere spent 1975-76 in Atlanta and was a quality addition to the Flames defense, but the following season he was traded along with Hilliard Graves to Vancouver for ex-Sabre team-mate John Gould, and the year after that, was sent to LA for the immortal Sheldon Kannegiesser.

When the Kings demoted him to their AHL club in Springfield, Imlach made good on his promise and rescued him from the minors late in the 1977-78 season and he played nine more games for the Sabres. He was not on the playoff roster, though, and after Buffalo had been eliminated in the second round by Philadelphia, Carriere announced his retirement.

He moved his family to Toronto, took a job working for Molson Breweries, and was perfectly content with his new life when he got a call from Imlach in February of 1980. Imlach had since been fired by the Sabres and was now back in Toronto as general manager. Floyd Smith had been coaching the Leafs, but he had been injured in a car accident, so Imlach called Joe Crozier up from Moncton of the AHL to take over behind the Leafs' bench. The old Buffalo hierarchy was back together, and recognizing that the

Toronto defensive corps was a little thin heading into the playoffs, Imlach decided to coax Carriere out of retirement.

"They were in a little trouble," Carriere said. "I was out of hockey, but Joe and Punch had seen me play in an alumni game. They were short a couple defensemen for the playoffs, and I was living in Toronto, so he called me up and said, 'Would you be interested in coming back in March for the playoffs?'"

"Punch was very loyal that way. I think he kind of remembered what he said to me, that he'd get me back, and he did it twice. I took a leave of absence from what I was doing, then played the rest of that year, but we got beat out by Minnesota in the first round. And that was it for me, 1980 was the last year."

Carriere eventually left Molson and moved back to his hometown of Montreal to take a position as vice-president of Canadian Cardiovascular Products. He yearned to get back into hockey, though, so he contacted the Sabres and worked out an arrangement where he would help Racicot – the man who had discovered him more than a decade earlier – scout the Ontario and Quebec regions.

For 10 years Carriere spent many long, lonely nights on the road. He sat in chilly arenas in various Canadian outposts, listening to droning organ music, trying to gauge the abilities of hundreds of teen-age hockey players, and he loved every minute of it.

"Scouts are very dedicated people who put in a tremendous amount of time, and they're under a lot of pressure," Carriere said. "It used to be you were drafting 20-year-olds and you knew what you were getting. Now you're drafting 17- and 18-year-olds, and you're not going to see this guy for at least two years, so there's a lot more projecting that has to go on.

"I enjoyed it. I saw a lot of former players scouting so that was fun to run into a lot of old friends who you played with and against. It's a tough grind, and it can really wear on you. The life of a scout is very intense from September 1 to the end of May, so you have to have a passion for the game. But when the organization is winning, it's all worth it because it's a real positive experience."

Carriere had always made it clear to the Sabres that he hoped for an opportunity to climb the management

ladder and that chance came about in August of 1993 when Ramsay – who had been serving as assistant to general manager Gerry Meehan – left Buffalo to take an assistant coaching job with the Florida Panthers. Carriere was brought in to fill Ramsay's chair, and he still holds that position.

"I'm pretty much involved in everything, from travel and immigration to working closely with Rochester, working with our coaches here to make sure we support them in every way we can," he said. "Every day in the hockey business, we're constantly trying to improve the hockey club."

Those efforts came to fruition last season as the 1996-97 Sabres rose far beyond expectations, winning the Northeast Division title, finishing fifth overall in points, and advancing into the second round of the playoffs. In many ways, that Sabres team reminds Carriere of the 1972-73 club.

"I think it's a good parallel," he said. "The '73 team was early in its development stage, month to month it changed and you got excited. I think what was so important was the way that team was built. Punch's vision was to build a contender through the draft, picking up quality young people. The first year you had Perreault, the second year you had Martin and Ramsay, and the third year you had Schoenfeld and myself.

"They had some high picks, Punch made some trades, and all of a sudden they had accumulated 10 to 15 quality players that were the nucleus of the team. And then Punch plugged in some tremendous veterans, and we had the goaltending of Roger Crozier and Dave Dryden. It was a great combination. We had some hungry, young, aggressive people who were trying to create careers for themselves and be part of something really good, combined with veterans like Tim Horton, Larry Mickey and Larry Hillman. You could see things were starting to come.

"That's a lot like this team. You see the good, young, quality people who were drafted, you look at the young guys like Mike Peca, Jay McKee, Mike Wilson, and then we have some older veterans mixed in like Garry Galley and Randy Burridge. The guys on this team today, and that team in the 70s, they had that passion for the game. It's exciting."

The Sabres left Los Angeles with a valuable point in their pocket and flew up the coast to Oakland for a game the next night against their surprising nemesis, the Seals, and Rick Smith's goal with 4:09 left gave California a 2-2 tie. The Sabres blew a 2-0 first-period lead and thus closed their five-game season series against the pitiful Seals with just one win.

"It was tougher playing this club than it would be playing a contender," said Meehan, who had one of the goals. "They have nothing to lose and they just relaxed. They just wheel and wheel and wheel. We should have picked up two points."

Instead, Detroit was picking up two points with a win over Atlanta, reducing the Red Wings' deficit to one point. Joe Crozier was visibly upset with the officiating in this game, and he was even more infuriated a couple nights later when the Sabres saw their winless streak reach five with a 5-2 loss in Vancouver.

Referee Ron Wicks drew Crozier's ire when he awarded the Canucks a first-period penalty shot, ruling that Roger Crozier had thrown his stick at the puck. And in the second, he whistled Perreault and Pratt for questionable penalties 50 seconds apart, and Vancouver capitalized on the two-man advantage when Andre Boudrias – who had scored on the penalty shot – flipped in a backhand rebound three seconds before the period ended.

As the Sabres made the cross-country flight back to Buffalo, a glance at the standings revealed that they had earned a mere two points in three games against teams that possessed a combined record of 57-117-33.

"Part of our problem is the pressure," Imlach said, trying to explain the sudden inability to win. "The majority of our players are young, they've never played under this kind of pressure. When they get a couple of goals, they don't keep going at the other guys. They play defense, hold back a little bit, and when you play like that, you make mistakes."

Ramsay's recollection of the March slump echoed Imlach's thoughts.

"Sometimes you put too much pressure on yourself and you don't perform at your best, or there's times that coaches put so much pressure on the team and the team starts to falter because they don't have that huge reservoir of experience to say, 'We've done that before, we've done this before, don't worry, it'll all work out.' We had to find a way to relax and just go play and whatever happens, happens."

Despite the troubles the team was having, Carriere remembered being struck by the change in the team's attitude and confidence during the two months he had been away in Cincinnati.

"When I left to go to Cincinnati, I had a feeling that we had a pretty good team in Buffalo, but when I went back there in early March, I saw that we really had something special and we were capable of beating some of the better teams," he said. "I saw the potential and the improvement, the desire and the confidence. We had that confidence of young people thinking we could win every game."

While the Sabres were idle over the weekend, the Red Wings played twice, and after a 2-0 loss to Montreal, Detroit defeated St. Louis, 3-1, to jump back into fourth place, one point ahead of the Sabres.

"We should be a lot better off than we are right now," Joe Crozier said. "If

NHL STANDINGS THROUGH SUNDAY, MARCH 11

EAST	W	L	T	PTS
Montreal	46	9	14	106
NY Rangers	44	17	7	95
Boston	43	20	5	91
Detroit	34	23	11	79
Buffalo	33	23	12	78
Toronto	23	35	9	55
Vancouver	18	43	8	44
NY Islanders	9	57	5	23

WEST	W	L	T	PTS
Chicago	38	23	8	84
Philadelphia	33	26	10	76
Minnesota	33	27	8	74
St. Louis	29	29	10	68
Los Angeles	28	31	10	66
Pittsburgh	27	35	7	61
Atlanta	24	32	13	61
California	11	43	15	37

SCORING THROUGH MARCH 11

PLAYER	G	A	PTS
Perreault	24	52	76
Robert	36	39	75
Martin	33	30	63
Lorentz	25	33	58
Meehan	29	25	54
Luce	15	23	28
Harris	12	24	36
Hillman	5	22	27
Ramsay	10	13	23
Mickey	11	9	20
Atkinson	9	9	18
Robitaille	3	15	18
Schoenfeld	4	13	17
Pratt	1	15	16
Horton	1	14	15
Gratton	7	7	14
Terbenche	0	6	6
Wyrozub	3	3	6
Carriere	1	5	6
Rombough	1	0	1
Gould	0	1	1

things had gone right, we'd be finishing in second place. Imagine, we've won only six of 33 games on the road. If we'd won three or four more away, it would be no contest, not for fourth place."

St. Louis was next on Buffalo's schedule, and the Blues weren't as accomodating as they had been to Detroit. Jacques Caron stopped 23 shots to post a 2-0 shutout victory, stretching the winless streak to six.

After watching the Red Wings lose in Montreal, the Sabres had a chance to pull back into fourth place when they hosted the Bruins in what was, to this point, the most important NHL game played at the Aud. It was so big, that the Century theater was set up for a closed-circuit television hookup and about 1,200 fans paid $5 to watch the game. What they saw was Buffalo's finest effort in weeks, but it wasn't nearly enough against the powerful Bruins who scored three times in the final 10 minutes to pull away for a 4-1 victory.

"I can't expect my hockey club to play any better," Joe Crozier said. "They gave me all they had. The score didn't indicate the game. That was the best our hockey club has played in some time."

Bobby Orr, who scored twice including an empty net goal from about 180 feet away, was impressed by the Sabres, saying, "The Sabres are still the same good team we played earlier this season. Buffalo is still skating hard, and they have a good enough team to get up some steam, make it into the playoffs and be tough."

Robert did not dress due to a charley horse, so Gratton took his place on right wing and scored the first goal of the game off a nifty setup by Perreault. However, Boston goalie Jacques Plante stopped everything else the Sabres fired his way, making 33 saves in all.

Orr tied the game with a low slap shot from 50 feet away early in the second period, and then the teams played a tense standoff until midway through the third when Gregg Sheppard won a faceoff from Perreault, got the puck back to the point and Carol Vadnais teed up a slapper from just inside the blue line that hit the post and caromed into the net behind Roger Crozier. Just 53 seconds later, Phil Esposito circled the net and slipped a backhander home to make it 3-1, and with Crozier out for an extra attacker in the final minute, Orr scored the longest goal in Aud history.

Boston flew home that night and, showing no ill effects from playing on back-to-back nights, knocked off Detroit, 5-4, on a goal by Doug Roberts with 18 seconds left, preventing the Red Wings from adding to their lead. And then Buffalo put forth another strong effort to steal a 3-3 tie in Montreal that pulled the Sabres even with Detroit at 79 points apiece. Dave Dryden outplayed his brother, Ken, making 38 saves, and Gratton, again filling in for the injured Robert, scored the tying goal with 3:22 left when he swatted in the rebound off a shot by Robitaille.

When the team flew back to Buffalo after the game, they were a spirited bunch. Despite going winless in eight games, they were tied for fourth place and had played marvelously for two games in a row against perhaps the two best teams in the league. Also, there was good news on the injury front as Schoenfeld – who had missed every game during the slump – and Robert would both be ready to go when the Sabres took on the Maple Leafs at the Aud.

Robert promptly snapped an 11-game goal-less drought, Martin, Ramsay, Meehan and Carriere also scored, and Perreault dished out three assists in a solid 5-1 victory over Toronto.

"This was like old times tonight," Meehan said concerning the Sabres' free-wheeling style that produced 33 shots and five goals. "We had about 10 good chances in the first period and couldn't score, but we kept blasting away, and we finally did score."

Although Detroit kept pace with a 2-0 victory over Chicago, Joe Crozier again boasted, "If we play like we did tonight and against Montreal, there is no question that we'll make the playoffs. I used everybody on the bench, and everybody played well."

Perreault, Roger Crozier and Schoenfeld were selected as the three stars against Toronto, but Ramsay could have very easily been chosen as well. Not only had he scored the first goal of the game, but he and his linemates, Luce and Mickey, frustrated Toronto's top line, centered by Darryl Sittler, all evening.

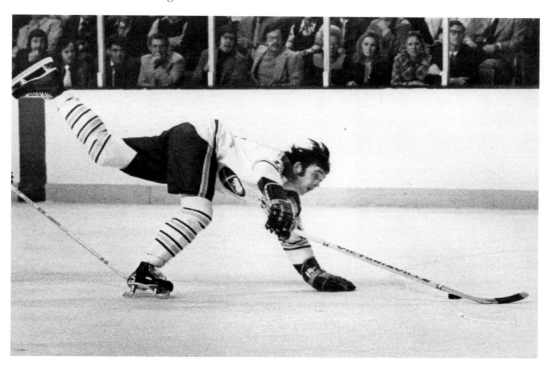

Captain Gerry Meehan, who finished the season with 31 goals, scored one against Toronto that helped the Sabres snap a season-high eight-game winless streak on March 18.

But that type of performance had become a common occurence, and Joe Crozier said of the checking line, "I don't know where we'd be without them. Those three guys work so hard night after night."

"We honestly thought that we controlled the destiny of our team before every game, that's the way we looked at it," Ramsay recalled. "Every single night, Donnie and I and whoever was with us, usually Larry Mickey, we had to play against the best players on the other team, so there was never a night off. We'd have (Phil) Esposito one night, Yvan Cournoyer the next night, (Jean) Ratelle, (Rod) Gilbert and (Vic) Hadfield the next night. So we felt very strongly that we had to play our best every night to give our team a chance to win.

"If we could stop those guys from scoring and maybe get one ourselves, then we should win the game because our other guys are going to play well, The French Connection is going to score, Meehan and Lorentz are going to make something happen. We knew that if we took a night off against one of those lines, they were going to fill the net. That year was no different than any other year in terms of our approach to the game. We had to go out and play our best and if we didn't, we were letting us and the team down."

PROFILE - Craig Ramsay

Every day growing up in Rexdale, a suburb of Toronto, Ramsay was still asleep when his father, Bill, went to work at Bell Telephone. He'd leave the home before six in the morning and wouldn't return until after six at night, and then he'd do it again the next day. A husband and father of three, Bill Ramsay had responsibilities that he did not take lightly. He had a job to do, so he did it. Every day.

There was a consistency to Bill Ramsay as well as a toughness, a desire to work, a knowingness that to be respected, you had to earn it. Every one of those attributes he passed on to his only son, Craig.

"I never saw my dad miss a day of work," Ramsay said of his father, who passed away in 1993.

And very rarely did Bill ever see his son miss a day of work.

From March 27, 1973, to February 10, 1983, Craig played in 776 consecutive games for the Sabres, a streak that ranks as the fourth-longest in NHL history. It was a streak that was defined by consistency, toughness, desire and respect. It was defined by Bill Ramsay.

"You can't grow up and watch that without thinking, 'Geez, that's the way you're supposed to do it,'" Craig said when recalling the memory of his father punching that daily time clock. "My father was a hard worker. And I think that rubbed off on me. I always felt that if you get paid to play hockey, you go play. And if I could play, then I was going to play."

Of course Cal Ripken's consecutive games streak is a monumental feat that stands alone in the annals of sport. But Ramsay's streak, as well as the three in the NHL that are longer – Doug Jarvis (964), Garry Unger (914) and Steve Larmer (884) – have to be considered somewhat miraculous when you consider the often violent nature of hockey.

"I was lucky," Ramsay said, "and you have to be with something like that. In some cases, I'd get a flu and I couldn't play, but we'd happen to have that day

off, and the next day I'd be OK. I always thought if I had a day, I could play no matter what the injury was. I would never play a game if I didn't think I could help the team, but in those days you didn't carry a lot of extra players. Today, there are some nights where a coach might say, 'Take a night off and be ready for the next game.' In our case we didn't have a lot of extra players.

"I remember one game in Atlanta

when my back was really bad, I couldn't even sit on the bench it hurt so much, so I just stood at the end. I wasn't playing, but after about eight minutes we were so bad, Joe Crozier looked down at me and I said, 'I'll try it,' and I ended up playing. Once you got in the game, you just got it going and you forgot about whatever it was and on you went."

As the streak lengthened, Ramsay admitted that the pressure to play grew, and he couldn't help but think that taking some time off might have been beneficial.

"I think at some point it was a burden,"

he said. "I would see guys who had an injury and they would miss a week or two weeks, then they'd come back refreshed and all excited and jumping to play, and here I was playing every night. The pressure was always there, you always had to perform, and there were times I almost thought, wouldn't it be nice if the doctor said, 'You know, I really think you should miss two weeks.' But to be honest, that was in the back of my mind. I wanted to play, so I played."

The Sabres were on a West Coast trip when the invincible Ramsay was finally gunned down. Los Angeles' Dave Lewis ripped a slap shot off Ramsay's left foot at the Great Western Forum, and two nights later, Ramsay was not in the lineup when Buffalo traveled to Calgary. Ramsay wound up missing 16 games that season, missed only five more games in the next two years combined, and then retired at the end of 1984-85.

When he was finished, he had played in 1,070 NHL games – all with the Sabres – to rank second on the team's all-time list behind Perreault. He also ranks fifth in goals (252), third in assists (420), fourth in points (672) and first in short-handed goals (27).

Not bad for a 5-foot-10, 170-pound guy who wasn't a very fast skater, wasn't a great shooter and wasn't an intimidating body checker. All Ramsay did was play good, steady hockey every night, and Imlach summed it up best when he once said of the Rammer, "We had plenty of personal differences, but I have never had any doubts about his hockey ability."

Ramsay began playing organized hockey when he was 10 years old. Nick Durbano, the father of one of Ramsay's friends, Steve Durbano, who went on to play six years in the NHL, gathered the kids in Rexdale and formed a team that played in the B Division of the Toronto Hockey League. The boys were coached by Ramsay's neighbor, Bert Turnkey.

"We played against teams that were

sponsored and who picked players from all over Toronto, but we were just a bunch of kids from our little area, and we had a pretty talented group," Ramsay said. "We had two lines and four defensemen, so there was lots of ice time. I had a great opportunity to play. And I was so lucky that I had a coach who believed in teaching the game, winning wasn't his priority. Certainly our focus was to win, but Bert's focus was to teach the game, know the game, understand the game."

With Turnkey's help, Ramsay became Rexdale's most promising prospect, so when he was 16, he moved north to Peterborough to play junior hockey for the Petes, who were then coached by Roger Neilson.

Neilson was a school teacher who believed education was every bit as important as hockey. Because Neilson planted the seed, Peterborough has long been recognized as one of the best junior organizations in terms of schooling, and Ramsay found this out right away.

"I was always a pretty good student, but now I was living on my own with a lady named Mrs. Crocker in Peterborough, so I missed a few days of school and within the first month Roger had the attendance report sent to him," Ramsay said. "He called me in one day and said, 'Excuse me, are you missing a couple days? That won't happen again.'"

"They stressed that you had to go to school, had to keep your marks up. Peterborough had a guy who was dedicated to his craft, coaching, but he was also a school teacher and he believed that you had to keep the boys busy as well as teach them how to play the game.

"We never stayed overnight for road trips, we always came back after every game because you had to be at school the next day. I remember one trip from Montreal, we got home at 5:30 in the morning and it was a $10 fine if you didn't go to school the next day. For kids making $10 a week spending money, that was a pretty substantial fine, so with two hours sleep, we were up and in school."

Ramsay was a good scorer in Peterborough and in his final season there, he had 30 goals and 76 assists for 106 points. But under Neilson's tutelage, he became a strong two-way forward, able to play defense as well as

offense. It was for this reason that Ramsay believed he was going to be a first-round choice in the 1971 amateur draft.

He wasn't. And if John Andersen hadn't talked Imlach into picking him in the second round, Ramsay may have dropped further down the board.

"I was disappointed that I wasn't drafted in the first round, and then when I was drafted by Buffalo, I knew I now had a 50-50 chance of dying in a fire because they seemed to have 10 a day in Buffalo," Ramsay said with a laugh. "I grew up in Toronto and I saw the Buffalo news reports, and the coverage gave such a bad impression of Buffalo, so there was some concern. I thought 'What kind of place is this?'

"And then there was Punch Imlach. I had grown up watching his tenure with the Toronto Maple Leafs and I knew how tough he was and what he put the players through, and I was quite concerned that after having the coaches I had, now I was going to have this real tough guy to deal with."

Ramsay rejected the first contract Imlach proposed, which showed some guts, but also got him off to a rocky beginning with the coach and general manager.

"We didn't see eye-to-eye right away," Ramsay said. "When the Sabres asked for my contract, I told them I wouldn't sign it because I knew it wasn't fair. It took a few more days of negotiations with myself and John Andersen, and he would go back to Punch because Punch wouldn't talk to me. I ended up getting another contract, it wasn't a very good contract, but it was a little bit more than they had offered in the first place.

"Then when I finally signed, we had a picture taken at the rink and Punch asked me 'When are you going to get a haircut?' I said, 'Gee, I just did.' It wasn't the best of starts. He was a tough guy, there's no question about it. There was always a feeling of apprehension and uncertainty when Punch was around."

During his first training camp, Ramsay knew he'd have a hard time making the Sabres. They had picked another left winger, Martin, in the first round, and Ramsay figured it was unlikely they'd keep two rookies on that side.

"I went into camp hoping for the best, and I thought I was doing OK, but I

wasn't given much of a chance to play on the team. I think I played in two exhibition games and then I was pushed over to the Cincinnati side of the camp."

However, Ramsay got off to a good start in Cincinnati when the season began, and the Sabres were hit with injuries, retirements and generally inadequate play early in 1971-72, so Ramsay was recalled to the Sabres in November. He had played 19 games with the Swords. He never played in the minor leagues again.

Ramsay was paired with Luce almost instantly, beginning a nearly 10-year playing relationship that benefitted both men.

"Donnie helped me right away both on the ice and off," Ramsay said. "He'd been in the league a little bit, he'd been in the minors, so it was good for me to be around him and learn."

Said Luce, "Craig was an extremely intelligent player. He wasn't big, he didn't have all the skills of some other players, but he was incredibly gifted at the hockey sense of the game. Our line was a hard-working line and we added quite a bit to that team. What a pleasure he was to play with."

Although Ramsay's first three goals in the NHL came in the same game against Minnesota on December 5, 1971, one of his first appearances with Buffalo, he knew his role with the Sabres was not to be a high scorer.

"I was more of a playmaker than a shooter, I didn't possess an overpowering shot," he said. "When I scored those three goals against Minnesota that was certainly out of the blue. They (fans) were thinking, 'Wow, we've got another scorer.' But I was never going to be an easy goal scorer, I wasn't nifty with the puck. Guys like Perreault and Robert, they were tricky. I was just a grinder, chase it up and down and get it to somebody. I could see that I wasn't going to score a ton."

Instead, Ramsay's primary job was to make sure the best players in the NHL didn't score a ton against the Sabres. In addition to his regular shift, Ramsay was also given the responsibility of playing on the penalty-killing unit, and he thrived on those duties.

"First of all, I wanted to do it, I loved it," he said. "It was a great challenge to go out there and be that guy. The team is shorthanded, you need somebody to step up, and I wanted to be that guy. We were aggressive about it, more aggressive than most any team at that time other than maybe Boston.

"Those guys, Ed Westfall, Derek Sanderson, they were trying to score goals as well. That's what we tried to do, we tried to score goals, we looked at it as an offensive situation for us. We didn't get a chance to play on power plays or in any great offensive situations, so Donnie and I looked at penalty-killing as a chance to really go for it, and that's why we scored shorthanded goals (48 combined). We gambled, took some chances."

Westfall, who was a Bruin in Ramsay's rookie season, then joined the expansion Islanders in 1972-73 and finished his career in New York, remembers a running battle he had with Ramsay.

"There was always this quiet rivalry I had with Craig in penalty-killing," Westfall said. "When I was playing against Buffalo, I always thought about how he was doing. I always gave him the credit for Buffalo's out-standing penalty-killing stats. He was the guy who was always out there. Back then, we prided ourselves on killing the entire two-minute penalty. We didn't want any-one on the ice, we wanted to do it."

What was the secret to Ramsay's success?

"I think I read the plays, I knew where the puck was going, and I anticipated very well," Ramsay said. "There was the old box, but there were times when I would go into the far corner because I thought I saw a chance. That's what I try to pass on to my players now, you go for it because you think you see it, you think you can make it work. If they make great plays around you or through you, they win, but they have an extra man, so they're supposed to do that."

Ramsay had a bagful of tricks, one of

which was switching hands with his stick, a skill that is commonplace today, but was unique when he played.

"I would do lots of different things with my stick, moving it around into the passing lanes. One of the best defensive plays you can make is often nothing more than a stall. By changing sides with my stick, often I would confuse that point man who thought he had an open guy and suddenly my stick was in a different place and before he could recover, I'd throw it back in my other hand.

"Very often if you just make a guy wait that second, your other players are going to recover, they can make a better read, and force them into a play they don't want to make. In order to do that effectively, you have to know what they want to do, and I think that's part of the fact that Don and I were pretty good offensive juniors, we knew what teams were trying to do.

"And you can't forget that we had great defensemen behind us. We had Tim Horton behind us killing penalties and he was as good as it got. And after

that, there was Schony and Bill Hajt and Mike Ramsey. They allowed us to take the chances and risks that we took."

In his 14th and final season in the NHL, Ramsay was named winner of the Selke Trophy, presented annually to the league's best defensive forward, and he helped the Sabres finish No. 1 in the NHL in penalty-killing efficiency (82.4 percent). Yet while he was clearly still a productive player, he decided to retire to concentrate on coaching, since he had spent the 1984-85 season as a player-assistant under Scotty Bowman. Upon reflection, he thinks he made a mis-take.

"I regret retiring when I did. I thought it was the right thing at the time because I was going to start coaching and I thought I could help the team as a coach, but it probably wasn't the best thing for me, or the team. I won the Selke, I could have played, and I probably should have played. But the team was not very good, we were drifting, and one of the things that bothered me was that nobody wanted to take my job over as the penalty-killer, the checker. There were times we wanted to try someone else for the job, but as long as I was there, it seemed no one was going to step forward, like Michael Peca has for them this season (1996-97). I thought maybe if I retired and coached, I could teach someone else that part of the game."

Ramsay's coaching career began in 1985 as an assistant, first under Schoenfeld and then under Bowman after Schoenfeld was fired 43 games into his tenure. The following season, Bowman decided to relinquish the head coaching chores in November, and Ramsay was promoted to the position. Bowman was fired a couple of weeks later, was replaced by Meehan, and Meehan decided after 21 games – of which Ramsay had won just four – to bring in Ted Sator to coach the team. Ramsay was re-assigned to the front office, and remained in an executive role with Buffalo until he left to become an assistant coach with the expansion Florida Panthers in 1993.

"I was the third coach in a matter of months, the team wasn't going anywhere, it was confusion around the team, and I felt my biggest job was to get these players to want to come down to the rink and play again," Ramsay said of his brief head coaching stint in Buffalo. "Guys didn't want to play, and it had been such a mess with all the changes and the player movement. But by the end of that time when Gerry hired Ted Sator, that was a big disappointment for me because I thought the team was finally having some fun. We started to have some trust between the coach and the players. They were starting to play the way I wanted them to, with enthusiasm."

Ramsay worked first as Director of Professional Evaluation & Development, then served as Assistant General Manager to Meehan, handling such tasks as the schedule, immigration work, transportation and managing the budgets. But it wasn't until he was given the added responsibility of overseeing the operation in Rochester in 1992-93 that Ramsay was truly happy because that gave him an opportunity to get out of the office and get back down to the ice and interact with coaches and players.

However, as much as he enjoyed working with the Amerks, Ramsay knew he wouldn't be in Buffalo too much longer. He had been pining for a chance to return to coaching, but when John Muckler joined the Sabres organization in 1991, Ramsay realized coaching in Buffalo was probably out of the question. Sure enough, Muckler – who was hired as Director of Hockey Operations but had won a Stanley Cup as coach of the Edmonton Oilers in 1990 – was in town less than six months when he stepped behind the bench to replace the fired Rick Dudley in December of 1991, and he stayed there until Ted Nolan was hired in 1995.

"When they brought John Muckler in,

I knew there was nowhere for me to go," Ramsay said. "I worked one year with Rochester, and then I called Roger Neilson and said, 'If you get anything, give me a call.' And he did."

Neilson – who had been Ramsay's head coach in Buffalo during the 1980-81 season – was chosen to be the first head coach of the Panthers. So, tapping into a friendship that went back nearly a quarter of a century to the days when Neilson coached Ramsay in Peterborough, he hired Ramsay to be his assistant coach.

For the first time since Ramsay entered the NHL, he was not going to be a part of the Sabres organization. And after 22 years of living in Western New York, Ramsay was going to move his wife Susan and their four children, Travis, Jad, Brendon and Tristin. As it turned out, though, the departure from Buffalo took a little longer than expected.

On August 13, 1993, the day the movers finished packing his home in Williamsville for the trip to Miami, a bleeding ulcer exploded in Ramsay's stomach and he nearly died. Doctors at Buffalo General Hospital performed an operation that they thought had taken care of the problem, but it didn't. As Ramsay lay in his hospital bed a week later, he experienced another near fatal bleed, and this time, the doctors had to remove his stomach.

"I woke up and they told me my stomach was gone, and I was wondering, 'How do you eat, how do you live?' and the doctor said 'You'll be OK.'"

Ramsay's esophagus is attached to his large intestine, so when he swallows, the food sits there until it gets digested through his small intestine.

"I have to eat often and in small portions, I take B-12 shots every three weeks, and I work out six days a week to keep myself in shape because that's the only reason I survived in the first place," he said.

After his stomach was taken out, he spent more than a month in Buffalo General, then was transferred to the Cleveland Clinic in Miami where he spent another month, and endured a third operation.

"It wasn't a lot of fun," Ramsay said.

"We had wonderful support here from my friends and from the Sabres' organization. We didn't have a place to live, Susan stayed with friends, and my in-laws took the kids to Florida and got them organized in school down there. I was almost dead a few times, but people kept coming around and pushing and pushing, giving Susan the help she needed to get through it.

"What was so disheartening was the fact that I wasn't getting better. It was quite a battle. After my stomach was out, I was supposed to get better, and I wasn't. I certainly was going downhill, and people still talk about how they came to see me and how disheartened I appeared. What I really hated was that my family had to see me like that, for my wife to come every day and almost see me die twice. To them, seeing me fade and fade into a downward spiral was very tough."

His condition finally began to improve, and when it did, that fire that fueled his marvelous playing career kicked in. "I told the doctor, 'Give me a day and I'll show you what I can do,'" Ramsay said. By December 26, 1993, he was working full-time behind the Panthers bench, side-by-side with his good friend, Neilson.

Ramsay and Neilson were fired after the 1994-95 season, but Ramsay was able to hook on for a year as a scout with the Dallas Stars, and then before the 1996-97 season, he was hired as an assistant coach by Ottawa.

It was Ramsay's desire, his will, his toughness, the same attributes that marked his playing career, the same traits bequeathed to him by his father Bill – who had died just before Ramsay went into the hospital – that pulled him through this traumatic period in his life.

"I remember when I was a kid, my dad had two discs in his back fused and when he got out of the hospital, we went on a camping trip about three weeks later," Ramsay said. "There he was carrying the tent and putting it up after having this major back operation. He was one tough son of a bitch."

If Bill were alive today, he'd say the same thing about his son.

Buffalo had six games to go, Detroit seven, and the teams were tied with 81 points apiece. Thanks to a quirk in the schedule, the Sabres and Red Wings were each playing their next four games on the road, on identical nights, over the coming eight days. So while they were playing, they would know what the other was doing simply by looking up at the message boards in each arena where out-of-town scores were posted.

Neither team looked like they deserved a playoff berth when their respective road swings began. The Sabres were thumped in Chicago, 6-2, while St. Louis flattened Detroit, 6-3.

The Sabres played one of their worst periods of the year as Chicago scored five times in the middle 20 minutes against Dryden, though Dryden was not to blame. "In the second period, Dave could have sued the rest of the team for non-support," Joe Crozier fumed afterward. "I thought Dave gave up one bad goal, but other than that he played a fine game. We checked pretty well in the first period, but we had no life, we were just hanging on. It's up to the players now. They simply have to decide they want to win these road games and go out and play like we do at home."

Dryden said he had an inkling the second period was not going to be a good one. "I was the first one on the ice and after I finished scraping the ice in front of my net, I looked around to yell encouragement to the players skating by, but I couldn't find anybody. I looked down at the other end and they were just stepping onto the ice and I thought right then it was going to be a long period."

Larry Mickey scored both Buffalo goals against the Blackhawks, though both were meaningless as they came in the third period when the game was already decided. However, three nights later in Pittsburgh, Mickey scored again, and this time it was a humongous goal, coming with eight seconds left to play to forge a 4-4 tie with the Penguins.

With Detroit losing again, this time 5-3 in Los Angeles, the Sabres took a one-point lead, and though they didn't know it at the time, it was a lead they would never relinquish.

The Sabres were up 2-1 entering the third period, but Al McDonough and Jean Pronovost scored on Roger Crozier to give the Penguins a 3-2 lead with 8:35 left. Robert tied the game with 4:08 to go when he backhanded a shot past Andy Brown after taking a pass from Perreault, but the Penguins regained control when former Sabre Jean-Guy Legace ripped a shot from the point past Crozier with 1:53 remaining.

In the final minute, the Sabres pulled Crozier in favor of an extra attacker and blitzed the Penguins. On the tying goal, Carriere made a nice play to keep the puck in the Pittsburgh zone, then passed to Lorentz who fired a shot on net that Mickey tipped in, keeping the Sabres unbeaten all-time in the Civic Arena (3-0-5). And in 18 games against the Penguins, Buffalo had still lost only one (7-1-9).

The euphoria over regaining fourth place was tempered by a miserable trip to Boston after the game, and by an injury to Ramsay – which would force him to miss the game against the Bruins, just his second absence of the season and his last for nearly 10 years.

The team's chartered plane was late taking off and didn't land at Logan International until 1:30 a.m. When the players finally got to the Sheraton

Plaza Hotel in Boston, some were assigned rooms that weren't ready for occupancy due to a refurbishing project. Those players were sent to another Sheraton hotel, with one stipulation: They had to check out by 1 p.m., even though the game with the Bruins wasn't scheduled to start until 7 p.m. So by mid-morning, after getting very little sleep, they re-packed their bags and were bused out to a Marriott hotel in Newton, Mass., where they spent the rest of the day until leaving for the game.

Needless to say, this was no way to get ready to play the big, bad Bruins, and Boston won its ninth game in a row, crushing the Sabres, 6-1. Fortunately, the Red Wings' disastrous road trip reached a new low when Detroit was routed by hapless California, 8-5, so Buffalo stayed one point ahead.

Phil Esposito scored two goals, enabling him to surpass the 50-goal plateau, and Bobby Orr also scored twice before being ejected in the second period for being third man in a fight between Mike Walton and Sabre rookie Ron Busniuk, who had been recalled to replace Ramsay.

Busniuk, who was in Jacksonville, Fla., that morning with Cincinnati, flew all the way in to Boston after receiving a call from Imlach, and he made his NHL debut a memorable one. He was Buffalo's only bright spot as he spent the entire night smashing into Bruins. He drew two Boston penalties in the first five minutes, although the Sabres failed to capitalize on either power play, and then during his fight with Walton, he basically drew Orr's game misconduct.

"I think one of the biggest mistakes I made all season was leaving this lad in the minors," said Joe Crozier. "He did a real job for me tonight."

Sadly, no one else did much of anything. The Bruins played shorthanded for six and a half minutes in the first period, yet came away with a 3-0 lead as Orr helped set up Esposito's first goal, then scored his pair 1:13 apart late in the period. Dryden replaced Roger Crozier in the second, and he was greeted by goals from Fred O'Donnell and Johnny Bucyk. Lorentz scored Buffalo's lone goal in the third, but Boston answered that when Esposito tallied his second of the game.

The Sabres had now won just one of their last 12 games, but the damage had been minimal because the Red Wings were playing just as poorly down the stretch. "Fourth place has been sitting there, just waiting for one of us to take it and wrap it up for weeks and neither of us has done much about it," Pratt said. "We can't hope that Detroit will go on losing, not with two games left against Toronto."

Pratt was right. The Red Wings' three-game losing streak came to a screeching halt when Mickey Redmond scored twice to become just the seventh player in NHL history to reach the 50-goal mark for one season, leading an 8-1 rout over the Maple Leafs. At the same time, though, the Sabres were scratching their way to a 3-2 victory over the Islanders in their final road game of the year to maintain their one-point lead.

Although Boston was Buffalo's most hated rival, fans at the Aud had to feel privileged to watch a player like Bobby Orr weave his magic when the Bruins came to town.

EAST	W	L	T	PTS
Montreal	49	10	16	114
Boston	50	20	5	105
NY Rangers	47	21	7	101
Buffalo	34	27	14	82
Detroit	35	28	11	81
Toronto	25	40	9	59
Vancouver	22	45	8	52
NY Islanders	12	58	5	29

WEST	W	L	T	PTS
Chicago	42	25	8	92
Minnesota	36	30	9	81
Philadelphia	35	28	11	81
St. Louis	31	33	11	73
Los Angeles	30	34	11	71
Pittsburgh	30	36	9	69
Atlanta	25	36	14	64
California	14	46	16	44

Roger Crozier, making his 16th start in the last 20 games, stopped 29 shots while Martin, Robitaille and Robert scored the goals.

"There's so much pressure, but we felt good when we scored on our first shift," Robert said of Martin's goal, which Perreault set up just 33 seconds into the game.

While Detroit got the next night off, Buffalo had to fly home to take on rugged Philadelphia. After meeting the Flyers on Wednesday, March 28, the Sabres had only one more game left, at home against St. Louis on Sunday. Meanwhile, the Red Wings would have three to play, so the Sabres were in a must-win situation. If they lost to the Flyers, Detroit would be in position to clinch the final playoff spot if it won its games against Toronto on Thursday and Chicago on Saturday.

"We can't worry about what Detroit is doing, we just have to win our games," Mickey said.

And so, that's what the Sabres did. Following up their solid effort in New York, the Sabres tore through the Flyers, 6-3, in a fight-filled game that had the Aud's walls buckling from the excitement.

Fred Shero's Flyers hadn't yet been dubbed the Broad Street Bullies, but they were on their way to earning that sobriquet, and this game was an example of why. The Flyers waited exactly 67 seconds to start throwing punches, but the Sabres stood tall, threw them back, and more importantly, won the game.

Hillman and Dave Schultz high-sticked each other to start the festivities, and when Pratt skated over to help Hillman, all hell broke loose. After a 20-minute delay, referee Bruce Hood sorted out the brawlers and decided that Pratt, Lorentz, Schultz and Don Saleski deserved game misconducts. Later in the period, Schoenfeld squared off with Bob Kelly in a spirited fight, and when the nearly hour-long blood bath of a period finally ended, 104 penalty minutes had been meted out, but no goals had been scored.

"As far as I'm concerned, it was deliberate," said Joe Crozier, who at one point shed his sport coat and wanted a piece of Schultz. "The fights were Philadelphia's game plan, they've done this type of thing before. I don't think he (Shero) could beat me in my building, that's why he sent two guys out there (Schultz and Saleski) to be rough."

Crozier may have had a point because once the goonery stopped in the second period and the teams actually played hockey, Buffalo erupted for four goals, two by Perreault in the first 2:27.

With a 4-2 lead entering the third, Martin scored a critical goal that gave the Sabres some breathing room, and after Terry Crisp narrowed the margin to 5-3 at the 6:19 mark, Buffalo buckled down and played tight defense the rest of the way. Luce was credited with the game's final goal with 18 seconds left to play when he broke in alone on an empty net after Shero pulled goalie Doug Favell and had the puck deflected away when Flyers defenseman Barry Ashbee threw his stick. That constituted an automatic goal.

Meehan, who had gotten into a scrap with Andre Dupont late in the second period, said he believed the Flyers were still trying to exact a measure of revenge on Buffalo dating to the previous year when Meehan's goal with four seconds remaining in the season finale beat the Flyers, 4-3, and knocked them out of the playoff picture.

"It's got to be in the back of their minds," Meehan said. "They've got a few guys that are still kind of bitter. I think there's always going to be bad blood between our two clubs."

Even with the victory and the three-point lead it provided, the Sabres still needed help in order to be able to control their own destiny. They got it on Thursday from an ironic source: the rival Maple Leafs. Toronto went into the Olympia and whipped Detroit, 6-4, meaning that the Sabres could now clinch the playoff berth by winning their season finale at the Aud against St. Louis.

"I remember listening to that game on the radio," Joe Crozier recalled of the pivotal Maple Leafs-Red Wings game. "I was living in Tonawanda and I couldn't get the reception that well, so I went outside and walked around so I could get it a little clearer. I was listening and listening and when Toronto won, I threw that damn radio as far as I could throw it, that's how excited I was. I was so damn happy that night."

The Sabres' booster club wasn't too happy Friday night when it held its annual testimonial dinner at the Hearthstone Manor to honor the team, and none of the players showed up because Crozier wouldn't allow them to. He wanted them in their homes resting for the showdown against St. Louis.

Gilbert Perreault and Philadelphia's Bobby Clarke went at it pretty good during their careers. In the second-to-last game of the regular season, Perreault scored two goals to key the Sabres' pressure-packed 6-3 victory over the Flyers. (Photo courtesy of Ron Moscati)

"Making the playoffs is the only thing that matters," Crozier said in explaining his decision. "Everything else is secondary. This dinner just happened to come at the wrong time."

Because the players weren't in attendance, Horton was unable to pick up the Wayne Larkin Memorial Trophy, given to the player deemed most valuable to the team in a vote by his teammates; Perreault couldn't receive the Frank Eddolls Memorial Trophy, presented to the most popular player as voted on by the booster club; and Lorentz wasn't handed the Unsung Hero trophy, also chosen by the booster club.

The Sabres could have clinched the playoff berth by sitting on their couches on Saturday night, March 31, if Detroit had lost to Chicago. But it only seemed appropriate that the Red Wings beat the Blackhawks, 6-4, meaning the race would indeed be decided on the final night of the season.

Despite being one point behind, the Red Wings were still not in dire straits because if Buffalo lost to St. Louis, all the Red Wings would have to do is tie the Rangers in New York. That would have pulled them even with the Sabres in points, and the Red Wings would finish fourth because the first tiebreaker was number of wins, and Detroit would hold a 37-36 advantage.

"We don't have to worry about what Detroit does as long as we win our game on Sunday," Joe Crozier said in the simplest possible terms.

On April 1, 1973, the final night of the regular season, the Sabres needed a victory over St. Louis to clinch a playoff berth. Here they gathered for a pep talk at the start of the third period. (Photo courtesy of Ron Moscati)

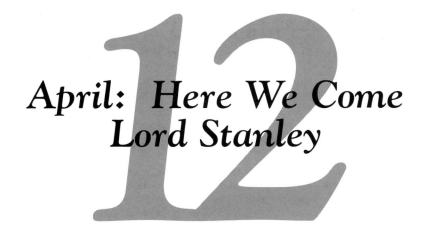

April: Here We Come Lord Stanley

Normally, Sunday night games at the Aud started at 7:05, but Imlach changed the starting time of the game with St. Louis to 8:35 when he learned that, due to an afternoon NBA contest at Madison Square Garden, Detroit's game there against the Rangers wasn't slated to begin until 8:30. Imlach reasoned that late-game strategy might hinge on what was happening in New York, so the NHL and the Blues rightfully agreed to the switch.

The delay was certainly a masterful stroke of genius by Imlach, but it also forced the already-nervous players to have to sit around an extra hour and a half before the most important game of their lives.

"I remember that last night when we had to beat St. Louis," said Ramsay. "The pressure was really on."

Especially for Roger Crozier. Crozier was jittery before every game he played, but the tension was almost unbearable on this night, and the extra 90 minutes he had to wait had his teammates concerned for his well-being.

"Roger was a very nervous goalie the day of a game," Meehan recalled. "I felt bad for him in that regard because he would get so agitated before the game. I guess it was his way of getting ready to play. I just assumed that was one of the quirks of being a goalie, and that goalies were a different type of player who had different ways of preparing for a game. The thing was, he was a very personable guy off the ice for the most part, he didn't let it affect him on off days."

Said Ramsay, "Roger hated the game, it seemed. He was so intense that it was certainly no fun for Roger before the game. I was like that a little, too, but to see Roger, it was actually a little intimidating. You saw him and you wondered how he could go out and play. But he did, and he was usually spectacular."

The fans in the jam-packed Aud were feeling the pressure, too. As they filed into the building, the air seemed to hang heavy with trepidation, and when Wayne Merrick scored just 1:54 into the game for the Blues, a year's worth of hard work was seemingly about to go down the drain.

A ray of hope beamed through the tense arena when the first update from

New York came in: Rangers 1, Red Wings 0. And just a few minutes later, that became 2-0 as Jean Ratelle scored for New York, bringing a tremendous roar from the crowd.

The Sabres, however, had said all along they didn't want to back in to the playoffs, they wanted to win their way in, and at the 15:35 mark of the first period, they began that quest in earnest when Perreault tied the game with a backhander off a rebound of a shot by Martin.

Then, within a span of 3:45 in the second period, the Sabres took control as Mickey swatted in his own rebound for the go-ahead goal, and Lorentz took a pass from Meehan and beat Jacques Caron from a tough angle to make it 3-1.

From that moment on, the Sabres played confidently, and they dominated the Blues, who had already secured the fourth playoff spot in the Western Division and really had nothing to play for. The Red Wings battled back to tie New York at 2-2, and after Vic Hadfield put the Rangers ahead midway through the third, Tim Ecclestone again tied it for Detroit, but it became a moot point as St. Louis was unable to break through on Crozier and Buffalo's sturdy defense.

"I remember we had the 3-1 lead with about 1:30 to go in the game and they pulled their goaltender," Ramsay said. "Rene took a shot from our side of center at the open net and he missed, and I had to race down to try to touch it to prevent the icing and Barclay Plager just about killed me. I beat him to the puck, but he was going to make sure I never did that again. But I remember it was worth it. We wanted to win so badly, and we battled and battled."

Punch Imlach and his wife, Dodo, spent a nervous evening at the Aud during the regular-season finale against St. Louis.

When the horn sounded to end the game, the fans went wild, the players streamed onto the ice and buried Roger Crozier in a sea of humanity, and Joe Crozier led his boys into the dressing room where he presented them with six bottles of champagne that he had been saving a couple of months for just this occasion.

Gerry Meehan assisted on the Sabres' last goal in their 3-1 victory over the St. Louis Blues. (Photo courtesy of Ron Moscati)

"It was like a balloon that was busting and all that pressure was gone," Joe Crozier said, remembering the feeling of finally clinching the playoff berth. "We had worked so hard, and now we were the first expansion team from the East Division to go into the playoffs."

Said Lorentz, "We were determined that we were going to make the play-offs and that was it. There was pressure, sure, but in the excitement of everything, we got carried along with it and sometimes that overcomes the pressure part of it. We had a great bunch of players and Joe did a tremendous job to keep us heading in the right direction."

Added Meehan, "We had gone through this daily grind for several months, and having accomplished what we had accomplished, we were pretty proud of ourselves."

FINAL NHL STANDINGS THROUGH SUNDAY, APRIL 1

EAST	W	L	T	PTS
Montreal	52	10	16	120
Boston	51	22	5	107
NY Rangers	47	23	8	102
Buffalo	37	27	14	88
Detroit	37	29	12	86
Toronto	27	41	10	64
Vancouver	22	47	9	53
NY Islanders	12	60	6	30

WEST	W	L	T	PTS
Chicago	42	27	9	93
Philadelphia	37	30	11	85
Minnesota	37	30	11	85
St. Louis	32	34	12	76
Pittsburgh	32	37	9	73
Los Angeles	31	36	11	73
Atlanta	25	38	15	65
California	16	46	16	48

Right: Seymour Knox seemed to be telling someone "I told you so" after the Sabres clinched their first playoff berth by beating St. Louis. (Photo courtesy of Ron Moscati)

Below: The team mobbed winning goalie Roger Crozier at the conclusion of the momentous game. (Photo courtesy of Ron Moscati)

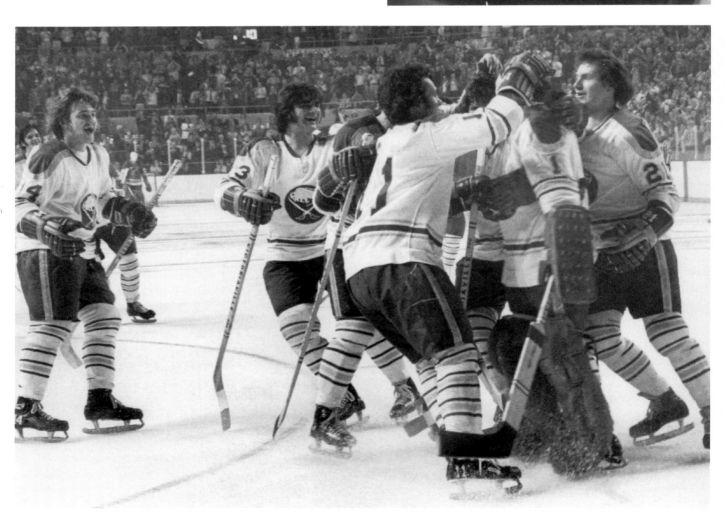

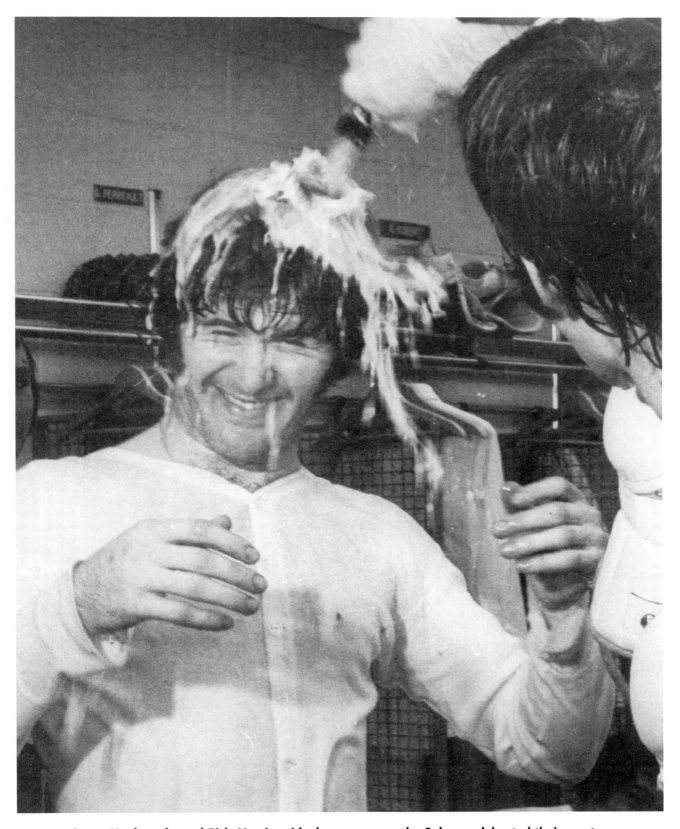

Gerry Meehan doused Rick Martin with champagne as the Sabres celebrated their most important victory to date. (Photo courtesy of Ron Moscati)

Sportscaster Van Miller interviewed The French Connection in the jubilant Buffalo locker room following the win over the St. Louis Blues.

Rene Robert, Gilbert Perreault and Rick Martin, The French Connection, got ready to board the flight that took them to Montreal for the start of the Sabres' first playoff series. (Photo courtesy of Ron Moscati)

THE PLAYOFFS: Montreal Knew It Was in a Battle

The Sabres' entry into the postseason was national news because their rise from expansion whipping boys to playoff participant was so unexpected. But the players were not surprised at all.

"Most of us had felt this was our year to do it," Meehan recalled. "We had gone through a pretty good first year, an uneven second year when the results didn't match our expectations, and then in the third year, it all came together."

Said Robert, "There was never any pressure put on us by management because we were a young team, but we knew ourselves that we had the potential to get to the playoffs."

And now that they were in the playoffs, the enthusiasm they had played with all season boiled over into youthful foolhardiness when they began to think they could actually beat the Montreal Canadiens in the first round.

"What we're going to do next is take Montreal," Perreault said in a rare display of bravado.

Said Martin, "If we pick up a game in Montreal, I think we can win the series. I like that rink in Montreal. It's a big one and I can move there. And we've played well there this season."

Even Joe Crozier was caught up in the frenzy when he said, "I'm not taking anything away from the Canadiens. They are without a doubt a super hockey club. But anything can happen in the playoffs. A team can get hot, a goaltender can get hot. I won't predict anything. We intend to take this series one game at a time. The thing is, we're here because we deserve to be here. And we'd like to show everyone that."

Today, Robert smiles as he looks back on that pre-playoff exuberance.

"When we played the Montreal Canadiens, let's be honest, we were hoping to play anyone but them that year," Robert said. "We were just hoping to do well. We knew our chances of beating them were very, very slim. They were so much more experienced and talented than we were all the way around. They had three all-star defensemen (Guy Lapointe, Jacques Laperriere and Serge Savard) and an all-star goalie (Ken Dryden), so right there, you haven't even gotten to their forwards."

What about those forwards? How about a group that included Guy Lafleur, Frank and Peter Mahovolich, Jacques Lemaire, Yvan Cournoyer, Marc Tardif, Henri Richard and Rejean Houle. Montreal coach Scotty Bowman said he was considering playing four lines in the series against Buffalo, and Joe Crozier quipped, "He has enough talent to play six lines."

In truth, the Sabres really didn't have a chance against the Canadiens, and Peter Mahovolich knew it when he said on the eve of the opener at the Forum, "Really, I hope we don't win by big scores. That hurts a team. I'd like to see 3-1 or 4-2 games where we're working all the time and not getting high on ourselves."

Don Luce (left) and Jim Schoenfeld enjoy a game of cards during the flight to Montreal. (Photo courtesy of Ron Moscati)

Mahovolich got his wish in Game One as the Sabres played marvelously and took Montreal right to the wire before losing, 2-1.

"I was a young guy, an intense guy, but I remember thinking, 'We're in the playoffs against Montreal, how am I going to do this?'" Ramsay said. "'If this (the last game against St. Louis) was the pressure, what's it going to be like in the playoffs?' Well, what happened is when we went in to play Montreal in that first game, I didn't feel pressure, I felt excitement. It was completely different, an incredible feeling and a wonderful experience.

"Joe told us, 'Show them no respect, just go,' and we did. We tried to show them no respect. As good as they were, as good as that defense was, we attacked them and chased them. I don't think they liked it or understood it. That first game, we legitimately had a chance to win it."

Joe Crozier made a surprise decision and started Dave Dryden in goal, and in his first start since March 21 in Chicago, Dryden was superb, stopping 33 shots. With Ken Dryden playing for the Canadiens, it was the first time in NHL history that goaltender brothers opposed each other in a playoff game.

"Dave played a super hockey game," Joe Crozier said afterward. "Roger has played so many big games lately that I decided to go with Dave. To win, you have to have everybody going. I thought Dryden could do a good job and he did. He made some excellent saves. I thought the goaltending at both ends was absolutely super."

The Sabres had a two-man advantage for 47 seconds in the first period, but couldn't capitalize as Ken Dryden turned away Martin, then stopped rebound attempts by Perreault and Gratton in the only flurry. Just after Savard's penalty expired, the Sabres had an apparent goal by Mickey disallowed when the goal judge ruled that the puck never crossed the line.

"More than half the puck was over the line," said Luce, who was standing right at the goal mouth and had a perfect view. "The puck went over the top of his glove and Dryden's hand was in the net when he grabbed it. And when he grabbed it, his hand was driven farther back. (Referee Art) Skov was out at the blue line, so he couldn't tell."

Later in the first, Montreal saw two good scoring chances die when Richard hit the post, then Dave Dryden foiled Cournoyer on a breakaway.

Early in the second period, Ramsay broke the scoreless tie when his shot from the faceoff circle to Ken Dryden's right found its way into the net for Buffalo's first postseason goal. "We talked about getting the puck high on Dryden, I put it high, and it went in," Ramsay said.

With both teams playing a man short, the Canadiens pulled even at 17:01 when Lemaire's low drive from 35 feet out glanced off Dave Dryden's right pad and went into the net. "I thought if they ever get another goal against us, it'll really get tough because in the playoffs when you get behind by two goals, it's difficult to catch up," Lemaire said. "I knew we needed it (his goal) to take the pressure off."

Perreault was stopped on a breakaway late in the period, and that proved to be a huge miss because at the 4:27 mark of the third, Cournoyer scored the game-winner on a power play. Carriere and Pratt had both been penalized, so for 18 seconds, the Canadiens had a two-man advantage. It was during that brief window of opportunity that Cournoyer weaved his way through the open space and fired a 20-foot slap shot. The puck entered the net two seconds after Carriere had returned to the ice, so in effect, the Sabres were still defending with only three players.

"They had a two-man disadvantage in the first period, but it's different than having it in the third period," Joe Crozier said. "A club is always stronger in the first than in the third. We got beat on a double penalty. That double penalty cost me the hockey game."

The Canadiens came away very impressed by Buffalo's performance, but Bowman reminded everyone that this was not a surprise. "They've been playing that way all season," said Bowman. "They have a good team that works very hard. They're a strong defensive club and they have some great scorers.

"He (Dave Dryden) played four of the five games against us (in the regular season) and I don't think there was a bad game in the bunch."

STANLEY CUP PLAYOFFS
GAME TWO
CANADIENS 7, SABRES 3
Thursday, April 5, 1973
Attendance – 16,558 at the Forum

Buffalo	2	0	1	– 3
Montreal	0	5	2	– 7

BUFFALO
Goalie: Dave Dryden
Defense: Tim Horton, Mike Robitaille, Tracy Pratt, Larry Hillman, Jim Schoenfeld, Paul Terbenche, Larry Carriere
Forwards: Rick Martin, Jim Lorentz, Norm Gratton, Craig Ramsay, Gil Perreault, Larry Mickey, Rene Robert, Gerry Meehan, Don Luce, Hugh Harris.

MONTREAL
Goalie: Ken Dryden
Defense: Jacques Laperriere, Guy Lapointe, Serge Savard, Bob Murdoch, Pierre Bouchard, Jim Roberts
Forwards: Guy Lafleur, Marc Tardif, Yvan Cournoyer, Rejean Houle, Claude Larose, Henri Richard, Murray Wilson, Pete Mahovolich, Chuck Lefley, Jacques Lemaire, Frank Mahovolich.

FIRST PERIOD
Scoring: 1, Buffalo, Perreault 1 (Schoenfeld), 1:06. 2, Buffalo, Martin 1 (Perreault, Lorentz), 16:48 (pp).
Penalties: Luce, Buf (high-sticking), 7:11; Lapointe, Mont (high-sticking), 7:11; Lefley, Mont (slashing), 16:27; Mickey, Buf (major-fighting), 17:19; Savard, Mont (major-fighting), 17:19; Lorentz, Buf (high-sticking), 19:51; Lapointe, Mont (high-sticking), 19:51.
SECOND PERIOD
Scoring: 3, Montreal, Savard 1 (Lafleur, Houle), 4:48. 4, Montreal, Cournoyer 2 (Savard, Lemaire), 6:07. 5, Montreal, Tardif 1 (Lafleur), 10:39. 6, Montreal, Lapointe 1 (Tardif), 16:26 (pp). 7, Montreal, Lemaire 2 (Cournoyer, F. Mahovolich), 17:29.
Penalty: P. Mahovolich, Mont (roughing), 7:12; Martin, Buf (slashing), 15:21.
THIRD PERIOD
Scoring: 8, Montreal, Cournoyer 3 (F. Mahovolich), 3:10. 9, Montreal, Cournoyer 4 (F. Mahovolich, Savard), 15:31. 10, Buffalo, Schoenfeld 1 (Gratton), 17:45.
Penalties: Wilson, Mont (tripping), 10:02.

SHOTS ON GOAL: Buffalo 8-4-11 - 23 Montreal 11-14-10 - 35.
POWER-PLAY OPPORTUNITIES: Buffalo 1-for-3; Montreal 1-for-1.
THREE STARS: 1. Cournoyer; 2. Savard; 3. Perreault.

There was a pretty bad one, though, in Game Two the following night. Despite Dryden's success in the opener, Imlach wanted Joe Crozier to start Roger Crozier, and the coach was going to defer to the general manager. But during the pregame skate, Joe changed his mind, played a hunch and chose Dryden.

All was well for one period as Dryden stopped 11 Montreal shots, and Perreault scored 1:06 into the game, then set up Martin at 16:48 on a power play to give the Sabres a 2-0 lead.

But in the middle period, Montreal showed why it lost only 10 games in the regular season, pummeling the Sabres mercilessly for five goals to blow the game open en route to a 7-3 victory.

"When they start coming, they hit you like a tidal wave," said Pratt.

Said Joe Crozier, "The Canadiens can explode at any time, any game, any period and tonight they exploded in the second period. They really exploded. That's the kind of hockey club the Montreal Canadiens can be. His club was so good, Scotty Bowman didn't even have to coach. One time there, I thought he was going to sit down and let them play without a coach."

The evening had begun with so much promise as Schoenfeld dove to block a shot, Perreault gathered the loose puck at his own blue line, deked Laperriere to the ice, and cruised in alone to beat Ken Dryden before some of the Forum faithful had even been seated. The Sabres looked much less tense than they had early in Game One, and they carried the play for the entire period.

Dave Dryden made a big save on Chuck Lefley at 7:05, and robbed Lemaire with his glove two minutes later to keep Buffalo in front, and then the Sabres took a 2-0 lead when Martin ripped one past Ken Dryden after Perreault's pass from the backboards.

During the first intermission, Bowman switched Frank Mahovolich to a line with Lemaire and Cournoyer, and then he tried to match that line against Buffalo's French Connection whenever he could. "That opened up the game," Bowman said, explaining that his high-scoring trio forced The French Connection to play both ends of the rink. This was an uncommon strategy because most teams had used checkers whose sole purpose was to play defense and shut down The French Connection, then get off the ice. The Mahovolich-Cournoyer-Lemaire trio shut out Perreault, Martin and Robert the rest of the way, and produced four goals of their own, including three by Cournoyer.

The Montreal offensive avalanche began at 4:48 of the second period. Savard kept a Buffalo clearing attempt in at the blue line, then fired one past a screened Dave Dryden that seemed to deflect off a Sabre in front of the net. Just 1:19 later, another Savard drive was stopped by Dryden, but Cournoyer cleaned up the rebound. The Sabres protested that the play was offsides because it appeared Savard failed to hold Lemaire's drop pass in at the blue line.

"It's pretty tough getting rooked out of a goal in the first game and in the second game, having an offside call like that," Joe Crozier fumed afterward. "I thought that goal was offside. The play started in their end with Frank Mahovolich batting the puck with his hand to Cournoyer. Starting a play by batting the puck with your hand is illegal, so there should have been a

One of the most frightening sights any defenseman could ever encounter: Gilbert Perreault stickhandling in open ice.

faceoff right there, but there wasn't. Then the puck got into our end, but it came back out over the blue line and the offside wasn't called."

Midway through the period, Lafleur won a faceoff from Meehan, the puck squirted to Tardif and he beat Dryden with a 20-footer to put the Canadiens ahead for good. Lapointe's 20-footer on a power play made it 4-2, and then Cournoyer faked a shot, sent a pretty pass to Lemaire and he fired it in from 10 feet out to complete the second-period barrage.

"The first two goals were bad goals," Mickey said. "We left the points open, especially on the second one. We played three good periods last night and one tonight. They played 10 minutes and got five goals. Savard and Lapointe were open at the points all night. And they were more or less responsible for three of the first four goals."

Roger Crozier replaced Dryden in the third period, and Cournoyer scored twice more to complete his first career playoff hat trick before Schoenfeld closed the scoring with 2:15 left to play.

"I guess we tried to nurse a two-goal lead through two periods instead of trying to increase it," said Meehan, who played only one shift in the final two periods – the one on which he lost the draw that resulted in Montreal's third goal – due to a hip injury suffered in Game One. "You can't sit back against the Canadiens. If they score one goal, they can quickly score six or seven. You can't play hockey in your own end against the Canadiens.

"We didn't get here just to lay down and die. If you're satisfied with just being in the playoffs, you're going to lay down in the first game and we didn't do that. We're confident we can win at home, and the big test is Saturday. We have to win that one."

The lopsided loss did not dampen the Sabres' collective spirit. They felt going back to the Aud, where they had posted a record of 30-6-3 and had outscored their opposition, 162-80, would give them the edge they needed to get back into the series.

"We still feel we can play with Montreal and this series is going seven games," Robert said.

Said Pratt, "They only pay us from gate receipts from the first four games, but we intend to go seven games just to prove we belong in the playoffs. If we win Saturday, we should have enough momentum to win Sunday and tie up the series. We can't afford to be down three games. It's almost impossible to win four straight against Montreal. We get a lift playing at home and I think we're going to take both games and get back in it."

In a perfect world, Pratt's prognostication would have been right on the money. But the guys in the red sweaters with the famous CH inscribed in the middle weren't buying into it. Goals by Peter Mahovolich and Murray Wilson 16 seconds apart midway through the second period snapped a 1-1 tie and propelled Montreal to a 5-2 victory and a three-game lead in the best-of-seven series. The usual sellout crowd was noisier than an earthquake and they certainly energized the Sabres. Buffalo unleashed a 44-shot assault on Ken Dryden, but Dryden was fabulous, and Roger Crozier was not.

"I thought we dominated in Game Three, but we couldn't score because Dryden was so great," Ramsay recalled. "We just couldn't find a way to put the puck into the net against him."

In the first period, it looked as if Crozier was going to match Dryden save for save. Crozier robbed Cournoyer twice and Lapointe once as Montreal put the pressure on early. Dryden answered the call by stuffing Ramsay twice within five seconds, and then Lorentz and Perreault from point-blank range a little later on. At the 16:56 mark, Crozier finally cracked when Lafleur scored off a rebound after Crozier had stopped Tardif's deflection of a shot from the point by Lapointe on a power play.

The Sabres tied the game just 1:13 into the second period as Mickey whacked in a rebound off a Horton shot that had been tipped by Ramsay, and the Aud was rocking like it never has. But at 8:44, the play that illustrated the difference between these two teams occurred.

With the Canadiens on a power play, Schoenfeld gained control of the puck at center ice and in an effort to kill time off the penalty, rather than quickly ice it, he tried to pass back into his own zone to his defensive partner, Pratt. Linesman Neil Armstrong, perhaps surprised that Schoenfeld went backward, couldn't get out of the way and the puck deflected off his skate and went directly to Cournoyer. Cournoyer wasted no time passing to Mahovolich who went in unchallenged and beat Crozier for a 2-1 lead.

"That play probably turned the game around," Bowman said. "We wanted to get the lead because the Sabres protect leads well in their own building. Getting that goal and going in front gave us a lift and took the pressure off."

It was the kind of mistake that a young team was apt to make in a pressure-packed atmosphere, and the kind of mistake that a veteran team was expected to capitalize on.

"He (Armstrong) told me later he tried to move, but he couldn't," Schoenfeld said of his miscue. "I guess he was too close to the boards. If it hadn't hit him, the puck would have gone to (Pratt) on a slight bank. That was the big one, too, but Armstrong was just doing his job. He certainly didn't try to get in the way."

The Sabres' heads were still hanging in despair, the vibration from the shock not even fully subsided, when Murray Wilson blasted a 30-footer past Crozier 16 seconds later for a demoralizing goal that dropped Buffalo into a hole it never dug itself out of.

"I'll tell you, we've played the Canadiens three games and there's no way they should be up three games to none," Joe Crozier said, lamenting his team's unfortunate luck. "If we'd had a few breaks in this series, we wouldn't be in this situation. The officiating has been terribly one-sided in this series. I think my club has been given a hosing. I think there are two sets of rules – one for the Canadiens and one for us.

"Tonight, Ramsay is moving in on a near breakaway and he's grabbed, and no penalty is called. If Craig scores, it's 2-2 and a new game. Instead, a few seconds later the Canadiens go down and score to make it 3-1 and we're out of it. I know it's going to cost me some money when Mr. (Clarence) Campbell hears this, but I don't care. What can you do, though? These (officials) are hired by the National Hockey League and there's nothing you can do but try and live with them."

To their credit, the Sabres did not quit. They pulled within 3-2 just 54 seconds into the third when Robert whistled a drive from the point off the

Tracy Pratt was the target of a Jim Schoenfeld pass during the second period of Game Three, but the puck inadvertently caromed off a linesman and led directly to a critical Montreal goal.

post and into the net. And less than a minute later on a power play, Lorentz tipped a Martin shot just wide of an open net. The Sabres continued to press, but Dryden repeatedly turned them away, and then at 12:15 Frank Mahovolich beat Crozier with a 40-foot blast to give the Canadiens a comfortable 4-2 lead. The final score came with 48 seconds left when Richard dumped one into an empty net.

Like Joe Crozier, Meehan was despondent over the Sabres' bad luck. "I'm not one to cry, but we definitely haven't had any breaks in this series," the captain said. "We've played well in two of the three games and yet we still haven't won. We're not finished yet."

The Canadiens, though, felt the Sabres were cooked. And in the locker room after the game, the veteran Habs made an uncharacteristic mistake by talking as if the series was over.

"Experience is the only thing holding Buffalo back," Peter Mahovolich said. "Playoff hockey means pressure hockey and this is something new for them. If they improve next year like they have this year, I don't want to face them."

Added Ken Dryden, "Stanley Cup experience is a bit new for the Sabres. They have confidence, but it's not the kind of confidence built by proving yourselves over the years. They're a good team and should acquire that confidence quickly. There used to be a time when we looked forward to playing the Sabres, but not anymore. The Buffalo Sabres' rise has definitely been the story of the year."

But the year wasn't over. The Canadiens still had one more game to win, and as Joe Crozier said, "Montreal is going to play hell winning that fourth game Sunday."

And hell it was.

After the first game, Savard had remarked how difficult it was to play against Perreault. "He's the toughest guy to stop in the NHL," Savard said.

"He's like a great punt returner, you've got to stop him before he gets started."

In Game Four, Perreault got started right away, and the Canadiens never had a chance of stopping him. He hit the ice as if he had rockets attached to his blades and he toyed with the Canadiens, putting on a dazzling display of skating, passing and shooting. With Perreault leading the way and his French Connection linemates following dutifully in his skate tracks, the Sabres simply overpowered Montreal, firing 50 shots at Dryden on their way to a 5-1 victory, the first postseason triumph in club history.

"It seemed like they always had control of the puck," an impressed and exhausted Dryden said afterward.

The French Connection finished with 24 shots – as many as the entire Montreal team – and they combined for seven points with Perreault scoring two goals and one assist.

"He (Perreault) is one super hockey player," said Joe Crozier, who had been criticized for not using The French Connection more in Game Three.

Crozier had been trying to match lines against Bowman in Game Three, and as it turned out, The French Connection played less than 10 minutes in the first two periods. Crozier had been disappointed by the way the Frank Mahovolich-Lemaire-Cournoyer line controlled play in Game Two, so being at home with the last line change, he made sure his checking unit of Luce-Ramsay-Mickey was on the ice whenever that line played. Crozier also reasoned that he was trying to give Perreault, Martin and Robert some much-needed rest, and he expected that the three would have more spark for Game Four and therefore dominate play. That's exactly what happened.

"You want to talk about the time they put on the ice?" Crozier said. "Well, write about the awful lot of time they were on the ice tonight. In fact I was double-shifting them. Some of you writers use the pen too quickly and you'd better swallow it. Perreault was a fresh Perreault tonight. He, Robert and Martin controlled play. Tonight I knew I had them a lot fresher. They played extra hard all night.

"We only had seven forwards in Montreal (after Meehan was hurt) and I'm thinking in terms of playing four games in five nights. They're a tired hockey club."

By contrast, Crozier said, the Canadiens went four lines deep, so with Bowman able to give his players ample rest, they always had an advantage no matter what line Crozier had on the ice.

Although Perreault was flying from the drop of the first puck, it took awhile for his teammates to catch up to him and Cournoyer broke a scoreless tie with 1:23 left in the first period. Roger Crozier had made a number of difficult stops, so it was frustrating for the Sabres that he didn't stop Cournoyer's shot from the slot as the puck glanced in off his glove.

More than half the second period had been played before the Sabres finally scored on Dryden to tie the game. Meehan won a draw back to Lorentz at the left point, he sent the puck to the opposite point to Schoenfeld and his low 50-foot blast through a screen eluded Dryden.

With the building in an uproar, the Sabres began congregating all around

Jim Lorentz had one assist during the Sabres' 5-1 victory in Game Four, the first playoff win in Buffalo history. (Photo courtesy of Ron Moscati)

the Montreal net and just 3:16 later on a power play the relentless pressure paid off as Perreault ripped a slap shot from the blue line past Dryden to make it 2-1.

The Sabres finished the period with 19 shots, and then they fired 20 more in the third. At the 1:28 mark, Perreault took the puck away from Frank Mahovolich behind the net and fed Robert in the slot for a critical goal that gave Buffalo a 3-1 lead. Rather than retreat into a defensive shell, though, the Sabres kept up the attack and never let Montreal threaten. The Canadiens took only four shots in the third period.

Luce scored on a breakaway to make it 4-1 with 41 seconds remaining, and Perreault added some flair to the victory when he scored 22 seconds later.

"No, no more pressure," Perreault said when asked about the Sabres' 3-0 deficit coming into the game. "We just try to go on the ice, make some plays and score goals."

Added Luce, "You've got to see what you're made of when you go into the fourth game three behind. It was either do or die for us – just like last week – and we did it tonight. We knew we could do something against Montreal. I just hope it can continue that way."

Still, no one was giving the Sabres much of a chance in Game Five back at the Forum. In fact, Peter Mahovolich said, "Give Buffalo credit, but this was a bad game for us, we got worse as we went along. I don't think we'll repeat it."

Before Game Five, Crozier remarked that there would be no more rest for The French Connection. "They will see plenty of ice time tonight," Crozier said the day of the game. "We'll win with Gil Perreault because that's the way we have to win. He's the best player in the National Hockey League. We'll go with our best and I'll play the Perreault line as much as I can. We can play with the Montreal Canadiens, I believe it and my players believe it. And if the Perreault line is going, we'll beat them."

The Perreault line was going.

And indeed, the Sabres won the game.

In what remains one of the most dramatic nights in Sabres' history, The French Connection scored all three goals including Robert's winner at 9:18 of the first overtime for a 3-2 victory that sent the series back to Buffalo with the Sabres trailing just three games to two.

It was Buffalo's first win in the Forum in three years after going 0-8-3 to that point, and it came in the first overtime game in franchise history.

"All we wanted to do is prove to the world that we were a team on the upswing and we were there to stay, that we weren't a fluke," Robert recalled. "When we beat them in overtime, I think we opened a lot of eyes, especially because we beat them in Montreal."

The Canadiens took a 1-0 lead at 16:22 of the first period when Frank Mahovolich beat Crozier with a blast from just outside the blue line. The stout Montreal defense had contained The French Connection throughout the opening period, and as a team, the Sabres had managed only six shots. However, Perreault was a whirling dervish in the middle period, and he set up a pair of goals that put Buffalo in front.

At 12:03, Robert stole a pass and sent Perreault and Martin in on a two-on-one break against Savard. Savard slid over to challenge Perreault, so Perreault passed to Martin who fired in a 15-foot wrist shot for the tying goal.

Just 1:08 later, Perreault won a faceoff from Lemaire, the puck squirted to Robert in the slot, and he fired a backhander past Dryden from 20 feet and suddenly the Sabres were ahead, 2-1.

In the third, the Canadiens began to feel a sense of urgency. They did not want to have to go back to Buffalo for a sixth game, and they came out determined to make sure that wasn't going to happen. However, they didn't count on Roger Crozier acting like Ken Dryden. Crozier made 15 saves in the third period, and although he did allow the Canadiens to tie the game with 7:14 left when Henri Richard set up Guy Lapointe at the goal crease, he refused to let them win the game.

"It was a long night, even before we went into overtime," Roger said that night. "The Canadiens never let up, they just keep coming. But our team played well. When you consider the pressure on these guys we have who haven't been in the Stanley Cup playoffs before, you have to say we played exceptionally well. The type of club Montreal is, you have to be at the peak of your game to beat them. And in overtime, that's especially tough."

Crozier's performance, and that of Horton's, left an indelible impression

STANLEY CUP PLAYOFFS GAME FIVE
SABRES 3, CANADIENS 2 (OT)
Tuesday, April 10, 1973
Attendance – 16,436 at the Forum

Buffalo	0	2	1	–	3
Montreal	1	0	1	0	–	2

BUFFALO
Goalie: Roger Crozier
Defense: Tim Horton, Mike Robitaille, Tracy Pratt, Larry Hillman, Jim Schoenfeld, Paul Terbenche, Larry Carriere
Forwards: Rick Martin, Jim Lorentz, Norm Gratton, Craig Ramsay, Gil Perreault, Larry Mickey, Rene Robert, Gerry Meehan, Don Luce, Hugh Harris

MONTREAL
Goalie: Ken Dryden
Defense: Jacques Laperriere, Guy Lapointe, Serge Savard, Bob Murdoch, Pierre Bouchard, Jim Roberts
Forwards: Guy Lafleur, Marc Tardif, Yvan Cournoyer, Rejean Houle, Claude Larose, Henri Richard, Murray Wilson, Pete Mahovolich, Chuck Lefley, Jacques Lemaire, Frank Mahovolich

FIRST PERIOD
Scoring: 1, Montreal, F. Mahovolich 2 (Laperriere), 16:22
Penalties: Pratt, Buf (interference), 3:38; P. Mahovolich, Mont (tripping), 4:17; Carriere, Buf (roughing), 11:03; Larose, Mont (slashing), 11:03; Pratt, Buf (holding), 13:59
SECOND PERIOD
Scoring: 2, Buffalo, Martin 2 (Perreault, Robert), 12:03. 3, Buffalo, Robert 3 (Perreault), 13:11.
Penalties: F. Mahovolich, Mont (high-sticking), 4:45; Crozier, Buf (tripping – served by Lorentz), 8:33; Cournoyer, Mont (slashing), 13:58; Carriere, Buf (tripping), 14:54
THIRD PERIOD
Scoring: 4, Montreal, Lapointe 2 (Richard, P. Mahovolich), 12:46
Penalty: Dryden, Mont (illegal equipment), 20:00
OVERTIME
Scoring: 5, Buffalo, Robert 4 (Perreault, Martin), 9:18
Penalties: None

SHOTS ON GOAL
Buffalo 6-15-9-4 – 34
Montreal 10-9-16-5 – 40
POWER-PLAY OPPORTUNITIES
Buffalo 0-for-4
Montreal 0-for-4
THREE STARS
1. Crozier
2. Perreault
3. Robert

In the late stages of Game Five, Tim Horton displayed the ultimate in leadership as he threw his 43-year-old body all over the ice in an effort to hold off the Canadiens. It was the 125th playoff game of his career. (Photo courtesy of Ron Moscati)

on Ramsay.

"Game Five was truly something special," Ramsay recalled. "When I saw Tim Horton and Roger Crozier, the way they played in that game, it was something that I'll never forget. I saw that night what veterans could do for a team and what it meant to have dedication and the willingness to go for it at all costs. Tim worked so hard and Roger was just unbeatable.

"I remember one shift late in the game, I was just exhausted, and I was out against the Cournoyer line and it was a shooting gallery in our end. I could barely put one foot in front of the other, and there's Timmy diving to block a shot, Roger knocking the puck away and making save after save. I'm thinking, 'If those guys can do it, I've got to find a way to do it, to play better. I've got to be better, I can't leave it all up to these guys.'"

Just before regulation time ran out, Joe Crozier called referee Bruce Hood over to the Buffalo bench to make an unusual request. He wanted Hood to measure the width of Dryden's leg pads because he knew they were wider than the mandated 10 inches.

The team's public relations director, Paul Wieland, had told Crozier almost a month earlier that he suspected the pads were illegal. Crozier and Imlach sat on the information, then had Wieland sneak into the Canadiens' locker room at the Aud prior to the start of Game Three, and sure enough Wieland found them to be a shade wider than 10 inches.

"In the Aud you could get into the other dressing room with a key, so we sent him (Wieland) in there, and he told us they were too wide," Crozier remembered.

The penalty for illegal goalie pads was a two-minute minor to be assessed at the start of the next period. Crozier and Imlach agreed to use the loophole to their advantage in a tie game near the end of regulation, so the Canadiens would have to start the overtime period shorthanded. That scenario did not present itself in Game Three, and the Sabres didn't need any help in Game Four. But with 29 seconds to go in Game Five, the time was right.

Had the Sabres waited until the end of regulation to ask, the penalty would not have been assessed until the start of a potential second overtime period. After time ran out, Hood put a tape measure on the pads and reluctantly slapped Montreal with a penalty.

"When Joe called the pads on Dryden, that was great because I thought Bowman's head was going to explode," Martin recalled with a laugh. "Whatever hair he had on his head, he was pulling it out, and Joe just stood there smiling. That was just beautiful. We were laughing our asses off."

Bowman immediately asked for a measurement of Roger Crozier's pads, but because he hadn't done so during the third period, that measurement couldn't be taken until the intermission after the first overtime. Therefore, any potential Montreal power play would not occur until the start of the second overtime. Now Bowman was really aggravated, and he continued to rant at Hood to no avail.

Hood was actually sympathetic toward Bowman, and at one point, threatened to call an even-up penalty on the Sabres because he deemed their tactic to be underhanded. But the referee eventually realized that a rule was a rule, and he was there to enforce them.

Paul Wieland, the Sabres' public relations director, played a key role in the goalie pads scandal in Game Five. It was Wieland who snuck into the Montreal locker room prior to Game Three and found Canadiens goalie Ken Dryden's leg pads to be too wide. The Sabres asked for a measurement near the end of the third period in Game Five, and Montreal was assessed a penalty at the start of overtime which infuriated Canadiens' coach Scotty Bowman.

Montreal's Frank Mahovolich jabbed his skate into Rick Martin's ribs, while Martin appeared ready to retaliate with his stick. (Photo courtesy of Ron Moscati)

The Sabres' plan almost had a storybook conclusion when, on the ensuing power play, Lorentz came within inches of ending the game. However his shot clanged off the goal post, and Montreal was able to ward off any further threats and killed the penalty. In a way, it was probably appropriate that the Sabres didn't score on that power play because there is no question many people would have considered the victory tainted.

Although they didn't score, the Sabres were in control because The French Connection – as they often did – flicked a switch and brought their level of play up that one extra notch where most players were incapable of reaching. As promised, Crozier had double-shifted them much of the game, and they were worn out. But the intermission had dragged on longer than usual because of the pads controversy, and that, coupled with the five-minute delay when Crozier had initially asked for the measurement late in the third period, provided Perreault, Martin and Robert with some much-needed rest. All the sitting around enabled them to re-charge their batteries, and they came out flying in the overtime.

"The delays gave The French Connection time to rest and gave me the opportunity to keep them on the ice more in the overtime," Crozier said. "I had The French Connection out there so long, Bowman didn't know how to check me. He didn't know what to do, he was all messed up."

Just before the team returned to the ice, Crozier had pulled aside Perreault and said, "You're better than anyone they've got on the ice, Gil. You can win this hockey game for me. Just take that puck and go through them all."

It didn't quite work out that way, but Perreault did make the pass that sent Robert in for the breakaway that resulted in the winning goal. Schoenfeld had gained control of the puck and fired it around the boards where Martin picked it up. He avoided a check by Lemaire, fed Perreault at center and he quickly relayed it to Robert breaking in on right wing at the Montreal blue line.

"The play developed in Rick's corner," Robert said, a twinkle in his eye evident as he recalled the momentous goal. "One of the defenseman pinched in, and Gilbert was able to get loose, and by the time he got loose, I had beaten Savard on the far side. When Gilbert saw me, he gave me a hard pass, and I knew once I got the puck nobody could catch me. I knew what I wanted to do, I was just hoping I could do it. I saw the opening, I had about a foot and a half to shoot at (on Dryden's stick side) and I knew from past experiences if you faked him high, he had a tendency of twitching and pulling up, so what I did was shoot the puck along the ice and he just had no chance. It was an absolutely perfect shot."

That night in the joyous locker room, Robert remembered thinking to himself as he skated in alone on Dryden, "I can't choke on this one. Laperriere was between me and the goal, but there was no way he was going to stop me. The move I used to get around him was purely instinct. Gil gave me a hard pass. If it had been a soft pass, Laperriere would have been able to check me. But it was good and hard and I was able to take it and go in cold turkey on the goalie."

Said Hillman, "All I could think of when I saw the play developing was, 'I can't think of a better guy to have busting in like that.' Rene is one of the surest shots on our team. I wasn't on the ice when he scored, but I got over those boards pretty fast as soon as I saw Dryden take one step toward the bench. He knew it was in, he never looked back."

For the first time all season, the Canadiens had lost two games in a row, and as the Sabres packed their gear for the flight back to Buffalo – where they would be greeted in the early morning by about 500 delirious fans – people were daring to believe that maybe that youthful foolhardiness the players had exuded before the series began wasn't so foolhardy. Maybe the Sabres could win this series.

"Montreal was under pressure to take four straight from us and when they won the first three, the heat had to be off a little," Meehan said before the team boarded the plane. "Now that we have won two in a row, the pressure has to be back on them to take the series. I think we'll be coming back to Montreal (for Game Seven)."

Gilbert Perreault and Rene Robert embraced after Robert's overtime goal won Game Five at the Montreal Forum. (Photo courtesy of Ron Moscati)

As Meehan looks back on that statement today, he realizes it was all wishful thinking. Two nights later, the usual standing-room-only crowd gave the Sabres one of the most stirring pre-game ovations in the history of sport, but it wasn't nearly enough to propel their young heroes past the now extremely agitated Canadiens. Montreal scored four times in the first 16 minutes and cruised to a 4-2 victory to wrap up the series and bring to an end Buffalo's glorious season.

"We believed we could win, and as the series went on, it looked like we had a chance, but I remember that sixth game in Buffalo and they just owned it from beginning to end," Meehan said. "They seemed to turn it up a notch just when the young upstarts were giving them a run for their money. It really wasn't much of a contest."

Said Luce, "We weren't thinking we could lose that game, we felt we'd win it. That's because of the confidence we had gained and the growing we had done as a team. We felt if we could beat them twice, we could beat them again. We were the underdogs, and here we were playing the Canadiens, the icons of hockey, and we were beating them. Even though we lost that series, we gained a lot of confidence that helped us in later years because we knew if we continued to work hard and get a little better, we could beat these people."

Martin's recollection of that sixth game is the way the Canadiens played once they got the lead. Sometimes lost in all of Montreal's offensive firepower, and the sheer brilliance of Dryden in goal, was the way the Canadiens played defense. They were impenetrable when they were at their best, and although Buffalo poured 44 shots on Dryden, most were harmless, and very few came on rebounds as Savard, Laperriere, Lapointe, Larry Robinson and the rest just cleared the loose pucks out of the zone.

"Montreal always had something that people don't understand," Martin said. "As much as they were an offensive powerhouse, when they got the lead, they were an incredibly disciplined defensive team. If they wanted to sit on a 3-1 lead, they could. They could either dump it in, or they also had the horses so if they wanted to, they could make it 4-1 or 5-1 or 6-1. We were able to counter some of that offensive ability, but they respected our offensive capabilities, so they didn't try to open it up.

"We were very high for that game, coming back into our own rink, but they were much more experienced than we were. And I think we had run out of steam by that time of the year. We always practiced hard, there weren't many days off, we were always 100 percent nose to the grindstone, and I think by the end of that series, it was starting to take its toll. We tried to go hard, but we didn't have that overdrive, we were stuck in a one-speed mode. We were so tired by then."

The fans hadn't even settled back in their seats after their memorable pre-game greeting when Terbenche lost the puck to Frank Mahovolich behind the net, Mahovolich got it out to the point to Savard, and he whistled one past Crozier to put the Canadiens ahead for good just 1:32 into the game.

Six minutes later, Houle's perfect pass set up Wilson for a 2-0 lead, and just 1:20 after that, Richard's pass from the backboards set up Lafleur from

---

**STANLEY CUP PLAYOFFS
GAME SIX
CANADIENS 4, SABRES 2**
Thursday, April 12, 1973
Attendance – 15,668 at the Aud

Montreal	4	0	0	– 4
Buffalo	0	0	2	– 2

BUFFALO
Goalie: Roger Crozier
Defense: Tim Horton, Mike Robitaille, Tracy Pratt, Larry Hillman, Jim Schoenfeld, Larry Carriere
Forwards: Rick Martin, Jim Lorentz, Norm Gratton, Craig Ramsay, Gil Perreault, Larry Mickey, Rene Robert, Gerry Meehan, Paul Terbenche, Don Luce, Hugh Harris

MONTREAL
Goalie: Ken Dryden
Defense: Jacques Laperriere, Guy Lapointe, Serge Savard, Larry Robinson, Bob Murdoch, Pierre Bouchard
Forwards: Guy Lafleur, Yvan Cournoyer, Rejean Houle, Claude Larose, Henri Richard, Murray Wilson, Pete Mahovolich, Jim Roberts, Chuck Lefley, Jacques Lemaire, Frank Mahovolich

FIRST PERIOD
Scoring: 1, Montreal, Savard 2 (P. Mahovolich, F. Mahovolich), 1:32. 2, Montreal, Wilson 2 (Houle), 7:33. 3, Montreal, Lafleur 2 (Richard, Savard), 8:53. 4, Montreal, Lapointe 3 (Roberts, Wilson), 16:03
Penalties: Wilson, Mont (roughing), 4:45; Martin, Buf (roughing), 4:45; Horton, Buf (tripping), 16:35
SECOND PERIOD
Scoring: None
Penalties: Roberts, Mont (high-sticking), 4:11; Gratton, Buf (holding), 6:34.
THIRD PERIOD
Scoring: 5, Buffalo, Robert 5, 11:41. 6, Buffalo, Martin 3 (Lorentz, Perreault), 19:48
Penalties: Lapointe, Mont (tripping), 15:04; Savard, Mont (delay of game), 19:32; Roberts, Mont (10-minute misconduct), 19:32.

SHOTS ON GOAL:
Buffalo 16-8-20 - 44
Montreal 13-7-4 - 24
POWER-PLAY OPPORTUNITIES:
Buffalo 1-for-3
Montreal 0-for-2
THREE STARS:
1. Lapointe
2. Wilson
3. Savard

Roger Crozier must have felt like he was all alone in the first period of Game Six as the Canadiens swarmed around him and scored four goals. (Photo courtesy of Ron Moscati)

10 feet out for an insurmountable 3-0 cushion. Still, the Canadiens continued their assault. Roger Crozier stopped breakaways 25 seconds apart by Wilson and Laperriere, but at 16:03, he couldn't stop Laperriere's screened drive from the point that made it 4-0 and rendered the final two periods inconsequential.

"They got four fast goals and that was the story of the game," Meehan said. "After that they always had bodies in front of the cage. But there's no embarrassment in this locker room tonight. We're happy that we had such a good year. We accomplished our objective – to reach the playoffs – and we now have confidence in our ability to do it from now on."

Dryden didn't make a mistake until just 8:19 remained in the game when Robert's 40-foot blast snuck by. Joe Crozier pulled Roger Crozier with 2:12 to go, and when Savard was penalized for delay of game, the Sabres had a two-man advantage. With the fans rocking the Aud with their "Thank You Sabres" chant, Martin banged in his own rebound with 12 seconds left for the final goal of the year.

"A little more time and a little more luck and there would have been an upset," Joe Crozier said, insisting to the end that his team could have pulled it out. "But the best team won. I love these kids of mine and these fans. They matured this year and I think we have a great future together."

Bowman had endured quite a struggle in this series. He had seen his heavily favored team lose twice, had been embarrassed by the goalie pads incident, and had listened to Joe Crozier take shots at him in the press. When it was over, he breathed a huge sigh of relief.

"We played Buffalo in five good games during the season and I felt a lot of pressure in this series," he admitted. "I feel like somebody has just taken a piano off my back. No matter who we face in the rest of the playoffs, they aren't going to be any tougher than the Sabres. This Buffalo team was badly underrated because it was only a third-year team."

On the constant sniping from Crozier, Bowman replied, "He was just trying to get the most out of his team. They played right to the end. He got a lot out of his team. He did a great job and he's a great coach. I said 'Thank you,' when he congratulated me and, 'I hope you didn't mean all those things you said.'"

Trailing 4-0 after the first period, the Sabres had to take chances on offense and even Jim Schoenfeld got into the act. Here he pinched in from his defensive position and tried to score from the slot. (Photo courtesy of Ron Moscati)

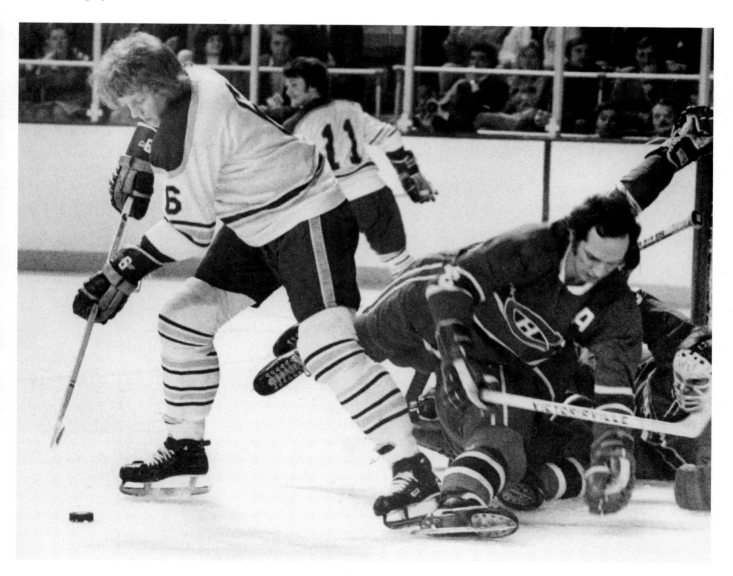

The Sabres became so popular in 1972-73, the fans treated them like rock stars. Here, Dave Dryden is mobbed as he tries to get into his car. (Photo courtesy of Ron Moscati)

Epilogue

Thank You Sabres!

They had all showered away the blood and sweat and sadness, and now the Buffalo Sabres stood around in clusters in their locker room, not wanting to leave for fear that the reality and finality would set in. They talked about how the Canadiens scored four times in the first period which pretty much sabotaged the night. They talked about Ken Dryden, about Montreal's airtight defense, about the Canadiens' speed and skill and glamour, and they talked about how they almost overcame all of that and scared the living daylights out of Les Habitants.

But what they talked about most was the fans of Buffalo, and about the outpouring of emotion and love and support they had received.

"Those fans are just terrific," Meehan said. "With those people behind us, we are really determined to come back next year and give 'em hell."

Said Pratt, "We played a hell of a team, but I'd rather talk about the fans. They were beautiful, weren't they? They upheld their half of it."

And said Robitaille, "I love this town and I love these people. I plan to use the playoff money to help buy a home here. That's what I think of Buffalo."

Meehan has been asked on numerous occasions through the years to share the feelings he had that night now nearly 25 years ago, when the fans stood and bestowed upon the beaten but unbowed Sabres that proud, passionate laudation.

"It's something that I don't think has ever been done for a professional team," he said. "It was pretty spine-tingling, it made the hair on the back of your neck stand on end. Usually, the series is over, you've lost, and the fans go home. Instead, they gave us a standing ovation before the game, another one that started before the game was over, and they continued it afterward. It was pretty remarkable."

Luce and Joe Crozier still work for the Sabres, and they attend home games at Marine Midland Arena regularly. The fans were loud and excited last season when the team won the Northeast Division and advanced to the second round of the playoffs, but it is asking too much to repeat what went on in Buffalo during that 1972-73 season.

"Back then, the fans were so important because it was a first-time thing for this franchise to be in the playoffs, and it was very exciting," Luce said. "As a player you were excited about being in the playoffs, and the fans were so excited about it, too. It was so great to go onto the ice at home games because they just cheered and cheered for you. That night we lost to Montreal that ended the series, that was just something that was very special. You don't see that very often, if ever. As a player, it was something that's hard to describe. It was like we had won the Stanley Cup."

Said Crozier, "The way they chanted and carried on, those fans were unbelievable. That last night when they started with the 'Thank You Sabres' you got a feeling in your gut that you've never felt before. I was so happy for those fans, and I was so happy for those players because they were great guys and they deserved it."

Last spring, Ramsay came back to Buffalo during the playoffs, this time as an enemy in his role as assistant coach of the Ottawa Senators. He lives in a different city and wears the colors of a different organization today, but Buffalo will always be his home, and the old blue and gold Sabres crest will always be dear to his heart. And of all the memories he built in Buffalo during his 22 years with the team, none can top what took place on April 12, 1973.

"Before the start of the game, they wouldn't stop cheering," Ramsay recalled. "I remember the referee looking at us and he wouldn't drop the puck. We were certainly disappointed the way the game had gone, we played hard, but we just didn't get it done. We had tried so hard, it was such a great year, and when the fans chanted, 'Thank You Sabres' it was so incredibly moving. It was truly a very special experience to be in that building that night.

"We were on the bench saying, 'What is this? Can you believe this? Is this the greatest?' We came out of that game feeling awful that we had lost, but we also felt how great it was to be in Buffalo, how great it was to be in this city, playing for this team in this building."

Photo courtesy of Ron Moscati

1972-73
Game by Game

GAME 1 - SABRES 5, FLAMES 3

| Atlanta | 1 | 2 | 0 | - | 3 |
| Buffalo | 2 | 1 | 2 | - | 5 |

Sunday, October 8, 1972
Attendance - 15,508 at the Aud

Goals Buffalo: Lorentz 2 (2), Ramsay (1), Robert (1), Perreault (1)
Atlanta: Bob Leiter (2), Bill MacMillian (1), Keith McCreary (1)
Shots Buffalo 36, Atlanta 27
Goalies Buffalo: Roger Crozier; Atlanta: Dan Bouchard

GAME 2 - SABRES 7, KINGS 3

| Los Angeles | 1 | 2 | 0 | - | 3 |
| Buffalo | 3 | 1 | 3 | - | 7 |

Wednesday, October 11, 1972
Attendance - 15,508 at the Aud

Goals Buffalo: Perreault (2), Atkinson (1), Martin 2 (2), Mickey (1), Robert (2), Hillman (1)
Los Angeles: Bob Berry 2 (2), Doug Volmar (1)
Shots Buffalo 39, Los Angeles 33
Goalies Buffalo: Roger Crozier; Los Angeles: Rogie Vachon

GAME 3 - SABRES 1, FLAMES 1

| Buffalo | 1 | 0 | 0 | - | 1 |
| Atlanta | 1 | 0 | 0 | - | 1 |

Saturday, October 14, 1972
Attendance - 14,568 at the Omni

Goals Buffalo: Lorentz (3)
Atlanta: Ernie Hicke (1)
Shots Buffalo 31, Atlanta 17
Goalies Buffalo: Roger Crozier; Atlanta: Phil Myre

GAME 4 - SABRES 3, MAPLE LEAFS 2

| Toronto | 0 | 2 | 0 | - | 2 |
| Buffalo | 1 | 2 | 0 | - | 3 |

Sunday, October 15, 1972
Attendance - 15,516 at the Aud

Goals Buffalo: Perreault (3), Atkinson (2), Wyrozub (1)
Toronto: Darryl Sittler 2 (2)
Shots Toronto 30, Buffalo 25
Goalies Buffalo: Roger Crozier; Toronto: Jacques Plante

GAME 5 - SABRES 6, CANUCKS 0

| Vancouver | 0 | 0 | 0 | - | 0 |
| Buffalo | 2 | 2 | 2 | - | 6 |

Thursday, October 19, 1972
Attendance - 15,516 at the Aud

Goals Buffalo: Perreault (4), Martin 2 (4), Atkinson (3), Ramsay (2), Robert (3)
Vancouver: None
Shots Vancouver 32, Buffalo 26
Goalies Buffalo: Roger Crozier; Vancouver: Dunc Wilson

GAME 6 - SABRES 1, BLUES 1

| Buffalo | 0 | 1 | 0 | - | 1 |
| St. Louis | 0 | 1 | 0 | - | 1 |

Saturday, October 21, 1972
Attendance - 18,526 at St. Louis Arena

Goals Buffalo: Martin (5)
St.Louis: Frank St. Marseille
Shots St.Louis 32, Buffalo 23
Goalies Buffalo: Roger Crozier; St. Louis: Wayne Stephenson

GAME 7 - SABRES 7, FLAMES 2

Atlanta   0   1   1 - 2
Buffalo   1   1   5 - 7
Sunday, October 22, 1972
Attendance - 15,516 at the Aud

Goals   Buffalo: Martin 4 (9), Perreault 2 (5), Robert (4)
          Atlanta: Bob Leiter (3), Lew Morrison (1)
Shots   Buffalo 32, Atlanta 29
Goalies   Buffalo: Roger Crozier; Atlanta: Phil Myre

GAME 8 - SABRES 2, BRUINS 2

Boston   2   0   0 - 2
Buffalo   0   2   0 - 2
Wednesday, October 25, 1972
Attendance - 15,516 at the Aud

Goals   Buffalo: Robert (5), Meehan (1)
          Boston: Ace Bailey (1), Johnny Bucyk (2)
Shots   Buffalo 36, Boston 31
Goalies   Buffalo: Roger Crozier; Boston: Ross Brooks

GAME 9 - SABRES 3, CANADIENS 3

Buffalo   2   0   1 - 3
Montreal   1   2   0 - 3
Saturday, October 28, 1972
Attendance - 17,037 at the Forum

Goals   Buffalo: Lorentz (4), Martin 2 (11)
          Montreal: Chuck Lefley (3), Yvan Cournoyer 2 (7)
Shots   Buffalo 31, Montreal 31
Goalies   Buffalo: Dave Dryden; Montreal: Ken Dryden

GAME 10 - SABRES 2, NORTH STARS 1

Minnesota   0   0   1 - 1
Buffalo   1   1   0 - 2
Sunday, October 29, 1972
Attendance - 15,516 at the Aud

Goals   Buffalo: Martin 2 (13)
          Minnesota: Bob Nevin (2)
Shots   Minnesota 36, Buffalo 28
Goalies   Buffalo: Roger Crozier; Minnesota: Cesare Maniago

GAME 11 - MAPLE LEAFS 7, SABRES 1

Buffalo   1   0   0 - 1
Toronto   1   3   3 - 7
Wednesday, November 1, 1972
Attendance - 16,362 at Maple
          Leaf Gardens

Goals   Buffalo: Perreault (7)
          Toronto: Errol Thompson 2 (3), Dave Keon 2 (5), George Ferguson (1),
           Pierre Jarry (3), Gerry Monahan (1)
Shots   Toronto 44, Buffalo 30
Goalies   Buffalo: Roger Crozier; Toronto: Ron Low

GAME 12 - FLYERS 5, SABRES 3

Buffalo   1   0   2 - 3
Philadelphia   1   2   2 - 5
Saturday, November 4, 1972
Attendance - 16,600 at the Spectrum

Goals   Buffalo: Deadmarsh (1), Lorentz (5), Hillman (2)
          Philadelphia: Bill Barber (1), Don Saleski (3), Tom Bladon (1),
           Rick MacLeish 2 (6)
Shots   Buffalo 33, Philadelphia 30
Goalies   Buffalo: Roger Crozier; Philadelphia: Bob Taylor

GAME 13 - SABRES 1, BLUES 1

St. Louis   0   1   0 - 1
Buffalo   1   0   0 - 1
Sunday, November 5, 1972
Attendance - 15,516 at the Aud

Goals   Buffalo: Robitaille (1)
          St.Louis: Frank St. Marseille (5)
Shots   St.Louis 36, Buffalo 31
Goalies   Buffalo: Dave Dryden; St.Louis: Jacques Caron

GAME 14 - SABRES 0, SEALS 0

California   0   0   0 - 0
Buffalo   0   0   0 - 0
Thursday, November 9, 1972
Attendance - 15,516 at the Aud

Goals   Buffalo: None
          California: None
Shots   Buffalo 28, California 23
Goalies   Buffalo: Roger Crozier; California: Marv Edwards

GAME 15 - FLYERS 3, SABRES 1

Buffalo   0   0   1 - 1
Philadelphia   1   2   0 - 3
Saturday, November 11, 1972
Attendance - 16,600 at the Spectrum

Goals   Buffalo: Robert (6)
          Philadelphia: Bill Barber (4), Rick MacLeish 2 (11)
Shots   Buffalo 32, Philadelphia 26
Goalies   Buffalo: Roger Crozier; Philadelphia: Doug Favell

GAME 16 - SABRES 1, PENGUINS 0

Pittsburgh   0   0   0 - 0
Buffalo   0   0   1 - 1
Sunday, November 12, 1972
Attendance - 15,668 at the Aud

Goals   Buffalo: Atkinson (4)
            Pittsburgh: None
Shots   Buffalo 41, Pittsburgh 18
Goalies   Buffalo: Roger Crozier: Pittsburgh: Jim Rutherford

GAME 17 - SABRES 3, KINGS 3

Buffalo   0   2   1 - 3
Los Angeles 1   1   1 - 3
Wednesday, November 15, 1972
Attendance - 9,183 at the Forum

Goals   Buffalo: Martin (14), Meehan (2), Atkinson (5)
            Los Angeles: Butch Goring (11), Don Kozak (4), Mike Corrigan (10)
Shots   Los Angeles 35, Buffalo 27
Goalies   Buffalo: Roger Crozier; Los Angeles: Rogie Vachon

GAME 18 - SEALS 5, SABRES 1

Buffalo   0   0   1 - 1
California 1   2   2 - 5
Friday, November 17, 1972
Attendance - 4,272 at Oakland Arena

Goals   Buffalo: Meehan (3)
            California: Joey Johnston 2 (8), Reg Leach 2 (4), Stan Gilbertson (2)
Shots   Buffalo 34, California 24
Goalies   Buffalo: Roger Crozier; California: Marv Edwards

GAME 19 - CANUCKS 9, SABRES 5

Buffalo   1   0   4 - 5
Vancouver 4   3   2 - 9
Sunday, November 19, 1972
Attendance - 15,570 at Pacific Coliseum

Goals   Buffalo: Perreault (8), Schoenfeld (1), Martin 2 (16), Harris (1)
            Vancouver: Bobby Lalonde (5), Gerry O'Flaherty (4), Jocelyn
            Guevremont (6), John Wright (2), Bobby Schmautz 4 (13),
            Andre Boudrias (6)
Shots   Buffalo 38, Vancouver 35
Goalies   Buffalo: Roger Crozier; Vancouver: Dunc Wilson

GAME 20 - RED WINGS 6, SABRES 2

Buffalo   0   1   1 - 2
Detroit   1   4   1 - 6

Wednesday, November 22, 1972
Attendance - 14,523 at the Olympia

Goals   Buffalo: Ramsay (3), Meehan (4)
            Detroit: Bob Cook (1), Ron Stackhouse (2), Guy Charron (7),
            Billy Collins (5), Marcel Dionne (9), Mickey Redmond (11)
Shots   Detroit 33, Buffalo 29
Goalies   Buffalo: Dave Dryden; Detroit: Roy Edwards

GAME 21 - SABRES 5, RANGERS 3

NY Rangers 1   1   1 - 3
Buffalo   0   2   3 - 5
Thursday, November 23, 1972
Attendance - 15,668 at the Aud

Goals   Buffalo: Ramsay (4), Luce 2 (2), Robert (7), Meehan (5)
            NY Rangers: Jean Ratelle 2 (8), Vic Hadfield (8)
Shots   NY Rangers 28, Buffalo 28
Goalies   Buffalo: Roger Crozier; NY Rangers: Ed Giacomin

GAME 22 - SABRES 9, ISLANDERS 2

NY Islanders 1   0   1 - 2
Buffalo   0   4   5 - 9
Sunday, November 26, 1972
Attendance - 15,668 at the Aud

Goals   Buffalo: Robert 2 (9), Lorentz 2 (7), Perreault (9), Martin 2 (18)
            Luce (3), Meehan (6)
            NY Islanders: Germain Gagnon (7), Tom Miller (4)
Shots   Buffalo 50, NY Islanders 16
Goalies   Buffalo: Roger Crozier; NY Islanders: Gerry Desjardins

GAME 23 - SABRES 7, ISLANDERS 2

Buffalo   2   4   1 - 7
NY Islanders 0   1   1 - 2
Tuesday, November 28, 1972
Attendance - 10,735 at Nassau Coliseum

Goals   Buffalo: Robert (10), Perreault 2 (11), Luce (4), Meehan (7), Harris (2)
            Martin (19)
            NY Islanders: Don Blackburn (2), Dave Hudson (4)
Shots   Buffalo 39, NY Islanders 29
Goalies   Buffalo: Roger Crozier; NY Islanders: Billy Smith

GAME 24 - BRUINS 5, SABRES 4

Buffalo	0	2	2	- 4
Boston	1	1	3	- 5

Thursday, November 30, 1972
Attendance - 15,009 at Boston Garden

Goals Buffalo: Robert 2 (12), Martin (20), Hillman (3)
Boston: Bobby Orr 2 (8), Ken Hodge (10), Johnny Bucyk (10), Don Marcotte (11)
Shots Buffalo 31, Boston 26
Goalies Buffalo: Roger Crozier; Boston: Ed Johnston

GAME 25 - NORTH STARS 8, SABRES 6

Buffalo	4	2	0	- 6
Minnesota	3	2	3	- 8

Saturday, December 2, 1972
Attendance - 15,357 at the Met Center

Goals Buffalo: Robert 3 (15), Meehan 3 (10)
Minnesota: Dean Prentice 2 (8), Danny Grant (8), Dennis Hextall (9), Murray Oliver (4), Jude Drouin 2 (8), Bob Nevin (4)
Shots Minnesota 45, Buffalo 35
Goalies Buffalo: Dave Dryden; Minnesota: Gilles Gilbert

GAME 26 - SABRES 7, NORTH STARS 4

Minnesota	1	1	2	- 4
Buffalo	2	3	2	- 7

Sunday, December 3, 1972
Attendance - 15,668 at the Aud

Goals Buffalo: Luce 2 (6), Lorentz (8), Perreault (12), Meehan 2 (12), Ramsay (5)
Minnesota: Jude Drouin (9), Dennis Hextall (10), Danny Grant (9), Bill Goldsworthy (11)
Shots Buffalo 33, Minnesota 20
Goalies Buffalo: Dave Dryden; Minnesota: Cesare Maniago

GAME 27 - SABRES 3, RANGERS 2

Buffalo	1	0	2	- 3
NY Rangers	1	1	0	- 2

Wednesday, December 6, 1972
Attendance - 17,500 at Madison Square Garden

Goals Buffalo: Wyrozub (2), Harris (3), Meehan (13)
NY Rangers: Bill Fairbairn (11), Jean Ratelle (12)
Shots NY Rangers 33, Buffalo 29
Goalies Buffalo: Dave Dryden; NY Rangers: Gilles Villemure

GAME 28 - SABRES 6, RED WINGS 1

Detroit	0	0	1	- 1
Buffalo	2	2	2	- 6

Thursday, December 7, 1972
Attendance - 15,668 at the Aud

Goals Buffalo: Meehan 2 (15), Robert 2 (17), Ramsay (6), Harris (4)
Detroit: Tim Ecclestone (7)
Shots Detroit 38, Buffalo 32
Goalies Buffalo: Dave Dryden; Detroit: Roy Edwards

GAME 29 - SABRES 4, CANADIENS 2

Montreal	2	0	0	- 2
Buffalo	2	0	2	- 4

Sunday, December 10, 1972
Attendance - 15,668 at the Aud

Goals Buffalo: Luce (7), Robert (18), Lorentz (9), Martin (21)
Montreal: Jacques Lemaire (25), Rejean Houle (4)
Shots Buffalo 38, Montreal 28
Goalies Buffalo: Dave Dryden; Montreal: Ken Dryden

GAME 30 - SABRES 7, BRUINS 3

Boston	2	1	0	- 3
Buffalo	2	3	2	- 7

Wednesday, December 13, 1972
Attendance - 15,668 at the Aud

Goals Buffalo: Hillman (4), Ramsay (7), Meehan (16), Perreault 2 (14), Atkinson (6), Luce (8)
Boston: Ken Hodge (16), Don Marcotte (16), Bobby Orr (9)
Shots Boston 32, Buffalo 30
Goalies Buffalo: Dave Dryden; Boston: John Adams

GAME 31 - SABRES 4, BLUES 3

Buffalo	3	0	1	- 4
St. Louis	2	0	1	- 3

Saturday, December 16, 1972
Attendance - 18,303 at St. Louis Arena

Goals Buffalo: Perreault 2 (16), Lorentz (10), Meehan (17)
St.Louis: Phil Roberto (8), Garry Unger (14), Pierre Plante (1)
Shots St.Louis 38, Buffalo 28
Goalies Buffalo: Roger Crozier; St.Louis: Jacques Caron

GAME 32 - SABRES 4, MAPLE LEAFS 0

Toronto	0	0	0 -	0
Buffalo	0	2	2 -	4

Sunday, December 17, 1972
Attendance - 15,668 at the Aud

Goals Buffalo: Robert (19), Meehan (18), Luce (9), Lorentz (11)
Toronto: None
Shots Buffalo 28, Toronto 21
Goalies Buffalo: Dave Dryden; Toronto: Jacques Plante

GAME 33 - SABRES 6, CANUCKS 3

Vancouver	0	2	1 -	3
Buffalo	1	2	3 -	6

Wednesday, December 20, 1972
Attendance - 15,668 at the Aud

Goals Buffalo: Martin 2 (23), Lorentz (12), Meehan (19), Harris 2 (6)
Vancouver: Richard Lemieux (5), Gerry O'Flaherty (7), Dan Tannahill (9)
Shots Buffalo 30, Vancouver 29
Goalies Buffalo: Roger Crozier; Vancouver: Bruce Bullock

GAME 34 - SEALS 4, SABRES 2

Buffalo	0	1	1 -	2
California	1	1	2 -	4

Friday, December 22, 1972
Attendance - 3,080 at Oakland Arena

Goals Buffalo: Atkinson (7), Robitaille (2)
California: Craig Patrick 2 (7), Joey Johnston (18), Hilliard Graves (8)
Shots Buffalo 27, California 20
Goalies Buffalo: Dave Dryden; California: Marv Edwards

GAME 35 - KINGS 2, SABRES 0

Buffalo	0	0	0 -	0
Los Angeles	0	2	0 -	2

Saturday, December 23, 1972
Attendance - 8,752 at the Forum

Goals Buffalo: None
Los Angeles: Mike Corrigan (17), Ralph Backstrom (16)
Shots Los Angeles 23, Buffalo 20
Goalies Buffalo: Roger Crozier; Los Angeles: Rogie Vachon

GAME 36 - SABRES 4, RANGERS 1

Buffalo	2	2	0 -	4
NY Rangers	0	0	1 -	1

Wednesday, December 27, 1972
Attendance - 17,500 at Madison Square Gardens

Goals Buffalo: Robert (20), Lorentz (14), Luce (10), Perreault (17)
NY Rangers: Bruce MacGregor (8)
Shots NY Rangers 33, Buffalo 30
Goalies Buffalo: Dave Dryden; NY Rangers: Gilles Villemure

GAME 37 - SABRES 8, BLACKHAWKS 2

Chicago	2	0	0 -	2
Buffalo	1	2	5 -	8

Thursday, December 28, 1972
Attendance - 15,668 at the Aud

Goals Buffalo: Pratt (1), Mickey (2), Robert 2 (22), Atkinson (8), Meehan 3 (22)
Chicago: J.P. Bordeleau (9), Lou Angotti (5)
Shots Buffalo 44, Chicago 20
Goalies Buffalo: Dave Dryden; Chicago: Gary Smith

GAME 38 - BLACKHAWKS 4, SABRES 2

Buffalo	0	1	1 -	2
Chicago	0	2	2 -	4

Sunday, December 31, 1972
Attendance - 17,700 at Chicago Stad.

Goals Buffalo: Lorentz (14), Robert (23)
Chicago: Dick Redmond (4), Jim Pappin (15), Pat Stapleton (3), Stan Mikita (18)
Shots Buffalo 32, Chicago 32
Goalies Buffalo: Dave Dryden; Chicago: Tony Esposito

GAME 39 - SABRES 4, ISLANDERS 1

NY Islanders	0	1	0 -	1
Buffalo	1	2	1 -	4

Wednesday, January 3, 1973
Attendance - 15,668 at the Aud

Goals Buffalo: Robitaille (3), Robert (24), Meehan (23), Martin (24)
NY Islanders: Brian Spencer (6)
Shots Buffalo 30, NY Islanders 18
Goalies Buffalo: Dave Dryden; NY Islanders: Gerry Desjardins

GAME 40 - RED WINGS 4, SABRES 2

Buffalo	0	0	2	-	2
Detroit	0	3	1	-	4

Thursday, January 4, 1973
Attendance - 15,532 at the Olympia

Goals Buffalo: Robert 2 (26)
Detroit: Al Karlander (7), Nick Libett (8), Alex Delvecchio (10), Marcel Dionne (18)
Shots Detroit 40, Buffalo 29
Goalies Buffalo: Rocky Farr; Detroit: Roy Edwards

GAME 41 - SABRES 4, RANGERS 1

Buffalo	0	0	4	-	4
NY Rangers	0	1	0	-	1

Saturday, January 6, 1973
Attendance - 17,500 at Madison Square Garden

Goals Buffalo: Harris (7), Martin (25), Meehan (24), Robert (27)
NY Rangers: Steve Vickers (12)
Shots Buffalo 29, NY Rangers 25
Goalies Buffalo: Dave Dryden; NY Rangers: Ed Giacomin

GAME 42 - SABRES 2, FLYERS 0

Philadelphia	0	0	0	-	0
Buffalo	0	1	1	-	2

Sunday, January 7, 1973
Attendance - 15,668 at the Aud

Goals Buffalo: Lorentz (15), Martin (26)
Philadelphia: None
Shots Buffalo 39, Philadelphia 35
Goalies Buffalo: Dave Dryden: Philadelphia: Doug Favell

GAME 43 - RANGERS 4, SABRES 2

NY Rangers	1	2	1	-	4
Buffalo	1	0	1	-	2

Thursday, January 11, 1973
Attendance - 15,668 at the Aud

Goals Buffalo: Mickey (3), Robert (28)
NY Rangers: Jean Ratelle (20), Pete Stemkowski 3 (12)
Shots Buffalo 31, NY Rangers 25
Goalies Buffalo: Dave Dryden; NY Rangers: Ed Giacomin

GAME 44 - BRUINS 6, SABRES 0

Buffalo	0	0	0	-	0
Boston	2	2	2	-	6

Sunday, January 14, 1973
Attendance - 15,003 at Boston Garden

Goals Buffalo: None
Boston: Johnny Bucyk (20), Phil Esposito 4 (29), Nick Beverly (1)
Shots Boston 40, Buffalo 20
Goalies Buffalo: Dave Dryden; Boston: Eddie Johnston

GAME 45 - SABRES 5, BLACKHAWKS 1

Chicago	1	0	0	-	1
Buffalo	2	1	2	-	5

Thursday, January 18, 1973
Attendance - 15,668 at the Aud

Goals Buffalo: Meehan 2 (26), Lorentz (16), Martin (27), Harris (8)
Chicago: Dennis Hull (22)
Shots Buffalo 31, Chicago 19
Goalies Buffalo: Roger Crozier; Chicago: Tony Esposito

GAME 46 - RED WINGS 4, SABRES 2

Buffalo	1	0	1	-	2
Detroit	0	3	1	-	4

Saturday, January 20, 1973
Attendance - 15,532 at the Olympia

Goals Buffalo: Luce (11), Atkinson (9)
Detroit: Nick Libett (10), Mickey Redmond (30), Marcel Dionne (20), Brian Lavender (7)
Shots Detroit 31, Buffalo 25
Goalies Buffalo: Roger Crozier; Detroit: Roy Edwards

GAME 47 - FLYERS 4, SABRES 3

Philadelphia	2	1	1	-	4
Buffalo	0	0	3	-	3

Sunday, January 21, 1973
Attendance - 15,668 at the Aud

Goals Buffalo: Martin (28), Robert (29), Harris (9)
Philadelphia: Bill Flett 3 (25), Rick MacLeish (28)
Shots Buffalo 45, Philadelphia 30
Goalies Buffalo: Dave Dryden; Philadelphia: Bob Taylor

GAME 48- SABRES 5, NORTH STARS 2

Minnesota	1	1	0	-	2
Buffalo	0	3	2	-	5

Thursday, January 25, 1973
Attendance - 15,668 at the Aud

Goals Buffalo: Schoenfeld (2), Meehan (27), Perreault 2 (19), Luce (12)
Minnesota: J.P. Prentice (13), Bill Goldsworthy (18)
Shots Buffalo 40, Minnesota 25
Goalies Buffalo: Roger Crozier; Minnesota: Gilles Gilbert

GAME 49 - FLAMES 8, SABRES 5

Atlanta	1	3	4	-	8
Buffalo	2	2	1	-	5

Sunday, January 28, 1973
Attendance - 15,668 at the Aud

Goals	Buffalo: Lorentz 2 (18), Robert (30), Mickey (4), Harris (10)
	Atlanta: Rey Comeau 3 (15), Keith McCreary 3 (16), Larry Romanchych (14), Ernie Hicke (11)
Shots	Buffalo 31, Atlanta 26
Goalies	Buffalo: Roger Crozier; Atlanta: Phil Myre

GAME 50 - SABRES 5, KINGS 3

Los Angeles	1	1	1	-	3
Buffalo	1	2	2	-	5

Thurday, February 1, 1973
Attendance - 15,668 at the Aud

Goals	Buffalo: Lorentz 2 (20), Harris (11), Perreault (20), Schoenfeld (3)
	Los Angeles: Vic Venasky (9), Mike Corrigan 2 (25)
Shots	Los Angeles 29, Buffalo 26
Goalies	Buffalo: Dave Dryden; Los Angeles: Rogie Vachon

GAME 51 - SABRES 1, ISLANDERS 1

Buffalo	1	0	0	-	1
NY Islanders	1	0	0	-	1

Saturday, February 3, 1973
Attendance - 13,612 at Nassau
    Coliseum

Goals	Buffalo: Mickey (5)
	NY Islanders: Terry Crisp (4)
Shots	Buffalo 37, NY Islanders 21
Goalies	Buffalo: Roger Crozier; NY Islanders: Billy Smith

GAME 52 - SABRES 5, ISLANDERS 1

NY Islanders	1	0	0	-	1
Buffalo	1	3	1	-	5

Sunday, February 4, 1973
Attendance - 15,668 at the Aud

Goals	Buffalo: Lorentz 2 (22), Perreault (21), Rombough (1), Mickey (6)
	NY Islanders: Craig Cameron (11)
Shots	Buffalo 49, NY Islanders 19
Goalies	Buffalo: Dave Dryden; NY Islanders: Billy Smith

GAME 53 - BLACKHAWKS 2, SABRES 1

Buffalo	0	0	1	-	1
Chicago	0	0	2	-	2

Wednesday, February 7, 1973
Attendance - 17,500 at Chicago Stad.

Goals	Buffalo: Schoenfeld (4)
	Chicago: Jim Pappin (30), Dennis Hull (27)
Shots	Chicago 33, Buffalo 21
Goalies	Buffalo: Dave Dryden; Chicago: Tony Esposito

GAME 54 - SABRES 4, SEALS 0

California	0	0	0	-	0
Buffalo	2	0	2	-	4

Thursday, February 8, 1973
Attendance - 15,668 at the Aud

Goals	Buffalo: Wyrozub (3), Rombough (2), Robert 2 (32)
	California: None
Shots	Buffalo 30, California 24
Goalies	Buffalo: Dave Dryden; California: Marv Edwards

GAME 55 - CANADIENS 2, SABRES 1

Buffalo	0	1	0	-	1
Montreal	1	0	1	-	2

Saturday, February 10, 1973
Attendance - 18,095 at the Forum

Goals	Buffalo: Robert (33)
	Montreal: Frank Mahovolich (29), Henri Richard (6)
Shots	Montreal 27, Buffalo 26
Goalies	Buffalo: Dave Dryden; Montreal: Michel Plasse

GAME 56 - RED WINGS 5, SABRES 2

Detroit	1	0	4	-	5
Buffalo	0	2	0	-	2

Sunday, February 11, 1973
Attendance - 15,668 at the Aud

Goals	Buffalo: Martin 2 (30)
	Detroit: Marcel Dionne 2 (27), Henry Boucha (9), Al Karlander (9), Billy Collins (17)
Shots	Buffalo 37, Detroit 23
Goalies	Buffalo: Dave Dryden; Detroit: Roy Edwards

GAME 57 - SABRES 3, MAPLE LEAFS 2

Buffalo 1 1 1 - 3
Toronto 1 0 1 - 2
Wednesday, February 14, 1973
Attendance - 16,485 at Maple
Leaf Gardens

Goals   Buffalo: Lorentz (23), Harris (12), Robert (34)
        Toronto: Norm Ullman (14), Rick Kehoe (23)
Shots   Buffalo 45, Toronto 30
Goalies   Buffalo: Roger Crozier; Toronto: Jacques Plante

GAME 58 - SABRES 4, RANGERS 1

NY Rangers 0 1 0 - 1
Buffalo 2 0 2 - 4
Thursday, February 15, 1973
Attendance - 15,668 at the Aud

Goals   Buffalo: Robert (35), Perreault (22), Mickey (7), Gratton (4)
        NY Rangers: Jean Ratelle (29)
Shots   NY Rangers 31, Buffalo 24
Goalies   Buffalo: Roger Crozier; NY Rangers: Ed Giacomin

GAME 59 - SABRES 3, PENGUINS 3

Buffalo 1 2 0 - 3
Pittsburgh 3 0 0 - 3

Saturday, February 17, 1973
Attendance - 13,100 at Civic Arena

Goals   Buffalo: Mickey (8), Martin 2 (32)
        Pittsburgh: Bryan Hextall (20), Syl Apps (24),
         Jean Pronovost (13)
Shots   Buffalo 33, Pittsburgh 33
Goalies   Buffalo: Roger Crozier; Pittsburgh: Jim Rutherford

GAME 60 - SABRES 4, PENGUINS 1

Pittsburgh 0 1 0 - 1
Buffalo 1 2 1 - 4
Sunday, February 18, 1973
Attendance - 15,668 at the Aud

Goals   Buffalo: Robert (36), Ramsay (8), Gratton (5), Meehan (28)
        Pittsburgh: Greg Polis (19)
Shots   Buffalo 27, Pittsburgh 25
Goalies   Buffalo: Roger Crozier; Pittsburgh: Jim Rutherford

GAME 61 - SABRES 3, CANUCKS 1

Vancouver 1 0 0 - 1
Buffalo 1 1 1 - 3
Thursday, February 22, 1973
Attendance - 15,668 at the Aud

Goals   Buffalo: Luce (13), Gratton (6), Mickey (9)
        Vancouver: Jim Mair (3)
Shots   Buffalo 33, Vancouver 31
Goalies   Buffalo: Roger Crozier; Vancouver: Ed Dyck

GAME 62 - NORTH STARS 4, SABRES 2

Buffalo 0 0 2 - 2
Minnesota 0 2 2 - 4

Saturday, February 24, 1973
Attendance - 15,434 at the Met Center

Goals   Buffalo: Mickey (10), Luce (14)
        Minnesota: Terry Holbrook (2), Buster Harvey 2 (17), Bill
         Goldsworthy (21)
Shots   Buffalo 35, Minnesota 26
Goalies   Buffalo: Dave Dryden; Minnesota: Cesare Maniago

GAME 63 - SABRES 2, PENGUINS 1

Pittsburgh 0 1 0 - 1
Buffalo 0 1 1 - 2
Sunday, February 25, 1973
Attendance - 15,668 at the Aud

Goals   Buffalo: Ramsay (9), Perreault (23)
        Pittsburgh: Nick Harbaruk (8)
Shots   Buffalo 31, Pittsburgh 23
Goalies   Buffalo: Roger Crozier; Pittsburgh: Jim Rutherford

GAME 64 - SABRES 4, FLAMES 4

Buffalo 0 2 2 - 4
Atlanta 2 2 0 - 4

Thursday, March 1, 1973
Attendance - 12,730 at the Omni

Goals   Buffalo: Luce (15), Lorentz (24), Martin (33), Mickey (11)
        Atlanta: Rey Comeau (19), Larry Romanchych (16), Bob Leiter (24),
         Curt Bennett (13)
Shots   Buffalo 27, Atlanta 25
Goalies   Buffalo: Roger Crozier; Atlanta: Dan Bouchard

GAME 65 - CANADIENS 4, SABRES 2

Montreal	1	1	2	-	4
Buffalo	1	1	0	-	2

Sunday, March 4, 1973
Attendance - 15,668 at the Aud

Goals Buffalo: Hillman (5), Ramsay (10)
Montreal: Guy Lapointe (15), Marc Tardif (21), Jacques Lemaire (37), Frank Mahovolich (31)
Shots Buffalo 35, Montreal 32
Goalies Buffalo: Roger Crozier; Montreal: Ken Dryden

GAME 66 - SABRES 2, KINGS 2

Buffalo	0	1	1	-	2
Los Angeles	1	1	0	-	2

Tuesday, March 6, 1973
Attendance - 7,867 at the Forum

Goals Buffalo: Lorentz (25), Carriere (1)
Los Angeles: Frank St. Marseilles (13), Butch Goring (22)
Shots Los Angeles 34, Buffalo 26
Goalies Buffalo: Roger Crozier; Los Angeles: Rogie Vachon

GAME 67 - SABRES 2, SEALS 2

Buffalo	2	0	0	-	2
California	0	1	1	-	2

Wednesday, March 7, 1973
Attendance - 4,910 at Oakland Arena

Goals Buffalo: Gratton (7), Meehan (29)
California: Joey Johnston (23), Rick Smith (8)
Shots California 32, Buffalo 27
Goalies Buffalo: Dave Dryden; California: Marv Edwards

GAME 68 - CANUCKS 5, SABRES 2

Buffalo	1	1	0	-	2
Vancouver	2	1	2	-	5

Friday, March 9, 1973
Attendance - 15,570 at Pacific Coliseum

Goals Buffalo: Horton (1), Perreault (24)
Vancouver: Andre Boudrias 2 (26), Bobby Lalonde (16), Dale Tallon (13), Barry Wilkins (8)
Shots Vancouver 40, Buffalo 36
Goalies Buffalo: Roger Crozier; Vancouver: Dunc Wilson

GAME 69 - BLUES 2, SABRES 0

Buffalo	0	0	0	-	0
St. Louis	0	1	1	-	2

Tuesday, March 13, 1973
Attendance - 18,630 at St. Louis Arena

Goals Buffalo: None
St.Louis: Phil Roberto (18), Floyd Thomson (13)
Shots St.Louis 28, Buffalo 23
Goalies Buffalo: Dave Dryden; St.Louis: Jacques Caron

GAME 70 - BRUINS 4, SABRES 1

Boston	0	1	3	-	4
Buffalo	1	0	0	-	1

Thursday, March 15, 1973
Attendance - 15,668 at the Aud

Goals Buffalo: Gratton (8)
Boston: Bobby Orr 2 (22), Carol Vadnais (7), Phil Esposito (47)
Shots Buffalo 34, Boston 33
Goalies Buffalo: Roger Crozier; Boston: Jacques Plante

GAME 71 - SABRES 3, CANADIENS 3

Buffalo	2	0	1	-	3
Montreal	2	0	1	-	3

Saturday, March 17, 1973
Attendance - 18,853 at the Forum

Goals Buffalo: Meehan (30), Luce (16), Gratton (9)
Montreal: Peter Mahovolich 2 (15), Murray Wilson (15)
Shots Montreal 41, Buffalo 34
Goalies Buffalo: Dave Dryden; Montreal: Ken Dryden

GAME 72- SABRES 5, MAPLE LEAFS 1

Toronto	0	0	1	-	1
Buffalo	0	3	2	-	5

Sunday, March 18, 1973
Attendance - 15,668 at the Aud

Goals Buffalo: Ramsay (11), Martin (34), Carriere (2), Robert (37), Meehan (31)
Toronto: Darryl Sittler (26)
Shots Buffalo 33, Toronto 31
Goalies Buffalo: Roger Crozier; Toronto: Ron Low

GAME 73 - BLACKHAWKS 6, SABRES 2

Buffalo	0	0	2 -	2
Chicago	0	5	1 -	6

Wednesday, March 21, 1973
Attendance - 19,599 at Chicago
Stadium

Goals Buffalo: Mickey 2 (13)
Chicago: Cliff Koroll (31), Jerry Korab (9), Jim Pappin (39), Dick Redmond (11), Ralph Backstrom 2 (24)
Shots Chicago 33, Buffalo 29
Goalies Buffalo: Dave Dryden; Chicago: Tony Esposito

GAME 74 - SABRES 4, PENGUINS 4

Buffalo	2	0	2 -	4
Pittsburgh	1	0	3 -	4

Saturday, March 24, 1973
Attendance - 12,945 at Civic Arena

Goals Buffalo: Martin (35), Perreault (25), Robert (38), Mickey (14)
Pittsburgh: Daryl Edestrand (15), Al McDonough (32), Jean Pronovost (20), Jean-Guy Lagace (1)
Shots Pittsburgh 35, Buffalo 26
Goalies Buffalo: Roger Crozier; Pittsburgh: Andy Brown

GAME 75 - BRUINS 6, SABRES 1

Buffalo	0	0	1 -	1
Boston	3	2	1 -	6

Sunday, March 25, 1973
Attendance - 15,003 at Boston Garden

Goals Buffalo: Lorentz (26)
Boston: Phil Esposito 2 (51), Bobby Orr 2 (26), Fred O'Donnell (9), Johnny Bucyk (40)
Shots Boston 34, Buffalo 31
Goalies Buffalo: Roger Crozier; Boston: Ross Brooks

GAME 76 - SABRES 3, ISLANDERS 2

Buffalo	2	1	0 -	3
NY Islanders	0	1	1 -	2

Tuesday, March 27, 1973
Attendance - 14,250 at Nassau Coliseum

Goals Buffalo: Martin (36), Robitaille (4), Robert (39)
NY Islanders: Tom Miller (11), Billy Harris (27)
Shots NY Islanders 31, Buffalo 26
Goalies Buffalo: Roger Crozier; NY Islanders, Billy Smith

GAME 77 - SABRES 6, FLYERS 3

Philadelphia	0	2	1 -	3
Buffalo	0	4	2 -	6

Wednesday, March 28, 1973
Attendance - 15,668 at the Aud

Goals Buffalo: Perreault 2 (27), Robert (40), Luce 2 (18), Martin (37)
Philadelphia: Bobby Clarke (33), Bill Clement (13), Terry Crisp (4)
Shots Buffalo 29, Philadelphia 29
Goalies Buffalo: Roger Crozier; Philadelphia: Doug Favell

GAME 78 - SABRES 3, BLUES 1

St. Louis	1	0	0 -	1
Buffalo	1	2	0 -	3

Sunday, April 1, 1973
Attendance - 15,668 at the Aud

Goals Buffalo: Perreault (28), Mickey (15), Lorentz (27)
St.Louis: Wayne Merrick (10)
Shots Buffalo 42, St.Louis 20
Goalies Buffalo: Roger Crozier; St.Louis: Jacques Caron

A Sabres tradition: The open practice during the Christmas holiday.

Gilbert Perreault made a little girl's day by signing an autograph.

1972-73
Player Biographies

STEVE ATKINSON
Position: Right wing

Born: Toronto, Ontario on October 16, 1948
Height: 5-11; Weight: 170 pounds

- Was claimed on waivers from Boston on Nov. 2, 1970
- Was known for his ability to get off a quick wrist shot
- Left organization in 1974 Expansion Draft when claimed by Washington
- Spent four years playing junior hockey for the Niagara Falls Flyers of the Ontario Hockey Association where his best year was 1967-68 when he had 37-36-73 in 50 games
- Originally selected in 1966 amateur draft by Boston
- In 1968-69, he scored 40-40-80 in 65 games for Oklahoma City and was the Central League's rookie of the year and a first-team All-Star
- In 1969-70, had 29-23-52 for Oklahoma City and earned a one-game callup from Boston

PLAYING RECORD

YEAR	TEAM	GP	G	A	PTS	PIM
1968-69	Boston	1	0	0	0	0
1970-71	Buffalo	57	20	18	38	12
1971-72	Buffalo	67	14	10	24	26
1972-73	Buffalo	61	9	9	18	36
1973-74	Buffalo	70	6	10	16	22
1974-75	Washington	46	11	4	15	8
NHL TOTALS		302	60	51	111	104
SABRES TOTALS		255	49	47	96	96
NHL PLAYOFFS		1	0	0	0	0

LARRY CARRIERE
Position: Defense

Born: Montreal, Quebec on January 3, 1952
Height: 6-1; Weight: 190 pounds

- Was the Sabres second-round choice in the 1972 amateur draft
- Was a steady stay-at-home defenseman throughout his career
- Left organization in trade to Atlanta for Jacques Richard on Oct. 1, 1975
- Made a brief return as a player during 1978 season
- Rejoined organization as a scout in the Quebec region in 1985, and after eight years, was promoted to Director of Player Evaluation in 1993
- In 1995, he became Assistant General Manager

PLAYING RECORD

YEAR	TEAM	GP	G	A	PTS	PIM
1972-73	Buffalo	40	2	8	10	52
1973-74	Buffalo	77	6	24	30	103
1974-75	Buffalo	80	1	11	12	111
1975-76	Atlanta	75	4	15	19	96
1976-77	Atl-Van	74	3	12	15	71
1977-78	Van-LA-Buf	18	0	3	3	30
1979-80	Toronto	2	0	1	1	0
NHL TOTALS		366	16	74	90	463
SABRES TOTALS		206	9	43	52	284
NHL PLAYOFFS		27	0	3	3	42

ROGER CROZIER

Position: Goalie

Born: Bracebridge, Ontario on March 16, 1942
Height: 5-8; Weight: 165 pounds

- Was acquired in a trade with Detroit on June 10, 1970 for Tom Webster
- Is a member of the Sabres Hall of Fame
- Chosen by team members as the Sabres MVP in 1971-72
- Began his pro hockey career in the American Hockey League with the Buffalo Bisons in 1960
- While playing for Pittsburgh in the AHL, was chosen the outstanding goalie in 1964 and was named AHL rookie of the year
- Won the Calder Memorial Trophy as NHL rookie of the year in 1964-65 with the Detroit Red Wings
- In 1966, he won the Conn Smythe Trophy as MVP of the Stanley Cup playoffs as he helped Detroit to the Finals and nearly keyed an upset of Montreal
- Retired from hockey for about six weeks during 1967-68 season, but returned
- Had three shutouts for Detroit in the 1969 playoffs
- In the summer of 1971, underwent surgery for removal of his gall bladder
- Holds Sabres record for having faced most shots in a single season with 2,190 in 1971-72. His 34 losses that season are also the most in Sabres history
- Injuries and illness allowed him to play in just 46 games for Buffalo from 1973-74 to 1977
- Left organization on March 3, 1977 when he was sold to Washington
- When his career ended, he joined the Capitals front office and from Nov. 1981 to Aug. 1982, he served as interim General Manager
- Joined MBNA America Bank, N.A., a credit card operation based in Newark, Del. in 1983 as an Executive Vice-President and Director of Facility Management. Worked there for 12 years and was responsible for overseeing company's massive construction which saw square footage of its complex rise from 30,000 square feet to more than 2 million
- During his time with MBNA, he also operated the Roger Crozier Enterprises Hockey Schools in Barrie, Ont. for 10 years
- Died in 1995 after a long bout with cancer, and Sabres honored him by wearing a patch on their jerseys during the 1995-96 season

PLAYING RECORD

YEAR	TEAM	GP	MINS	GA	SO	GAA
1963-64	Detroit	15	900	51	2	3.40
1964-65	Detroit	70	4167	168	6	2.42
1965-66	Detroit	64	3734	173	7	2.78
1966-67	Detroit	58	3256	182	4	3.35
1967-68	Detroit	34	1729	95	1	3.30
1968-69	Detroit	38	1820	101	0	3.33
1969-70	Detroit	34	1877	83	0	2.65
1970-71	Buffalo	44	2198	135	1	3.69
1971-72	Buffalo	63	3654	214	4	3.51
1972-73	Buffalo	49	2633	121	3	2.76
1973-74	Buffalo	12	615	39	0	3.80
1974-75	Buffalo	23	1260	55	3	2.62
1975-76	Buffalo	11	620	27	1	2.61
1976-77	Washington	3	103	2	0	1.17
NHL TOTALS		518	28566	1446	30	3.04
SABRES TOTALS		202	10980	591	10	3.23
NHL PLAYOFFS		31	1769	82	1	2.78

BUTCH DEADMARSH

Position: Left wing

Born: B. Trail, B.C. on April 5, 1950
Height: 5-10; Weight: 185 pounds

- Was a second-round draft choice of the Sabres in 1970 and was a member of the original Sabres team
- Left organization in a trade with Atlanta on Feb. 14, 1973 for Norm Gratton

PLAYING RECORD

YEAR	TEAM	GP	G	A	PTS	PIM
1970-71	Buffalo	10	0	0	0	9
1971-72	Buffalo	12	1	1	2	4
1972-73	Buf-Atl	53	2	1	3	34
1973-74	Atlanta	42	6	1	7	89
1974-75	Kansas City	20	3	2	5	19
NHL TOTALS		56	12	5	17	155
SABRES TOTALS		100	2	2	4	39
NHL PLAYOFFS		4	0	0	0	17

DAVE DRYDEN

Position: Goalie

Born: Hamilton, Ontario on Sept. 5, 1941
Height: 6-2; Weight: 180 pounds

- Purchased for cash from Pittsburgh on Oct. 9, 1970
- Won the Sabres Most Improved Player award in 1972-73
- Played in the 1974 NHL All-Star game
- Is the older brother of former Montreal goalie and Hockey Hall of Famer Ken Dryden
- His .908 save percentage in 1972-73 was Sabres record until Dominik Hasek broke that mark in 1993-94
- Career goals against average of 3.06 is fourth-best in team history
- Left the organization following 1974 and finished his career in the WHA, first with Chicago, then with Edmonton. Was still with the Oilers when they joined the NHL in 1979-80

PLAYING RECORD

YEAR	TEAM	GP	MINS	GA	SO	GAA
1961-62	NY Rangers	1	40	3	0	4.50
1965-66	Chicago	11	453	23	0	3.05
1967-68	Chicago	27	1268	69	1	3.26
1968-69	Chicago	30	1479	79	3	3.20
1970-71	Buffalo	10	409	23	1	3.37
1971-72	Buffalo	20	1026	68	0	3.98
1972-73	Buffalo	37	2018	89	3	2.65
1973-74	Buffalo	53	2987	148	1	2.97
1979-80	Edmonton	14	744	53	0	4.27
NHL TOTALS		203	10424	555	9	3.19
SABRES TOTALS		120	6440	328	5	3.06
NHL PLAYOFFS		3	133	9	0	4.06

NORM GRATTON

Position: Left wing

Born: LaSalle, Quebec on Dec. 22, 1950
Height: 5-11; Weight: 165 pounds

- Was acquired in a trade with Atlanta on Feb. 14, 1973 for Butch Deadmarsh and provided an offensive spark late in the season
- Originally drafted by the New York Rangers in June 1970 after a successful junior career with the Montreal Junior Canadiens where he was a teammate of Gil Perreault and Rick Martin
- Went to the Atlanta Flames in June 1972 in the Intra-League Draft
- Was traded to Minnesota on Jan. 27, 1975, in exchange for Fred Stanfield, who became a key member of Sabres' only Stanley Cup Finals team

PLAYING RECORD

YEAR	TEAM	GP	G	A	PTS	PIM
1971-72	NY Rangers	3	0	1	1	0
1972-73	Atl-Buf	50	9	11	20	24
1973-74	Buffalo	57	6	11	17	16
1974-75	Buf-Minn	59	17	18	35	10
1975-76	Minnesota	32	7	3	10	14
NHL TOTALS		201	39	44	83	54
SABRES TOTALS		102	15	23	38	30
NHL PLAYOFFS		6	0	1	1	2

HUGH HARRIS

Position: Right wing

Born: Toronto, Ontario on June 7, 1948
Height: 6-1; Weight: 195 pounds

- Was chosen on June 6, 1971 from Montreal in the Intra-League Draft
- 1972-73 was the only year he spent in the NHL, as he joined New England of the World Hockey Association in 1973 and enjoyed five productive seasons in the WHA before retiring. He scored 107 goals and 280 points in the WHA

PLAYING RECORD

YEAR	TEAM	GP	G	A	PTS	PIM
1972-73	Buffalo	60	12	26	38	17
NHL TOTALS		60	12	26	38	17
SABRES TOTALS		60	12	26	38	17
NHL PLAYOFFS		3	0	0	0	0

LARRY HILLMAN
Position: Defense

Born: Kirkland Lake, Ontario on Feb. 5, 1937
Height: 6-0; Weight: 181 pounds

- Was acquired in a trade with Los Angeles on Dec. 16, 1971 along with Mike Byers for Doug Barrie and Mike Keeler
- Made his NHL debut with the Detroit Red Wings in 1955, but was taken by Chicago in the Intra-League Draft in June 1957. Four months later he was picked up off waivers by Boston
- Went to Toronto in Intra-League Draft in June 1960, and for the next eight years, he split time with the Maple Leafs and Rochester of the American League
- Spent time with Minnesota, Montreal, Philadelphia and Los Angeles before joining Buffalo
- In June 1971, he was traded from Philadelphia to Los Angeles in exchange for Larry Mickey, a future teammate in Buffalo
- Jumped to the WHA in 1973 and played three more seasons with Cleveland and Winnipeg before retiring after the 1976 season, his 22nd year in pro hockey

PLAYING RECORD
YEAR	TEAM	GP	G	A	PTS	PIM
1954-55	Detroit	6	0	0	0	2
1955-56	Detroit	47	0	3	3	53
1956-57	Detroit	16	1	2	3	4
1957-58	Boston	70	3	19	22	60
1958-59	Boston	55	3	10	13	19
1959-60	Boston	2	0	1	1	2
1960-61	Toronto	62	3	10	13	59
1961-62	Toronto	5	0	0	0	4
1962-63	Toronto	5	0	0	0	2
1963-64	Toronto	33	0	4	4	31
1964-65	Toronto	2	0	0	0	2
1965-66	Toronto	48	3	25	28	34
1966-67	Toronto	55	4	19	23	40
1967-68	Toronto	55	3	17	20	13
1968-69	Minn-Mont	37	1	10	11	17
1969-70	Philadelphia	76	5	26	31	73
1970-71	Philadelphia	73	3	13	16	39
1971-72	LA-Buf	65	2	13	15	69
1972-73	Buffalo	78	5	24	29	56
NHL TOTALS		790	36	196	232	579
SABRES TOTALS		121	6	35	41	114
NHL PLAYOFFS		74	2	9	11	30

TIM HORTON
Position: Defense

Born: Cochrane, Ontario on Jan. 12, 1930
Height: 5-10; Weight: 180 pounds

- Decided against retirement at the age of 42 when his former coach in Toronto, Punch Imlach, selected him from Pittsburgh in Intra-League Draft on June 5, 1972
- Was elected to the Hockey Hall of Fame in 1977
- Is a member of the Sabres Hall of Fame
- His No. 2 jersey was retired by the Sabres in a 1996 ceremony
- Played on four Stanley Cup-winning teams under Imlach with Toronto in the 1960s, including three in a row (1962-64)
- In 1962 playoffs, set records for most points (16) and assists (13) by a defenseman
- His 20-year stay in Toronto ended when he was traded to the New York Rangers for a player to be named later who turned out to be Denis Dupere
- Went to Pittsburgh in Intra-League Draft of 1971
- Chosen by team members as the Sabres MVP in 1972-73
- Was the owner of a successful chain of donut shops in Ontario and Western New York called Tim Horton Donuts
- Died in a one-car crash on the Queen Elizabeth Way while driving back to Buffalo after a game in Toronto on Feb. 21, 1974
- Sabres unsung hero award is now named the Tim Horton Memorial Award

PLAYING RECORD
YEAR	TEAM	GP	G	A	PTS	PIM
1949-50	Toronto	1	0	0	0	2
1951-52	Toronto	4	0	0	0	8
1952-53	Toronto	70	2	14	16	85
1953-54	Toronto	70	7	24	31	94
1954-55	Toronto	67	5	9	14	84
1955-56	Toronto	35	0	5	5	36

1956-57	Toronto	66	6	19	25	72
1957-58	Toronto	53	6	20	26	39
1958-59	Toronto	70	5	21	26	76
1959-60	Toronto	70	3	29	32	69
1960-61	Toronto	57	6	15	21	75
1961-62	Toronto	70	10	28	38	88
1962-63	Toronto	70	6	19	25	69
1963-64	Toronto	70	9	20	29	71
1964-65	Toronto	70	12	16	28	95
1965-66	Toronto	70	6	22	28	76
1966-67	Toronto	70	8	17	25	70
1967-68	Toronto	69	4	23	27	82
1968-69	Toronto	74	11	29	40	107
1969-70	Tor-NY Rangers	74	4	24	28	107
1970-71	NY Rangers	78	2	18	20	57
1971-72	Pittsburgh	44	2	9	11	40
1972-73	Buffalo	69	1	16	17	56
1973-74	Buffalo	55	0	6	6	53
NHL TOTALS		**1446**	**115**	**403**	**518**	**1611**
SABRES TOTALS		**124**	**1**	**22**	**23**	**109**
NHL PLAYOFFS		**126**	**11**	**39**	**50**	**183**

JIM LORENTZ

Position: Left wing

Born: Waterloo, Ontario on May 1, 1947
Height: 6-0; Weight: 180 pounds

- Was acquired by Sabres from the New York Rangers on Jan. 14, 1972 in exchange for second-round draft choice in 1972 which turned out to be Larry Sacharuk
- Joined the Boston Bruins in 1968 after winning the Central Hockey League scoring title and MVP award the previous season with 101 points as a member of the Oklahoma City Blazers. However, he was buried as the fourth center with the Bruins behind Phil Esposito, Derek Sanderson and Fred Stanfield
- Was dealt to St. Louis in exchange for the Blues No. 1 draft choice in 1970, which turned out to be Ron Plumb, but he grew frustrated by constant position switching and was dealt to the Rangers in 1971. He appeared in only seven games before coming to the Sabres
- Won Charlie Conacher Memorial Trophy in 1977
- Twice was chosen as Sabres unsung hero award-winner in 1973 and 1977
- One of the most versatile players to ever play for Sabres as he was a strong two-way forward who could play all three forward positions and also played on both the power play and the penalty-killing unit
- Retired after the 1978 season and joined the Sabres broadcast team in 1981, first on radio, and later on television, a position he still holds

PLAYING RECORD

YEAR	TEAM	GP	G	A	PTS	PIM
1968-69	Boston	11	1	3	4	6
1969-70	Boston	68	7	16	23	30
1970-71	St. Louis	76	19	21	40	34
1971-72	St.L-NYR-Buf	52	10	15	25	24
1972-73	Buffalo	78	27	35	62	30
1973-74	Buffalo	78	23	31	54	28
1974-75	Buffalo	72	25	45	70	18
1975-76	Buffalo	75	17	24	41	18
1976-77	Buffalo	79	23	33	56	8
1977-78	Buffalo	70	9	15	24	12
NHL TOTALS		**359**	**161**	**238**	**399**	**208**
SABRES TOTALS		**487**	**134**	**197**	**331**	**126**
NHL PLAYOFFS		**54**	**12**	**10**	**22**	**30**

DON LUCE

Position: Center

Born: London, Ontario on Oct. 2, 1948
Height: 6-2; Weight: 178 pounds

- Came to Sabres from Detroit along with Mike Robitaille on May 25, 1971 in a trade for goalie Joe Daley
- Is a member of the Sabres Hall of Fame
- Was one of the finest penalty killers in the NHL
- In 1975, won the NHL's Bill Masterton Trophy, presented to the player who exemplifies the qualities of perseverance, sportsmanship and dedication to hockey
- Chosen by team members as the Sabres MVP in 1973-74

- Won the Sabres Most Improved Player award in 1972-73
- Played in the 1975 NHL All-Star game
- Named Sabres unsung hero award-winner in 1972
- His plus-minus rating of plus 61 in 1974-75 remains a Sabres record
- His eight shorthanded goals in 1974-75 also remains a Sabres record, and it tied a then NHL record held by Toronto's Dave Keon
- Originally drafted by the New York Rangers in 1966, but was traded in November 1970 to Detroit for Steve Andrascik
- Led the Ontario Hockey Association in assists with 70 while playing junior hockey for the Kitchener Rangers
- Left organization on March 10, 1981, when he was traded to Los Angeles
- Rejoined organization in 1984 as an American scout
- Served as assistant coach during the 1985-86 season, and was elevated to Director of Player Personnel in 1987, a position he still holds
- Played a key role in Alexander Mogilny's defection from the Soviet Union in 1989 so he could play for the Sabres

PLAYING RECORD

YEAR	TEAM	GP	G	A	PTS	PIM
1969-70	NY Rangers	12	1	2	3	8
1970-71	NYR-Det	67	3	12	15	18
1971-72	Buffalo	78	11	8	19	38
1972-73	Buffalo	78	18	25	43	32
1973-74	Buffalo	75	26	31	57	44
1974-75	Buffalo	80	33	43	76	45
1975-76	Buffalo	77	21	49	70	42
1976-77	Buffalo	80	26	43	69	16
1977-78	Buffalo	78	26	35	61	24
1978-79	Buffalo	79	26	35	61	14
1979-80	Buffalo	80	14	29	43	30
1980-81	Buffalo-LA	71	16	13	29	21
1981-82	Toronto	39	4	4	8	32
NHL TOTALS		894	225	329	554	364
SABRES TOTALS		766	216	310	526	304
NHL PLAYOFFS		71	17	22	39	52

RICHARD MARTIN

Position: Left wing

Born: Verdun, Quebec on July 26, 1951
Height: 5-11; Weight: 179 pounds

- Was the Sabres first-round choice (fifth overall) in the 1971 amateur draft
- Is a member of the Sabres Hall of Fame, as well as the Greater Buffalo Sports Hall of Fame
- His No. 7 jersey was retired by the Sabres in a 1995 ceremony
- When he retired, he was the Sabres all-time leading goal scorer
- Played in seven consecutive All-Star games from 1972 to 1978. In the 1977 game, he scored two goals and was named the MVP
- Was selected an NHL All-Star four times, including three first-team selections
- Still holds Sabres rookie records for goals (44) and points (74) in a season
- Remains second on Sabres all-time goal-scoring list with 382, and third in points with 695
- His 21 power-play goals in 1974-75 is fourth-highest in team history
- Shares Sabres record with Alexander Mogilny for most hat tricks in a season with seven in 1975-76
- His 44 goals as a rookie was, at the time, an NHL record
- Had one of the hardest shots in the history of the game
- Left organization on March 10, 1981, when he was traded to Los Angeles for two draft choices, one of which was used to select Tom Barrasso in 1983

PLAYING RECORD

YEAR	TEAM	GP	G	A	PTS	PIM
1971-72	Buffalo	73	44	30	74	36
1972-73	Buffalo	75	37	36	73	79
1973-74	Buffalo	78	52	34	86	38
1974-75	Buffalo	68	52	43	95	72
1975-76	Buffalo	80	49	37	86	67
1976-77	Buffalo	66	36	29	65	58
1977-78	Buffalo	65	28	35	63	16
1978-79	Buffalo	73	32	21	53	35
1979-80	Buffalo	80	45	34	79	16
1980-81	Buffalo-LA	24	8	15	23	20
1981-82	Los Angeles	3	1	3	4	2
NHL TOTALS		685	384	317	701	439
SABRES TOTALS		681	382	313	695	437
NHL PLAYOFFS		63	24	29	53	74

GERRY MEEHAN

Position: Center

Born: Toronto, Ontario on Sept. 3, 1946
Height: 6-2; Weight: 200 pounds

- Was selected on June 10, 1970 in the NHL expansion draft from the Philadelphia Flyers
- Named Sabres unsung hero award-winner in 1971
- Was the second Sabres captain, wearing the C on his jersey from 1971-74
- His goal with four seconds left on the final night of the 1971-72 season prevented Philadelphia from qualifying for the playoffs
- Played his junior hockey for the Toronto Marlboros and made minor league stops in Rochester, Tulsa, Phoenix and Seattle
- Made his NHL debut with the Toronto Maple Leafs, but was traded to Philadelphia along with Mike Byers and Bill Sutherland for Forbes Kennedy and Brit Selby in March of 1969
- Left Sabres organization along with Mike Robitaille in a trade to Vancouver for Jocelyn Guevremont on Oct. 14, 1974
- After retiring from hockey in 1979, he completed his undergraduate degree at Canisius College and obtained a law degree from the University of Buffalo
- In 1984, he was named Assistant General Manager, the first ex-Sabre player to land a position in the team's front office
- He was named Sabres General Manager in December of 1986, replacing Scotty Bowman
- In his first full year as GM, he finished second in voting by *The Sporting News* for NHL Executive of the Year as the Sabres made a 21-point improvement in standings
- Was instrumental in helping Alexander Mogilny defect from Russia in order to join the Sabres in 1989. He also made the deals that brought Pat LaFontaine to Buffalo in 1991 and Dominik Hasek in 1992.
- Resigned his General Manager position in 1993 to assume duties as Executive Vice-President for sports operations
- Resigned that position in mid-1995 and left the organization
- Now lives in his native Toronto, practices law, does consulting work, and he helped build the St. Michaels College Majors, a junior team in the Ontario Hockey Association which debuted this fall

PLAYING RECORD

YEAR	TEAM	GP	G	A	PTS	PIM
1968-69	Tor-Phil	37	0	5	5	6
1970-71	Buffalo	77	24	31	55	8
1971-72	Buffalo	77	19	27	46	51
1972-73	Buffalo	77	31	29	60	21
1973-74	Buffalo	72	20	26	46	17
1974-75	Buf-Van-Atl	74	14	26	40	6
1975-76	Atl-Wash	80	23	35	58	18
1976-77	Washington	80	28	36	64	13
1977-78	Washington	78	19	24	43	10
1978-79	Washington	18	2	4	6	0
NHL TOTALS		670	180	243	423	111
SABRES TOTALS		306	94	114	208	60
NHL PLAYOFFS		10	0	1	1	0

LARRY MICKEY

Position: Right wing

Born: Lacombe, Alta. on Oct. 21, 1943
Height: 5-11; Weight: 180 pounds

- Came to Sabres from Philadelphia on Nov. 16, 1971 in a trade for left wing Larry Keenan
- A hard-working veteran player who General Manager Punch Imlach brought to Buffalo to provide leadership for a young team, much the way Tim Horton did
- Made his NHL debut with the Chicago Blackhawks in 1965, but was selected in the Intra-League Draft by the New York Rangers in June 1965
- While playing for the Rangers in the 1967 playoffs, was involved in a serious auto accident in which he suffered a broken arm. That injury forced him to miss most of the 1967-68 season. When he did play that year, it was for 30 games with the Buffalo Bisons of the American League.
- He went to Toronto in June 1968 through the Intra-League Draft, and then was chosen by Montreal in the same process in June 1969
- Was traded by Montreal in May 1970 along with Jack Norris and Lucien Grenier to the Los Angeles Kings in exchange for Leon Rochefort, Greg Boddy and Wayne Thomas
- Was traded by Los Angeles to Philadelphia in July 1971 in exchange for Larry Hillman
- Retired after the 1975 season
- Died of an apparent suicide

PLAYING RECORD

YEAR	TEAM	GP	G	A	PTS	PIM
1964-65	Chicago	1	0	0	0	0
1965-66	NY Rangers	7	0	0	0	2
1966-67	NY Rangers	8	0	0	0	0
1967-68	NY Rangers	4	0	2	2	0

1968-69	Toronto	55	8	19	27	43
1969-70	Montreal	21	4	4	8	4
1970-71	Los Angeles	65	6	12	18	46
1971-72	Phil-Buf	18	1	3	4	8
1972-73	Buffalo	77	15	9	24	47
1973-74	Buffalo	13	3	4	7	8
1974-75	Buffalo	23	2	0	2	2
NHL TOTALS		292	39	53	92	160
SABRES TOTALS		117	20	14	34	65
NHL PLAYOFFS		9	1	0	1	10

GILBERT PERREAULT

Position: Center

Born: Victoriaville, Que. on Nov. 13, 1950
Height: 6-1; Weight: 200 pounds

- Was the Sabres first player, chosen in the first round of the 1970 NHL entry draft
- In order to determine which expansion team - Buffalo or Vancouver - would make the first draft selection, a specially-constructed roulette wheel was spun, and it came up in favor of Buffalo. Oddly enough, it landed on No. 11, the jersey number Perreault wore as a junior player in Montreal
- He is the only Sabres player enshrined in the Hockey Hall of Fame, having been inducted in 1990
- Had his No. 11 jersey retired by the Sabres in a 1990 ceremony. He is the only player to ever wear that number for the Sabres
- Is a member of the Sabres Hall of Fame, as well as the Greater Buffalo Sports Hall of Fame
- Led Buffalo in goals scored four times, in assists nine times, and in points 12 times
- When he retired, he held team records for points in a season (113 in 1975-76), and assists in a season (69 in 1975-76)
- He still owns Sabres career marks for games played (1,191), goals (512), assists (814), points (1,326), game-winning goals (81) and shots (2,837)
- Also still owns career playoff records for games (90), goals (33), assists (70) and points (103)
- Scored his 500th goal on March 9, 1986 at the Aud, becoming the 12th player in NHL history to reach that milestone
- When he retired, he was sixth on the NHL's all-time points list, 11th in goals scored, and eighth in assists
- His seven points against California on Feb. 1, 1976, is the Sabres single-game scoring record
- Had an 18-game point scoring streak in 1971-72 that is still a team mark
- Served as Sabres captain from 1981-87
- Had 15 seasons of 20 goals or more, including 12 in a row
- Chosen by team members as the Sabres MVP in 1970-71 and 1983-84
- Won Calder Memorial Trophy in 1970-71 as NHL rookie of the year when he set a then NHL rookie record with 38 goals
- Won Lady Byng Memorial Trophy in 1973 for sportsmanlike conduct
- Was a second-team NHL All-Star selection in 1976 and 1977
- Played in eight NHL All-Star games, including the 1978 game in Buffalo where he scored the game-winning goal in overtime
- Played on NHL Challenge Cup (1979) and Team Canada (1981) squads that played against the Soviet Union
- Retired on Nov. 24, 1986, due to lingering injuries

PLAYING RECORD

YEAR	TEAM	GP	G	A	PTS	PIM
1970-71	Buffalo	78	38	34	72	19
1971-72	Buffalo	76	26	48	74	24
1972-73	Buffalo	78	28	60	88	10
1973-74	Buffalo	55	18	33	51	10
1974-75	Buffalo	68	39	57	96	36
1975-76	Buffalo	80	44	69	113	36
1976-77	Buffalo	80	39	56	95	30
1977-78	Buffalo	79	41	48	89	20
1978-79	Buffalo	79	27	58	85	20
1979-80	Buffalo	80	40	66	106	57
1980-81	Buffalo	56	20	39	59	56
1981-82	Buffalo	62	31	42	73	40
1982-83	Buffalo	77	30	46	76	34
1983-84	Buffalo	73	31	59	90	32
1984-85	Buffalo	78	30	53	83	42
1985-86	Buffalo	72	21	39	60	28
1986-87	Buffalo	20	9	7	16	6
NHL TOTALS		1191	512	814	1326	500
SABRES TOTALS		1191	512	814	1326	500
NHL PLAYOFFS		90	33	70	103	44

TRACY PRATT

Position: Defense

Born: New York, N.Y. on March 8, 1943
Height: 6-2; Weight: 195 pounds

- Selected on June 10, 1970 in the NHL expansion draft from Pittsburgh
- Is the son of former NHL great Babe Pratt, who played 12 seasons with the Rangers, Bruins and Maple Leafs from 1935-47
- Was a stay-at-home defenseman who excelled at taking the body
- Was nicknamed "Tree" because of his strength and size
- Set a record for most penalty minutes in the Central League playoffs when he accumulated 49 in 1964 while playing for St. Paul
- Was traded to the Chicago organization in June 1965, then was selected by the Oakland Seals in the Expansion Draft in June 1967, having never played for the Blackhawks
- Made his NHL debut with the Seals in 1967
- Started 1968-69 season with Vancouver of the Western League, but was traded to the Pittsburgh Penguins along with George Swarbrick and Bryan Watson in exchange for Earl Ingarfield, Dick Mattiussi and Gene Ubriaco in January 1969
- Missed part of the 1971-72 season with a broken leg
- Left Sabres organization along with John Gould in a trade to Vancouver for Jerry Korab on Dec. 27, 1973

PLAYING RECORD

YEAR	TEAM	GP	G	A	PTS	PIM
1967-68	Oakland	34	0	5	5	90
1968-69	Pittsburgh	18	0	5	5	34
1969-70	Pittsburgh	65	5	7	12	124
1970-71	Buffalo	76	1	7	8	179
1971-72	Buffalo	27	0	10	10	52
1972-73	Buffalo	74	1	15	16	116
1973-74	Buf-Van	78	3	15	18	96
1974-75	Vancouver	79	5	17	22	145
1975-76	Vancouver	52	1	5	6	72
1976-77	Col-Toronto	77	1	11	12	118
NHL TOTALS		580	17	97	114	1026
SABRES TOTALS		210	2	39	41	399
NHL PLAYOFFS		25	0	1	1	62

CRAIG RAMSAY

Position: Left wing

Born: Toronto, Ontario on March 17, 1951
Height: 5-10; Weight: 168 pounds

- Was a second-round choice in the 1971 amateur draft
- Is a member of the Sabres Hall of Fame, as well as the Greater Buffalo Sports Hall of Fame
- In 1984-85, won the NHL's Frank Selke Award, presented to the forward who best excels in the defensive aspects of the game
- Played in the 1976 NHL All-Star game
- Sabres all-time leader in shorthanded goals with 27
- His 1,070 games played is second on Sabres all-time list behind Gil Perreault. Like Perreault, every NHL game he played was with the Sabres.
- His 252 goals are fifth-most in Sabres history, and his 672 points are third-most
- From March 27, 1973, to Feb. 10, 1983, played in team record 776 consecutive games, which was then second in NHL history only to Garry Unger's streak of 914 games. It still ranks as the fourth-longest streak.
- Played entire 1973-74 season (78 games) without incurring a penalty
- His plus-minus rating of plus 51 in 1974-75 is third-best in team history
- Retired following the 1984-85 season, a year in which he also served as an assistant coach
- Upon retirement, he became a full-time assistant coach in 1985, and then served as interim head coach for one month in 1986 and posted record of 4-15-2
- After being relieved as head coach, served in a variety of front office positions including Assistant General Manager
- Ended his 22-year association with Sabres organization in the summer of 1993 when he joined the expansion Florida Panthers as an assistant coach
- After being fired in Florida, he worked as a scout for the Dallas Stars in 1995-96
- Became an assistant coach with the Ottawa Senators in 1996, a position he still holds

PLAYING RECORD

YEAR	TEAM	GP	G	A	PTS	PIM
1971-72	Buffalo	57	6	10	16	0
1972-73	Buffalo	76	11	17	28	15
1973-74	Buffalo	78	20	26	46	0
1974-75	Buffalo	80	26	38	64	26
1975-76	Buffalo	80	22	49	71	34
1976-77	Buffalo	80	20	41	61	20
1977-78	Buffalo	80	28	43	71	18
1978-79	Buffalo	80	26	31	57	10
1979-80	Buffalo	80	21	39	60	18
1980-81	Buffalo	80	24	35	59	12
1981-82	Buffalo	80	16	35	51	8
1982-83	Buffalo	64	11	18	29	7
1983-84	Buffalo	76	9	17	26	17
1984-85	Buffalo	79	12	21	33	16
NHL TOTALS		1070	252	420	672	201
SABRES TOTALS		1070	252	420	672	201
NHL PLAYOFFS		89	17	31	48	27

RENE ROBERT

Position: Right wing

Born: Three Rivers, Quebec on Dec. 31, 1948
Height: 5-10; Weight: 184 pounds

- Came to Sabres from Pittsburgh on March 4, 1972 in a trade for popular winger Eddie Shack
- Was the final link in the famed French Connection line
- Is a member of the Sabres Hall of Fame, as well as the Greater Buffalo Sports Hall of Fame
- His No. 14 jersey was retired by the Sabres in a 1995 ceremony
- Chosen by team members as the Sabres MVP in 1974-75
- Was an NHL All-Star selection in 1975
- Played in two NHL All-Star games and scored a goal in the 1973 game
- In 1975, he became the first Sabres player to reach 100 points for a season, leading team to the Stanley Cup Finals against Philadelphia
- Is sixth on Sabres all-time points list with 552 and seventh in goals with 222
- Was playing for minor league Vancouver Canucks in 1969-70 when he was traded to Toronto for Ron Ward in May of 1969, then was re-purchased by the Maple Leafs in May 1970
- Began 1970-71 with Tulsa of the Central League, then was loaned to Phoenix of the Western League before being recalled to Toronto in spring of 1971 for five games
- Was drafted by Sabres in Intra-League Draft of 1971, but was left unprotected momentarily as Punch Imlach was doing some wheeling and dealing, and Pittsburgh claimed him
- Left organization on Oct. 5, 1979, when he was traded to Colorado for John Van Boxmeer

PLAYING RECORD

YEAR	TEAM	GP	G	A	PTS	PIM
1970-71	Toronto	5	0	0	0	0
1971-72	Pitt-Buffalo	61	13	14	27	44
1972-73	Buffalo	75	40	43	83	83
1973-74	Buffalo	76	21	44	65	71
1974-75	Buffalo	74	40	60	100	75
1975-76	Buffalo	72	35	52	87	53
1976-77	Buffalo	80	33	40	73	46
1977-78	Buffalo	67	25	48	73	25
1978-79	Buffalo	68	22	40	62	46
1979-80	Colorado	69	28	35	63	79
1980-81	Col-Toronto	42	14	18	32	38
1981-82	Toronto	55	13	24	37	37
NHL TOTALS		744	284	418	702	597
SABRES TOTALS		524	222	330	552	401
NHL PLAYOFFS		50	22	19	41	73

MIKE ROBITAILLE

Position: Defense

Born: Midland, Ontario on Feb. 12, 1948
Height: 5-11; Weight: 195 pounds

- Came to the Sabres from the Detroit Red Wings along with Don Luce on May 25, 1971 in a trade for goalie Joe Daley
- Was voted the outstanding defenseman in the Central League in 1970 while with the Omaha Knights
- Made his NHL debut with the New York Rangers in 1970

- Was traded by the Rangers in February 1971 along with Arnie Brown and Tom Miller to Detroit in exchange for Bruce MacGregor and Larry Brown
- At the end of the 1971-72 season, was drafted and signed by the New York Raiders of the World Hockey Association, but was re-signed by the Sabres in July 1972
- Left organization along with Gerry Meehan in a trade to Vancouver for Jocelyn Guevremont on Oct. 14, 1974
- In 1983 he rejoined the organization as a broadcaster and served as the Sabres color commentator until 1994
- He still has a hand in hockey analysis as he co-hosts *Hockey Hotline* for the Empire Sports Network
- Is also the president of Fort Erie Race Track

PLAYING RECORD

YEAR	TEAM	GP	G	A	PTS	PIM
1969-70	NY Rangers	4	0	0	0	8
1970-71	NYR-Det	34	5	9	14	29
1971-72	Buffalo	31	2	10	12	22
1972-73	Buffalo	65	4	17	21	40
1973-74	Buffalo	71	2	18	20	60
1974-75	Buf-Van	66	2	23	25	31
1975-76	Vancouver	71	8	19	27	69
1976-77	Vancouver	40	0	9	9	21
NHL TOTALS		382	23	105	128	280
SABRES TOTALS		170	8	46	54	122
NHL PLAYOFFS		13	0	1	1	4

JIM SCHOENFELD
Position: Defense

Born: Galt, Ontario on Sept. 4, 1952
Height: 6-2; Weight: 200 pounds

- Was the Sabres first-round choice in the 1972 amateur draft
- Is a member of the Sabres Hall of Fame
- Played for three different junior clubs (London, Hamilton and Niagara Falls) in the Ontario Hockey Association from 1969-72
- His 225 penalty minutes were a league high for Niagara Falls in 1971-72
- Finished fourth in Calder Trophy voting for 1972-73 Rookie of the Year and was the top rookie defenseman in the NHL
- In 1978-79, he was chosen winner of the Seventh Player Award, presented to the player deemed to be most inspirational
- Was a second-team NHL All-Star in 1979-80 and played in the All-Star game in 1976-77 and 1979-80
- In 1979-80, he had a plus-minus rating of plus 60, second-best in Sabres history
- His three goals in 1981 game vs. Winnipeg is still tied for most by a Sabres defenseman in one game
- Served as Sabres captain from 1974-77
- Played for the NHL Challenge Cup team in 1979 against the Soviet Union
- Left organization on Dec. 2, 1981, in one of the biggest trades in Sabres history. Schoenfeld, Danny Gare, Bob Sauve and Derek Smith were sent to Detroit in exchange for Dale McCourt, Mike Foligno and Brent Peterson
- Returned to organization in 1984 as coach of the Sabres farm team in Rochester, then was promoted to Sabres coach in 1985. He was fired midway through his first season with a record of 19-19-5
- He returned to an NHL bench midway through 1987 as coach of New Jersey and led the Devils to the Wales Conference championship round where they lost to Boston
- Was fired during 1989-90 season and moved into the broadcast booth as an analyst for ESPN
- Midway through 1993-94, he was hired as head coach of the Washington Capitals
- In Spring of 1997, was hired as coach of the Phoenix Coyotes

PLAYING RECORD

YEAR	TEAM	GP	G	A	PTS	PIM
1972-73	Buffalo	66	4	15	19	178
1973-74	Buffalo	28	1	8	9	56
1974-75	Buffalo	68	1	19	20	184
1975-76	Buffalo	56	2	22	24	114
1976-77	Buffalo	65	7	25	32	97
1977-78	Buffalo	60	2	20	22	89
1978-79	Buffalo	46	8	17	25	67
1979-80	Buffalo	77	9	27	36	72
1980-81	Buffalo	71	8	25	33	110
1981-82	Buf-Det	52	8	11	19	99
1982-83	Detroit	57	1	10	11	18
1983-84	Boston	39	0	2	2	20
1984-85	Buffalo	34	0	3	3	28
NHL TOTALS		719	51	204	255	1132
SABRES TOTALS		584	45	183	228	1025
NHL PLAYOFFS		75	3	13	16	151

PAUL TERBENCHE

Position: Defense

Born: Port Hope, Ontario on Sept. 16, 1945
Height: 5-10; Weight: 170 pounds

- Was selected on June 10, 1970 in the NHL expansion draft from Chicago
- Made his NHL debut with Chicago in 1967-68 and played 68 games that year
- Was one of the six players who started Buffalo's first regular season game on Oct. 10, 1970 in Pittsburgh
- Was a versatile player who could also play on left wing
- Left organization in 1974 Expansion Draft when chosen by Kansas City

PLAYING RECORD

YEAR	TEAM	GP	G	A	PTS	PIM
1967-68	Chicago	68	3	7	10	8
1970-71	Buffalo	3	0	0	0	2
1971-72	Buffalo	9	0	0	0	2
1972-73	Buffalo	42	0	7	7	8
1973-74	Buffalo	67	2	12	14	8
NHL TOTALS		189	5	26	31	28
SABRES TOTALS		121	2	19	21	20
NHL PLAYOFFS		12	0	0	0	0

RANDY WYROZUB

Position: Center

Born: Lacombe, Alta. on April 8, 1950
Height: 5-11; Weight: 170 pounds

- Was a fourth-round draft selection in 1970 and was a member of the original Sabres team
- Was one of the first Sabres players who regularly wore a helmet
- Left organization when he was selected by Washington in 1974 Expansion Draft

PLAYING RECORD

YEAR	TEAM	GP	G	A	PTS	PIM
1970-71	Buffalo	16	2	2	4	6
1971-72	Buffalo	34	3	4	7	0
1972-73	Buffalo	45	3	3	6	4
1973-74	Buffalo	5	0	1	1	0
NHL TOTALS		100	8	10	18	10
SABRES TOTALS		100	8	10	18	10
NHL PLAYOFFS		0	0	0	0	0

1972-73
Statistics

STATISTICS

No.	PLAYER	GP	G	A	PTS	+/-	PIM	PP	SH	GW	GT	SHOTS
11	Gil Perreault	78	28	60	88	+11	10	8	0	7	0	234
14	Rene Robert	75	40	43	83	+16	83	9	0	6	0	265
7	Rick Martin	75	37	36	73	+4	79	11	0	4	3	299
8	Jim Lorentz	78	27	35	62	+6	30	11	0	5	1	175
15	Gerry Meehan	77	31	29	60	+4	21	3	1	6	2	208
20	Don Luce	78	18	25	43	+7	32	0	3	2	0	198
21	Hugh Harris	60	12	26	38	+9	17	0	0	0	0	121
5	Larry Hillman	78	5	24	29	-3	56	2	0	0	0	102
10	Craig Ramsay	76	11	17	28	+13	15	0	1	1	0	89
12	Larry Mickey	77	15	9	26	-6	47	1	0	2	3	160
3	Mike Robitaille	65	4	17	21	+9	40	0	0	0	1	182
6	Jim Schoenfeld	66	4	15	19	+12	178	1	0	0	0	91
19	Steve Atkinson	61	9	9	18	-5	36	2	0	1	1	96
2	Tim Horton	69	1	16	17	+12	56	0	0	0	0	73
4	Tracy Pratt	74	1	15	16	+9	116	0	0	0	0	63
9	Norm Gratton	21	6	5	11	+0	12	2	0	1	1	26
23	Larry Carriere	40	2	8	10	-1	52	1	0	0	1	34
18	Paul Terbenche	42	0	7	7	+7	8	0	0	0	0	20
16	Randy Wyrozub	45	3	3	6	-1	4	0	0	2	0	23
22	Doug Rombough	5	2	0	2	+2	0	0	0	0	0	3
9	Butch Deadmarsh	34	1	1	2	-3	26	1	0	0	0	15
17	Rick Dudley	6	0	1	1	-2	7	0	0	0	0	6
24	John Gould	8	0	1	1	+0	0	0	0	0	0	4
24	Ron Busniuk	1	0	0	0	+0	9	0	0	0	0	1
22	Ray McKay	1	0	0	0	+0	0	0	0	0	0	0
17	Bob Richer	3	0	0	0	+0	0	0	0	0	0	0

No.	GOALTENDER	GP	MIN	GAA	W	L	T	EN	SO	GA	SA	PCT
30	Dave Dryden	37	2018	2.65	14	13	7	3	3	89	968	.908
1	Roger Crozier	49	2633	2.76	23	13	7	3	3	121	1277	.905
28	Rocky Farr	1	29	6.21	0	1	0	0	0	3	-	-

RECORD BY MONTH	GP	W	L	T	GF	GA	PTS
October	10	6	0	4	37	18	16
November	14	4	7	3	43	51	11
December	14	10	4	0	63	39	20
January	11	5	6	0	34	35	10
February	14	8	4	2	40	27	18
March	14	3	6	5	37	48	11
April	1	1	0	0	3	1	2
TOTALS	78	37	27	14	257	219	88

TEAM-BY-TEAM SERIES BREAKDOWN

ATLANTA FLAMES

GP	W	L	T	GF	GA	PTS
5	2	1	2	22	18	6

GOALS BY PERIOD	1	2	3	T
Buffalo	6	6	10	22
Atlanta	5	8	5	18

SHOTS BY PERIOD	1	2	3	T
Buffalo	48	47	62	157
Atlanta	44	46	34	124

TOP SABRES SCORERS:
Perreault 3-7-10
Martin 5-3-8
Robert 3-5-8

TOP FLAMES SCORERS:
Comeau 4-2-6
McCreary 4-2-6
Hicke 2-4-6

BOSTON BRUINS

GP	W	L	T	GF	GA	PTS
6	1	4	1	15	26	3

GOALS BY PERIOD	1	2	3	T
Buffalo	3	7	5	15
Boston	10	7	9	26

SHOTS BY PERIOD	1	2	3	T
Buffalo	65	58	62	185
Boston	75	60	58	193

TOP SABRES SCORERS:
Perreault 3-3-6
Robert 5-3-8
Lorentz 1-4-5

TOP BRUINS SCORERS:
Orr 7-5-12
Esposito 7-3-10
Cashman 0-8-8

CALIFORNIA SEALS

GP	W	L	T	GF	GA	PTS
5	1	2	2	9	11	4

GOALS BY PERIOD	1	2	3	T
Buffalo	4	1	4	9
California	2	4	5	11

SHOTS BY PERIOD	1	2	3	T
Buffalo	47	39	60	146
California	42	40	41	123

TOP SABRES SCORERS:
Ramsay 0-4-4
Robert 2-1-3
Meehan 2-0-2

TOP SEALS SCORERS:
Patrick 2-4-6
Johnstone 4-1-5

CHICAGO BLACKHAWKS

GP	W	L	T	GF	GA	PTS
5	2	3	0	18	15	4

GOALS BY PERIOD	1	2	3	T
Buffalo	3	4	11	18
Chicago	3	7	5	15

SHOTS BY PERIOD	1	2	3	T
Buffalo	45	48	64	157
Chicago	42	51	44	137

TOP SABRES SCORERS:
Meehan 5-2-7
Lorentz 2-5-7
Robert 3-2-5

TOP HAWKS SCORERS:
D. Hull 2-4-6
Martin 0-6-6
Pappin 3-1-4

DETROIT RED WINGS

GP	W	L	T	GF	GA	PTS
5	1	4	0	14	20	2

GOALS BY PERIOD	1	2	3	T
Buffalo	3	5	6	14
Detroit	2	10	8	20

SHOTS BY PERIOD	1	2	3	T
Buffalo	48	43	61	152
Detroit	54	62	49	165

TOP SABRES SCORERS:
Robert 4-2-6
Martin 2-4-6
Meehan 3-2-5

TOP WINGS SCORERS:
Dionne 5-6-11
Ecclestone 2-4-6
Stackhouse 1-4-5

LOS ANGELES KINGS

GP	W	L	T	GF	GA	PTS
5	2	1	2	17	13	6

GOALS BY PERIOD	1	2	3	T
Buffalo	4	6	7	17
Los Angeles	4	7	2	13

SHOTS BY PERIOD	1	2	3	T
Buffalo	38	52	48	138
Los Angeles	47	53	54	154

TOP SABRES SCORERS:
Lorentz 3-5-8
Perreault 2-3-5
Meehan 1-4-5

TOP KINGS SCORERS:
Corrigan 4-1-5
Widing 0-5-5
Berry 2-2-4

MINNESOTA NORTH STARS

GP	W	L	T	GF	GA	PTS
5	3	2	0	22	19	6

GOALS BY PERIOD	1	2	3	T
Buffalo	7	9	6	22
Minnesota	5	6	8	19

SHOTS BY PERIOD	1	2	3	T
Buffalo	53	61	57	171
Minnesota	57	47	48	152

TOP SABRES SCORERS:
Robert 3-7-10
Meehan 6-0-6
Luce 4-1-5

TOP STARS SCORERS:
Hextall 2-5-7
Prentice 4-1-5
Drouin 3-2-5

MONTREAL CANADIENS

GP	W	L	T	GF	GA	PTS
5	1	2	2	13	14	4

GOALS BY PERIOD	1	2	3	T
Buffalo	7	2	4	13
Montreal	7	3	4	24

SHOTS BY PERIOD	1	2	3	T
Buffalo	62	43	59	164
Montreal	54	61	44	159

TOP SABRES SCORERS:
Martin 3-3-6
Robert 2-3-5

TOP CANADIENS SCORERS:
F. Mahovolich 2-2-4
Lemaire 2-2-4
Lapointe 1-3-4

NEW YORK ISLANDERS

GP	W	L	T	GF	GA	PTS
6	5	0	1	29	9	11

GOALS BY PERIOD	1	2	3	T
Buffalo	7	14	8	29
NY Islanders	3	3	3	9

SHOTS BY PERIOD	1	2	3	T
Buffalo	77	70	84	231
NY Islanders	45	45	44	134

TOP SABRES SCORERS:
Perreault 4-7-11
Martin 5-5-10
Robert 5-4-9

TOP ISLANDERS SCORERS:
B. Harris 1-3-4
Miller 2-1-3
Spencer 1-2-3

NEW YORK RANGERS

GP	W	L	T	GF	GA	PTS
6	5	1	0	22	12	10

GOALS BY PERIOD	1	2	3	T
Buffalo	6	4	12	22
NY Rangers	3	6	3	12

SHOTS BY PERIOD	1	2	3	T
Buffalo	45	55	70	170
NY Rangers	51	69	56	176

TOP SABRES SCORERS:
Meehan 3-3-6
Robert 5-0-5
Luce 3-2-5

TOP RANGERS SCORERS:
Ratelle 5-1-6
Gilbert 0-6-6
Stemkowski 3-1-4

PHILADELPHIA FLYERS

GP	W	L	T	GF	GA	PTS
5	2	3	0	15	15	4

GOALS BY PERIOD	1	2	3	T
Buffalo	1	5	9	15
Philadelphia	4	7	4	15

SHOTS BY PERIOD	1	2	3	T
Buffalo	56	53	69	178
Philadelphia	49	55	46	150

TOP SABRES SCORERS:
Perreault 2-7-9
Robert 3-3-6
Martin 3-3-6

TOP FLYERS SCORERS:
MacLeish 5-2-7
Barber 2-5-7
Flett 4-1-5

PITTSBURGH PENGUINS

GP	W	L	T	GF	GA	PTS
5	3	0	2	14	9	6

GOALS BY PERIOD	1	2	3	T
Buffalo	4	5	5	14
Pittsburgh	4	2	3	9

SHOTS BY PERIOD	1	2	3	T
Buffalo	49	68	50	167
Pittsburgh	46	45	44	135

TOP SABRES SCORERS:
Perreault 2-4-6
Martin 3-2-5
Robert 2-3-5

TOP PENGUINS SCORERS:
Polis 1-3-4
Pronovost 2-1-3

ST. LOUIS BLUES

GP	W	L	T	GF	GA	PTS
5	2	1	2	9	8	6

GOALS BY PERIOD	1	2	3	T
Buffalo	5	3	1	9
St. Louis	3	3	2	8

SHOTS BY PERIOD	1	2	3	T
Buffalo	43	53	51	147
St. Louis	52	61	41	154

TOP SABRES SCORERS:
Perreault 3-1-4
Lorentz 2-1-3
Meehan 1-2-3

TOP BLUES SCORERS:
Roberto 2-1-3
St. Marseille 2-0-2

TORONTO MAPLE LEAFS

GP	W	L	T	GF	GA	PTS
5	4	1	0	16	12	8

GOALS BY PERIOD	1	2	3	T		SHOTS BY PERIOD	1	2	3	T
Buffalo	3	8	5	16		Buffalo	57	58	46	161
Toronto	2	5	5	12		Toronto	37	53	56	146

TOP SABRES SCORERS: Perreault 2-5-7 Robert 3-2-5 Lorentz 2-3-5

TOP LEAFS SCORERS: Sittler 3-1-4 Keon 2-2-4

VANCOUVER CANUCKS

GP	W	L	T	GF	GA	PTS
5	3	2	0	22	18	6

GOALS BY PERIOD	1	2	3	T		SHOTS BY PERIOD	1	2	3	T
Buffalo	6	6	10	22		Buffalo	54	48	61	163
Vancouver	7	6	5	18		Vancouver	49	53	65	167

TOP SABRES SCORERS: Perreault 3-6-9 Martin 6-1-7

TOP CANUCKS SCORERS: Schmautz 4-2-6 Boudrias 3-2-5 Guevremont 1-3-4

PLAYOFFS VS. MONTREAL

GP	W	L	T	GF	GA	PTS
6	2	4	0	16	21	4

GOALS BY PERIOD	1	2	3	O	T	SHOTS BY PERIOD	1	2	3	O	T
Buffalo	2	6	7	1	16	Buffalo	67	75	81	4	227
Montreal	7	8	6	0	21	Montreal	66	64	51	5	186

TOP SABRES SCORERS: Perreault 3-7-10 Robert 5-3-8 Martin 3-2-5

TOP CANADIENS SCORERS: Cournoyer 5-3-8 Savard 2-5-7 F. Mahovolich 2-4-6

Author
Sal Maiorana

Sal Maiorana was born in Buffalo, New York, in 1962, attended Bishop Ludden High School in Syracuse, then returned to Buffalo and spent four years at Buffalo State College earning a bachelor of arts degree in journalism in 1984.

He has worked for The Associated Press, *The Leader* in Corning, New York, and for the last 11 years, the *Democrat and Chronicle* in Rochester, New York. With the *Democrat and Chronicle*, he covers as beats the National Football League's Buffalo Bills, amateur and professional golf and professional indoor lacrosse. He has also covered the National Hockey League's Buffalo Sabres, Syracuse University football and college lacrosse.

Maiorana is also the Bills correspondent for *The Sporting News*, he writes a weekly column for the internet service *CBS Sportsline* that chronicles great moments in sports history; and he is a regular contributor for the golf magazines *Golf World, Golf Week* and *PGA Magazine*.

THANK YOU SABRES is Maiorana's third book. His first was published in May of 1993 by St. Martin's Press Inc., New York, New York. *Through the Green – The Mind and Art of a Professional Golfer* was written with the cooperation of PGA Tour star Davis Love III and provided a unique behind-the-scenes look at life on the pro golf circuit.

His second, published by Quality Sports Publications, Coal Valley, Illinois, in September of 1994, was titled *RELENTLESS: The Hard-Hitting History of Buffalo Bills Football* and is a comprehensive history of the Bills.

Maiorana was the 1993 winner of the Charlie Wagner Sports Writer of the Year Award, presented annually by the Rochester Press-Radio Club. He was also honored as a distinguished citizen in Corning for his work covering area high school sporting events.

Maiorana lives in Walworth, New York, with his wife, the former Christine Charlton, their daughter, Taylor Marie, and son, Holden Joseph.